W9-CKI-837

Criminal Life

views from the inside

Edited by

DAVID M. PETERSEN
The Ohio State University

MARCELLO TRUZZI
New College

Prentice-Hall, Inc., Englewood Cliffs, New Jersey

For Linda and Pat

ISBN: P 0-13-192955-0
C 0-13-192963-1

Library of Congress Catalog Card Number: 70-178132

Printed in the United States of America

10 9 8 7 6 5 4 3 2 1

Prentice-Hall International, Inc., *London*
Prentice-Hall of Australia, Pty. Ltd., *Sydney*
Prentice-Hall of Canada, Ltd., *Toronto*
Prentice-Hall of India Private Limited, *New Delhi*
Prentice-Hall of Japan, Inc., *Tokyo*

Contents

Preface

We present in this book a collection of "inside" views by criminals themselves—from prostitutes and confidence men to organized mobsters—on their behavior, the world they move in, and their relationships to the larger society which tries to control them. Here are the feelings and experiences, the motivations and goals of the criminal—a human being rather than an abstraction in some theoretical scheme.

For a long time the literature on crime and criminals has been primarily represented by two kinds of work. One type includes those attemptedly objective appraisals conducted by people "outside" the world of the criminal. Most studies by criminologists, penologists, and social scientists fall into this class.[1] Many theories and empirical investigations have tried to account for crime through the years. These works are usually found in professional journals and textbooks in criminology, law, and the social sciences. The second source of data on criminals has included the many writings by wardens, psychologists, and others who have professional contact with criminals. Typical of such works are the autobiographical writings of such correctional personnel as Warden Lewis E. Lawes (1932; 1937), Warden Clinton T. Duffy (1962), prison psychologist Donald P. Wilson (1951), and the former director of the Federal Bureau of Prisons, James V. Bennett (1970). Most of these studies assess the "criminal mind" from the viewpoint of those having custody over, supervising, or treating offenders.

But most of these works ignore statements by criminals

[1] An exception is the well known study by Hans Reimer (1937). Reimer, a sociologist, by way of the deliberate commission of a criminal offense had himself imprisoned in order to obtain an "inside" view of the social life of inmates. A somewhat similar case of a sociologist writing about his past experiences as a prisoner can be found in a Scandinavian study done by Johan Galtung (1959).

themselves. There have, of course, been exceptions—most notably Edwin H. Sutherland's well known transcription of autobiographical commentary published in 1937 as *The Professional Thief*. However, as even a casual inspection of the bibliographic section at the end of this volume will demonstrate, a good number of such autobiographical statements existed before Sutherland's book, and many others are now available. Such personal reports have long been considered an important source of data for the sociologist,[2] but this large body of writings by criminals has generally been ignored by the criminologist.[3]

Why present first-person statements in a collection like this one? First, these documents reveal firsthand experiences in the life-histories of social violators. They are presented in the criminal's own words, not translated into scientific jargon. Though they may be "unobjective" from the scientist's standpoint, they show us the personal viewpoint that shapes the criminal's situation and his actions.[4] As Albert Morris (1941, p. 139) notes in his survey of criminals' views of themselves: "Even when they are lacking in penetration or sincerity, the verbalizations of criminals may have a diagnostic value as great as other overt behavior." Our attention is directed toward real cases rather than over-simplified theoretical models of human behavior. Though these reports could be used for quantitative study through techniques like content analysis, they are also important as qualitative data. There is much of theoretic value in such reports beyond that which is to be found in a statistical survey.

Second, these first-person statements expose the life styles of the various violators of law. This book is a first attempt to present in one volume a variety of personal accounts describing life as the criminal lives it; the traditions, customs, standards, activities, and personal contacts of his social

[2] The most notable of such uses in sociology is still the classic study by William I. Thomas and Florian Znaniecki, *The Polish Peasant in Europe and America* (1918).

[3] Exceptions which might be noted include the works of Clifford Shaw, *et al. Brothers in Crime* (1938), *The Natural History of a Delinquent Career* (1931), and *The Jack-Roller: A Delinquent Boy's Own Story* (1945).

[4] Relevant standard objective studies of the criminal by scientists can be found in the bibliography of this volume.

and cultural environment.[5] Reading these pieces may help many people to discard prejudices and misconceptions about criminals. These are reports by real people on the fringe of society. Many of them live in subcultures foreign to most members of the larger society, but the reports are relatively free of any attempt to glorify or sentimentalize the role of the criminal.

Third, the descriptions of the lives of criminals may help those searching for causes of criminality. The etiology of crime has been a main thrust of criminology since Lombroso's classic work in the mid-1880's. We do not intend that this volume replace the extensive work conducted by social scientists and others interested in explaining criminal behavior. However, expressions of the criminal "viewpoint" are more than simply ramblings by bitter men or outlets for personal frustrations. They contain a worth that cannot be ignored. Bringing these readings together in one source provides an interesting compendium for the reader's analysis of content through comparisons.[6] The rich potential available in autobiographical reports by criminals suggests that efforts toward explaining criminal behavior, the development of typologies, the process of being socialized into prison life (prisonization), and so on might be profitably investigated by examining the literature of the deviant or criminal. We include a lengthy bibliography of over 150 such statements at the end of this volume.

Finally, studying the criminal through his own self-reports adds humanity and compassion to the field of scientific criminology because they help the reader to identify with the criminal. The literary and intrinsic value of these accounts may motivate the reader's interest and concern. These readings, we hope, will also propel student interest in the broader issues of criminology. Thus, we hope this collection will vitalize those courses in criminology in which it is used as an adjunct to a text.

[5] A somewhat similar volume is the recent collection by McCaghy, Skipper, and Lefton (1968) which deals with autobiographical reports by a number of deviants such as nudists, the mentally ill, and political extremists.

[6] An interesting attempt at content analysis has been completed by Rogers and Alexander (1968) on another source of criminal writings largely unexplored, publications of the penal presses in our state and federal correctional institutions.

In *Criminal Life: Views from the Inside* we have included selections from individuals who have violated certain of society's rules. The behavior of our spokesmen differs from the standards of our society, and in that sense they are "deviants." All but two of the pieces included come from persons actually arrested and/or jailed. The readings emphasize the learning of "deviant norms" and the various subcultures of deviance, such as the juvenile gang. These choices can be explained as the product of the *bias* of the editors as *social* scientists. We don't maintain that these persons are "abnormal" or psychotic, but, rather, that they often behave normally *for their social and cultural groups.*

We have divided the statements into three general categories. Part One, Behavior Patterns of Offenders, includes pieces describing the learning of deviant norms and the subcultures of deviance through discussions of the lives of criminals prior to incarceration, including the social life of the criminal. Our second section, Prison, contains reports of life in prison, including punishment, violence, the deprivations of prison, and other aspects of prison life. The largest source of criminal writings by far comes from the previous prison experiences of criminals. The reactions of these violators to the existing penal system often constitute a major indictment of that system. Part Three, Issues in Criminology, includes statements on some (though not all) of the major issues in criminology today: rehabilitation, prison treatment, and capital punishment.

A fully exhaustive set of statements by criminals is impossible in one volume. But we think the readings presented do illustrate the wide diversity of criminal behaviors. A few words about our criteria for the selection of these readings: Using a behavior systems approach, we have tried to include every major type of criminal.[7] Unfortunately, it was not possible to find a good self-report for every type of criminal, though the only major category for which we were unable to obtain an appropriate selection was the white-collar criminal. Our selection was necessarily restricted by the kinds of self-reports available. Sometimes a single criminal represents several types of criminal behavior (Valachi, for example, was an organized criminal but was also a hired killer). In some instances in this volume a criminal talks about

[7] The scheme used for this book was that of Bloch and Geis (1962).

things other than his life of crime. In one selection Leopold talks about his prison life rather than his crime of murder. We have included several pieces dealing with prostitution and drug addiction, but this is not truly disproportionate since more of these self-reports exist than any other. Our inclusions were chosen to represent a large although lopsided and limited literature.

We used several other basic rules to select articles: (1) All persons presented in this anthology at some time violated an existing law. Not all spokesmen have been captured or jailed (some successfully evaded the laws) but all of them admit having committed acts that society defined as criminal. In some cases the statements we present come to us through third parties, themselves not criminals but rather transcribers or editors of the criminals' own statements. (2) All articles were selected for their sociological relevancy. They all concern social behavior or interaction. (3) Articles were chosen that might interest the general as well as the scientifically-trained reader. (4) With few exceptions, the articles come from recent sources, mostly post-1950 publications. (5) Articles were limited to those representing the English-speaking world (mostly from the United States, but a few from England). Readers should be most cautious in extrapolating these descriptions to criminals in other countries.

We wish to express our appreciation to the authors and publishers who graciously allowed us these materials. We would like to acknowledge the assistance of Mr. Lloyd Hooker and Miss Penny Doucette, Library, U.S. Bureau of Prisons and Miss Barbara Rubenstein during our research. We also wish to thank Mr. Roger Staples for his editorial assistance and Mrs. Dianne Breen for her excellent stenographic assistance.

DMP

MT

PART ONE

Behavior Patterns of Offenders

Our examination of criminal behavior patterns clusters around three interrelated problem areas: (1) the process of "induction" into criminal activity, (2) the deviant orientation (world view) of the professional criminal, and (3) the organization, life-style, and activities of the specialized criminal. Each of the writings in this section says something about all these areas, but we present them in a sequence that emphasizes these consecutive points.

Though theories abound (see Vold, 1958; Mannheim, 1965; Cohen, 1966), criminologists disagree about the prime causes involved in the making of a criminal. The first three selections illustrate variations in the "induction" process. Claude Brown demonstrates the importance of lower-class culture as a generator of criminal activities. His story epitomizes the view of crime as normal behavior learned through environmental subcultural processes (see, for example, Vold, 1958, pp. 209–18). Polly Adler, too, shows the importance of poverty as a contributing factor, but her interpretation of the causes implies a mixture of economic and psychological conditions. In contrast, William Burroughs describes his turning to criminal activity despite personal wealth and opportunity. His story is a good example of Sutherland's *theory of differential association* (1966, pp. 81–94), which explains the cause as social interaction with criminality and criminals.

Next, the orientation of the professional and systematic criminal is presented (Allerton, Conway, and Maxie the Goniff). This variety of lawbreaker engages in full-time pursuit of illicit, criminal income (constantly "grifting")*, and usually has complex occupational skills (techniques)

*A "grifter" is a criminal who employs skill rather than violence—one who lives by his wits.

and attitudes resulting from his long period of training. He usually takes great pride in his criminal skills, seeing himself and others like him as "professional." His activities are extensively organized, routinized, and complicated with safeguards ("fixes," pay-offs, etc.) and risks (pressures from other criminals and police unknown to the "amateur" criminal or the average citizen).

Finally, criminal activities are examined from the point of view of specialization and organization. Here, we include a wide range of behavior, an attempted "sampling" of the literally hundreds of possible criminal activities (see Clinard and Quinney, 1967). The readings take in criminal organizations and their activities: the juvenile gang (anonymously authored), the Cosa Nostra (from the Joseph Valachi hearings), the policy racket (recorded by James D. Horan), dope traffic (by "Ric"), and that important and necessary adjunct to organized crime, police cooperation (by the Ex-Deputy Sheriff). We turn then to a variety of more "independent" criminal offenders, including a disorderly alcoholic (Anonymous), a hustler (Henry Williamson), a tramp (George Orwell), a female prostitute (Anonymous), a male homosexual prostitute (Kenneth Marlowe), an insurance-racket man (David Schiffer), a confidence man ("Yellow Kid" Weil), and a safe-cracker (Herbert Emerson Wilson).

growing up in harlem

CLAUDE BROWN

Born and raised in the slums of Harlem, Claude Brown was thirteen when this incident took place. He had been involved in stealing, marijuana smoking, and gang fights for several years. Here he discusses his first attempt to use "horse" (heroin) after his release from Wiltwyck, a school for delinquents. Brown is rare in successfully emerging from the trapping slums of Harlem despite pressures to remain.[1] While writing this, he was a law student at an American university. This excerpt shows how a subcultural milieu itself can generate delinquent and criminal behavior.[2]

We started hanging out again. I was thirteen, so now it was okay for me to hang out. Nobody squawked. Butch and Danny used to take me to a place called the Lounge, and we'd dance. It was a cellar. It was dark in there, and we used to listen to records by the Orioles. We would dance the Grind, a dance that anybody could do. All you had to do was stand still and move a little bit.

Then I started staying out real late at night. Sometimes I'd come in at two or three o'clock in the morning, but Mama and Dad wouldn't squawk. They started treating me like I was old now, so whenever I was home, I didn't mind being there. But something else happened that summer—something that made things change, that made Harlem change.

When I came home, Kid and Butch and Danny weren't smoking reefers any more. I'd have a smoke, but they were doing other things. And the first thing that Danny told me was that they were using something that they called "horse." I remember Danny saying, "If I ever catch you messin' wit horse, I'll kill you." I had the feeling that he meant it, but it made me

[1]Other autobiographical accounts by minority members in slum areas include Thomas (1967), Williamson (1965), Malcolm X (1964), and Cleaver (1968).
[2]For a sociological look at the problem, see Cohen (1955), Cohen and Short (1958, pp. 20–36), and Miller (1958, pp. 5–19).

curious about horse. It seemed that they were saying this was something I wasn't old enough for. But I wanted to do the same things they were doing; I wanted to be as old as they were. All the older cats were using horse. The younger cats were still smoking reefers, drinking wine, and stuff like that. But I didn't want to be young. I wanted to be old. And the first time Danny spoke to me about it, I knew I was going to get some horse somehow, somewhere—soon.

Horse was a new thing, not only in our neighborhood but in Brooklyn, the Bronx, and everyplace I went, uptown and downtown. It was like horse had just taken over. Everybody was talking about it. All the hip people were using it and snorting it and getting this new high. To know what was going on and to be in on things, you had to do that. And the only way I felt I could come out of Wiltwyck and be up to date, the only way to take up where I had left off and be the same hip guy I was before I went to Wiltwyck, was to get in on the hippest thing, and the hippest thing was horse. It wasn't like the other time I came home and heard that the Orioles were singing at the Apollo and that guys were going around singing in little groups and trying to imitate them. These things had happened before. The first time I came home, it was still the gang fights. If you were in a gang, you were somebody, and you were doing things. The summer before this one, the Grind was the thing that was going on. But things kept changing, and I'd always been able to change with them and keep up with the neighborhood.

When I left New York that summer and went back to Wiltwyck, the thing I still wanted most was horse. I had been smoking reefers and had gotten high a lot of times, but I had the feeling that this horse was something that was out of this world. Back at Wiltwyck, I started telling everybody about horse. I told K.B. about horse; I told Tito about horse; I told Horse about horse. We just had to get some somehow. We knew that it was medicine and that you could get high off it and that it was better than reefers, but that was about all we knew.

For about six months or more, the guys in Aggrey House used to try to get high by taking a cigarette and sticking the teeth of a comb into it. All it did was stink when you smoked it. It didn't really get cats high, but you could make believe if you had enough imagination. Then I think it was Stumpy who came up with putting camera film into a cigarette. We tried this, and a lot of cats got sick, got headaches, and got everything else, but I don't think anybody ever really got high. When we heard about this horse thing, every cat who knew about it wanted to try some. I'd gotten some guys high off reefers when I took them home with me or when they came to visit me. Now we wanted to get some highs off horse.

K. B. had told me that this was something real big in Brownsville too. I wanted to turn him on before he could turn me on. He thought he was as hip as I was and was into as many things as I was, but I knew he wasn't. If he was the first one to come up with some horse, I would feel bad about that, so I really had to get some horse somehow. I wanted to turn K. B. and everybody else on and show them that I really knew how to get high. I started scheming and thinking that maybe we could steal some from the infirmary. But I didn't know what it was. All I knew was that it was medicine, that it was white, and that for a dollar, in the streets, you could get a capsule. But I didn't know what to look for if I went into the infirmary. So for some time, I had a lot of guys stealing all kinds of caps with white powder in them out of the infirmary. We got some of everything but horse.

Cats were getting sick around there from some of the stuff they were snorting in those white caps. We'd always get a guinea pig, and the guinea pig was usually Teddy D. He'd snort just about anything. He was from Harlem, too, and he'd heard a lot about horse. He was ready to try something new because it was time to move on. I think everybody up there had the feeling it was time to move on. It was time to stop smoking reefers and stop drinking wine; it was time to start really getting high. The old guys out on the streets were really getting high. They were snorting this horse, and this horse was making them bend; it was making them itch and nod and talk in heavier voices. It made you sound like a real gangster or like a real old cat. And everybody wanted to sound old.

I heard somebody talking about horse one night, but I didn't know it. It was Mr. Johnson. Mr. Johnson was one of the counselors, and he had heard some of the guys in our house talking about horse. He came in and told us that it was heroin and that heroin could kill you. He said that when he was going to college, he knew a boy who liked to use this horse. He said that they called it "snow" then but that the real name of it was heroin. And this heroin was something that you take a little bit of for a while, and then you would take more and more and more, and soon you have to take so much that you couldn't take anything else. You couldn't eat, you couldn't drink any water, and after a while, guys just dried up and died. And it was so expensive that you had to steal and rob and do a whole lot of other stuff. What Mr. Johnson was telling us about heroin really sounded frightening, but I knew that horse wasn't heroin; I knew that it was something altogether different. But Mr. Johnson sure scared the hell out of me.

The guys I had seen using it, like Butch and Danny and the others, had just started, of course, but it wasn't doing anything bad to them. It wasn't drying them up. They seemed to feel good. That's what really made me want to use it. Those guys seemed to feel like they were flying, like they were way up in the air; they felt a way that they'd never felt before. And to see so many people going around on those streets feeling so good—I just knew

I was missing out on something really big. It would be a drag for someone to come up to you and say, "Man, you ever snort any horse?" and you would have to say, "No." Hell, I wanted to be able to say, "Yeah, man."

I'd forgotten about everything but horse when I went back to Wiltwyck, but then something terrible happened. When I came back to Wiltwyck from that visit in 1950, I found out that K. B. was going home. I couldn't believe that. I panicked. I said, "No, man. You must be jokin'."

He said, "No, man, Stilly told me."

I ran to the office. I looked for Papanek. He wasn't around. I found Stilly. I said, "Stilly, I wanna go home. I gotta go home. If they don' let me outta this place, I'm gonna go crazy. I'm gon tear the place down."

"Don't get excited," Stilly said. "Didn't I promise you a year ago that you would be going home before I left?"

"Yeah," I said, but I had never paid too much attention to Stilly.

He said, "Look, I'm leaving here in a couple of months. I won't be here when school starts, and you won't be here either. Do you believe that?"

I said, "Yeah, man, I believe you." I did, but I still wanted to talk to Papanek. I wanted to scream and let everybody know how I felt about still being at that place after two years—two years and about four months. I had to get out of there.

But Papanek wasn't there, and nobody else was there, and after ranting and raving for a little while, I got used to the idea of being there and not having my old sidekick any more. It was okay when K. B. left. We made plans to see each other when I got out. And we kept those plans. K. B. told me to come to Brownsville when I got out and he would have some horse for me—all the horse I wanted.

I believed him. I knew K. B. would try damn hard and would probably succeed. He had a lot of older brothers, and they were hip guys. Most of them knew things. They'd been in the old gangs in Brooklyn—the Nits and the Robins and the Green Avenue Stompers, the real hip gangs. I couldn't wait. I kept dreaming about that horse that was waiting for me when I got out of Wiltwyck.

• • •

After I'd been out of Wiltwyck for about six weeks, a guy named Dunny and Tito and I stole some cigarettes from a grocery store's warehouse. We had something like a hundred cartons of cigarettes. We took them to Johnny, but he didn't want to give us too much money. Anyway, that's how he put it. He said, "Why don't I give you cats fifty dollars—and some of the best horse you ever tasted in your life?"

Everybody's eyes perked up. This was the first time anybody had ever offered us any horse, and we had been dying and trying so goddamn hard to get some horse, it was almost like a dream coming true. I don't think any of us even heard about the fifty dollars. We just heard the word "horse."

Dunny looked at me, and I looked at Tito, and we all looked at Johnny. We didn't want to seem too anxious. Maybe he would just give us a little bit of horse and take back twenty-five dollars. So I hesitated.

I said, "Man, I don' know."

Johnny said, "That's some good horse, Sonny." And he took up one of the bags and shook it.

I had never seen horse in bags before, and it seemed like a whole lot. All I'd ever seen was caps; that's what everybody was snorting back then. They were buying dollar caps; they'd snort half a cap, get high, and save half a cap for some other time. You could stay messed up all day long. All you did was nod; you didn't want to eat anything, you didn't want to do anything. I wanted some horse so bad I could taste it. I'd been tasting it for months.

So we said, "Okay, okay, man," after we had waited a while, long enough not to seem like we wanted it real bad. We said, "Okay, man, we'll take that."

We went up on the roof, and I picked up a matchbook. Everybody was crowding real close, and I said, "Like, be still, man; you don't want to waste this stuff, 'cause this stuff cost a whole lotta money." We didn't know it at the time, but Johnny had only given us a five-dollar bag. He had said that it was twenty-five dollars worth of horse. We didn't know that much about horse. All we knew was that it was good and that it was expensive. And since we were going to get to snort some, we didn't care anyway. We just wanted to get high off some horse, and here it was.

Tito said, "Give me some first."

Dunny said, "Let me. . . . Look man, let me get that. Man, it's gon spill." And everybody was grabbing.

I said, "Look man, here; here, you cats, just take it, man, and take what you want." This was how I used to always calm these cats down. I'd say, "Here," and walk away, and they'd start acting like some niggers with some sense.

Everybody cooled down then, and they said, "No, you go on, Sonny. You get straight, man. Here, you take some first."

I knew this was what had to come. Everybody looked at me. I scooped a little bit out of the bag into a piece of matchbook cover the way I'd seen Kid do it so many times. He always looked like he'd hit the ceiling and gone right into another world after a snort. I was anxious. I almost wasted it, I was trying so hard. My hands were shaking because I was trying to do it too fast. And when I put it up to my nose, I couldn't believe it was really happening. I almost wanted to break out and laugh for joy, but I held it back, and I snorted.

Something hit me right in the top of the head. It felt like a little spray of pepper on my brain. But I didn't pay too much attention to it just then.

I took some more and put it in the other nostril. The other cats were looking; they were real quiet, everything was real quiet.

Dunny grabbed me and said, "Sonny, give me some," and Tito did the same thing. And I just dropped it; I forgot about them. It seemed like I had left them. Everything was getting rosy, beautiful. The sun got brighter in the sky, and the whole day lit up and was twice as bright as it was before. It looked like Tito and Dunny were arguing and scrambling, trying to get some stuff, but they weren't in the same world I was in. I could reach out and touch them, but everything slowed down so much.

Everything was so slo-o-o-w. And then my head started. My head seemed to stretch, and I thought my brain was going to burst. It was like a headache taking place all over the head at once and trying to break its way out. And then it seemed to get hot and hot and hot. And I was so slow; I was trying to grab my head, but I couldn't feel it. I tried to get up, but my legs were like weights. I got scared. I'd never felt this way in my life before. I wanted to fall down on my knees and say, "Oh, Mama, Mama, help me."

I couldn't seem to talk to Tito. I couldn't seem to talk to Dunny. They were right there in front of me, but they seemed to be so far away that I couldn't reach them. I fell down on my knees and crawled over to them. They were down there scrambling for some horse; they seemed to be talking and hollering about horse and horse and horse, and they couldn't hear me. They couldn't feel me. They didn't know if I was here dying or if something had a hold on me.

My guts felt like they were going to come out. Everything was bursting out all at once, and there was nothing I could do. It was my stomach and my brain. My stomach was pulling my brain down into it, and my brain was going to pull my guts out and into my head. And I said, "O Lawd, if you'll just give me one more chance, one more chance, I'll never get high again."

And then it seemed like everything in me all of a sudden just came out, and I vomited. I vomited on Tito, and he didn't even feel it. He didn't even know it. The cats were still getting high. I was so scared. I thought we'd just killed ourselves. I wanted to pray. I wanted to tell these guys to pray. And they were so wrapped up in this thing; they were still snorting and snorting and talking about nodding and nodding. And it seemed like this went on for years. . . . I couldn't talk to them. I tried to touch them, but I couldn't reach them. I was trying to say something. I was trying to yell, and all these cats could do was nod, nod, nod, nod. I was dying, I was dying. I seemed to roll over fifty times, and every time I rolled over, I thought my guts were going to pour out on the floor.

I threw up, and I threw up. It seemed like I threw up a million times. I felt that if I threw up one more time, my stomach was just going to break all open; and still I threw up. I prayed and I prayed and I prayed. After a while, I was too sick to care.

The next thing I knew, Danny had me in his arms, and he was pouring some buttermilk down me, and he was slapping me and calling, "Sonny, Sonny, Sonny—"

I'd heard his voice for a long time, and then I started feeling the slap, and I was wondering, What the hell is he doin' slappin' me? I was never so glad to see anybody in all my life. And I felt maybe it was the work of the Lord, because Danny's mother was a preacher, and it seemed like I had been in hell and he had come and saved me.

After I was wide awake, Danny slapped me again, real hard. I wanted to hit that nigger then—I didn't go for that big brother thing any more. But I knew I couldn't beat him yet—Danny was more than six feet tall—so I just took it. And after he hit me, he held my collar, real tight, and he said, "Sonny, if I ever again, as long as I live, hear about you usin' drugs, I'm gon kill you. I'm gon git my gun, and I'm gon beat you wit it. I'm gon beat you wit my gun in your head, nigger, until you go in the hospital. 'Cause I'd rather see you there than see you on shit."

I didn't know how to take it. But I had a feeling that Danny meant good, that he meant damn good. Or maybe it was just that I was grateful because I'd almost died, or I thought I'd almost died, and he'd saved me. So I listened. I kind of felt that this was the last time that he was ever going to tell me anything or play that big brother bit with me—and that he knew it. And since it was the last time, maybe it was something to listen to.

I said to Danny, "Look, man, you don't ever, long as you live, have to worry about me messin' wit any more horse as long as I live."

I was sick for about two days after that. I didn't even want a reefer. I didn't want anything, anything, that was like a high. I started drinking some of Dad's liquor after that, but I was scared of those dry highs.

Anyway, that was the big letdown with horse. For a long time, I just looked at other people and wondered how the hell they could go through that. Dunny still liked it. He said it was pretty good. He said he had a real boss feeling. But Tito felt about the same way I did. He said he wasn't going to fuck with any more of that stuff as long as he lived. The horse had turned out to be a real drag.

on becoming a prostitute

POLLY ADLER

Polly Adler, perhaps the most famous madam in American history, ran for twenty-five years some of the most successful houses of prostitution in New York City. In 1945 she closed the doors of "New York's most famous bordello," ending a career in which she had contact with hundreds of prostitutes. Here Miss Adler directs her attention to the question of why girls enter prostitution.[1]

Inevitably, there is one question which every customer puts to a prostitute—what might be called the sixty-four-dollar question: "How did you get into this business?" As a rule men ask it, expecting to hear a tale of woe, but the sort of answer they would prefer to hear is implicit in a well-known joke. According to this story a man sleeps with a beautiful girl who, though a prostitute, is rich, well-bred, well-educated, and intelligent. Amazed that a girl with all these endowments and advantages should stoop to whoring, he asks how she got into the business. "Oh, I don't know," the tart answers. "I'm just lucky, I guess."

Men particularly relish this joke because it feeds their egos, and also because it would lessen their pleasure to think that a girl was submitting to them strictly from necessity. Actually, of course, despite all the feigned transports of ecstasy (for purposes of increasing the tip), to ninety-nine out of a hundred girls going to bed with a customer is a joyless, even distasteful, experience. Nothing could be farther from the truth than the "just lucky" explanation—unless the girl meant bad luck.

No girl, as a social worker once said, sets out to be a prostitute. Such stupidity would be incredible. Who wants to be a pariah, a social outcast—treated with contempt, jailed, beaten, robbed and finally kicked into the gutter when she is no longer salable? A prostitute can count on no more than ten money-making years. Then she is through—if not dead or diseased,

[1]Another relevant autobiography is that of Stanford (1966). For major sociological statements on prostitution, see Davis (1937, pp. 744–55), Bryan (1965, pp. 287–97), Hirschi (1962, pp. 33–49), and Lemert (1951, pp. 236–80).

so broken by drugs, alcohol and the steady abuse of her body that no one will hire her again. And since the sordid and pitiful fate of the prostitute is far from being a secret, no wonder people ask what propels a girl into this short and unhappy life.

No doubt there are as many answers to this question as there are sociologists, psychiatrists, philosophers and doctors of divinity. But in my opinion the greatest single factor—and the common denominator in an overwhelming majority of cases—is poverty. It is true that, though many girls are poor, only a small percentage of them take to hustling. But there is more than one kind of poverty—there is emotional poverty and intellectual poverty and poverty of spirit. As well as material lacks, there can be a lack of love, a lack of education, a lack of hope. And out of such impoverishment the prostitute is bred.

When a fifteen-year-old girl looks around her with the new awareness of adolescence and sees only poverty and ugliness, the groundwork is laid. She doesn't want to wind up like her mother, wornout from too much childbearing, slopping around in an old ragged dress, beaten by a drunken stupid husband every Saturday night. She wants a chance at the kind of life she's seen in the movies, with becoming frocks to wear and handsome men to pay her court, a house on a pretty street, clean, smiling children. . . . And suddenly she sees that she might not get all this, nor even any part of it, that in fact she does not even know how to go about getting it.

But she's heard that wishing will make it so, and she keeps on hoping that someday Jimmy Stewart or Dana Andrews will come through town and see her. And she does her hair the way Rita Hayworth does, and walks with a strut the way Lana Turner does, and she wears a tight sweater designed to emphasize she's a woman. And maybe she begins to get a bad name in the neighborhood because she makes such a parade of her nubility, and one of the guys outside the drugstore tells his pals he's had her and he'll line her up for them some night. And the story gets back to her parents and they call her a bum and she sasses them back, and after that there's a new defiance and don't-careness in her manner.

Then one day she meets Jimmy Stewart. Well, not exactly Jimmy Stewart, but a guy with a new convertible and sharp clothes and a snap-brim hat and a fast, easy line. And he wants to know what a pretty kid like her is doing without a boyfriend. He tells her she's beautiful, and he can see she's got too many brains to stay in this little tank town, and how would she like to take a trip? So why not? He says he loves her—and anyway what's she got to go home to? So she goes away with him in his shiny car, and he buys her some flashy clothes, and she thinks the pretty house on the pretty street comes next.

He has told her he's a salesman, but before long she finds that his line is selling underwear and junk jewelry to girls who work in joints. When she's gotten used to that idea, she meets some of the girls and the madams, and it seems that he's kind of in love with one of the girls in one joint. When she questions him, he tells her he owes a lot to Dolores. She's helping him get the money together to buy a shop of his own so he can settle down. Soon she understands that he would love her more if she helped him, too.

He takes her to the madam and she goes to work. She stays there all week, and at the end of the week he comes and collects the money she's made. She gets a card, which she wears fastened inside her working dress (with a zipper down the front, easy to get out of, which is important since no man can spend more than fifteen minutes with her, according to house rules), and every time she takes a customer, she opens the door and holds out her card so it can be punched. When it looks like a lace curtain, she's made her quota.

At first she's little offended that the men don't even take off their shoes, but pretty soon she stops noticing those things. When the girls kid her about her "sister-in-law," she learns that they mean Dolores, and that other girls working for pimps have their "sisters-in-law," too. She makes about a hundred and fifty dollars a week, at two dollars a customer. She's glad when her period intervenes to keep her from working, and she can spend the time with her sweetheart.

She loves him. He's all she's got to love. The other girls are competition, and the madam is a slave driver. She does without everything—new clothes, underwear—to get the money faster. She lives for that week with him. Only, after a while, he tells her he knows a way she can work that week, too. When she cries, he tells her to forget about it. But she learns that her sister-in-law does it, so, since she can't lose him to her sister-in-law, she agrees to work the full month, and then he loves her again. When they're raided and she's thrown in jail, he gets her out. When she has to move on because they're tired of her in that house, he gets her in another. When she gets pregnant, he pays the doctor who takes care of it. She can't do without him.

But one day she rebels. She screams and yells and flies out at him because suddenly she's gotten a vision of how it really is and what's really happening to her. She threatens to turn him in to the cops for transporting her across the state line, and he quiets her down with a needle. And then for the first time since she was a kid (now she's seventeen), she's happy.

The time goes by and she isn't shocked any more at what she's doing. She almost forgets that there's any other way of living, and when she remembers, there's always the needle and the immediate happiness she can get from it—and from him. But now he says she's got to work harder. On the dope she costs him more, and he withholds the dose, won't give her that, won't give her anything, tells her she's an old bag he's ashamed of, that he can't sell her in the houses any more, and she can get out and walk the pavements for the money to pay for her stuff.

So she hits the small hotels, the beer gardens, the street corners, learns how to stand in the shadow so the man won't see her too clearly. After a while she can't kid herself any more, she knows she's sick. She has pains that shoot up from the groin so sharply that she staggers and people stare at her as if she were drunk. One day on her beat she walks up a dirty stairway to the doctor's office, afraid all the time that her sweetheart will find out she's spending the money on this, or that the doctor will say she has something that will keep her from working. And the doctor does say that. He tells her she must have an operation or she'll die, and she says it's got to be some other way—she can't take the time. Only there's no other way.

She's almost calm when she stumbles down the wooden stairs. Now she doesn't have to worry any more because tomorrow (and she knows when she's charged it'll be easy to go through with it) she's going to step into the East River. She likes the idea of death by water. There won't be any blood or noise or pain, and the river will feel cool and it will be dark and solemn as death should be. But first there is tonight, and maybe tonight he'll be nice to her.

my first days on junk

WILLIAM BURROUGHS

This section was written by a man who described himself as a drug addict, pusher, and thief.[1] Originally interested only in the possibility of reselling drugs, Burroughs tells about his first experiments with morphine, his further involvement as a pusher, and his resulting immersion in the drug subculture.

My first experience with junk was during the War, about 1944 or 1945. I had made the acquaintance of a man named Norton who was working in a shipyard at the time. Norton, whose real name was Morelli or something like that, had been discharged from the peacetime Army for forging a paycheck, and was classified 4-F for reasons of bad character. He looked like George Raft, but was taller. Norton was trying to improve his English and achieve a smooth, affable manner. Affability, however, did not come natural to him. In repose, his expression was sullen and mean, and you knew he always had that mean look when you turned your back.

Norton was a hard-working thief and he did not feel right unless he stole something every day from the shipyard where he worked. A tool, some canned goods, a pair of overalls, anything at all. One day he called me up and said he had stolen a Tommy gun. Could I find someone to buy it? I said, "Maybe. Bring it over."

The housing shortage was getting under way. I paid fifteen dollars a week for a dirty apartment that opened on to a companionway and never got any sunlight. The wallpaper was flaking off because the radiator leaked steam when there was any steam in it to to leak. I had the windows sealed shut with a caulking of newspapers against the cold. The place was full of roaches and occasionally I killed a bedbug.

I was sitting by the radiator, a little damp from the steam, when I heard Norton's knock. I opened the door, and there he was standing in the dark hall with a big parcel wrapped in brown paper under his arm. He smiled and said, "Hello."

Reprinted with permission of Ace Books, Inc. from Junkie *by William Burroughs (New York, 1953).*

[1]Similar accounts of addicts include Street (1953), Fiddle (1967), and Hirsch (1968).

I said, "Come in, Norton, and take off your coat."

He unwrapped the Tommy gun and we assembled it and snapped the firing pin.

I said I would find someone to buy it.

Norton said, "Oh, here's something else I picked up."

It was a flat yellow box with five one-half grain syrettes of morphine tartrate.

"This is just a sample," he said, indicating the morphine. "I've got fifteen of these boxes at home and I can get more if you get rid of these."

I said, "I'll see what I can do."

• • •

At that time I had never used any junk and it did not occur to me to try it. I began looking for someone to buy the two items and that is how I ran into Roy and Herman.

I knew a young hoodlum from upstate New York who was working as a short-order cook in Jarrow's, "cooling off," as he explained. I called him and said I had something to get rid of, and made an appointment to meet him in the Angle Bar on Eighth Avenue near 42nd Street.

This bar was a meeting place for 42nd Street hustlers, a peculiar breed of four-flushing, would-be criminals. They are always looking for a "setup man," someone to plan jobs and tell them exactly what to do. Since no "setup man" would have anything to do with people so obviously inept, unlucky, and unsuccessful, they go on looking, fabricating preposterous lies about their big scores, cooling off as dishwashers, soda jerks, waiters, occasionally rolling a drunk or a timid queer, looking, always looking, for the "setup man" with a big job who will say, "I've been watching you. You're the man I need for this setup. Now listen. . ."

Jack—through whom I met Roy and Herman—was not one of these lost sheep looking for the shepherd with a diamond ring and a gun in the shoulder holster and the hard, confident voice with overtones of connections, fixes, setups that would make a stickup sound easy and sure of success. Jack was very successful from time to time and would turn up in new clothes and even new cars. He was also an inveterate liar who seemed to lie more for himself than for any visible audience. He had a clean-cut, healthy country face, but there was something curiously diseased about him. He was subject to sudden fluctuations in weight, like a diabetic or a sufferer from liver trouble. These changes in weight were often accompanied by an uncontrollable fit of restlessness, so that he would disappear for some days.

The effect was uncanny. You would see him one time a fresh-faced kid. A week or so later he would turn up so thin, sallow and oldlooking, you would have to look twice to recognize him. His face was lined with suffering in which his eyes did not participate. It was a suffering of his cells alone.

He himself—the conscious ego that looked out of the glazed, alert-calm hoodlum eyes—would have nothing to do with this suffering of his rejected other self, a suffering of the nervous system, of flesh and viscera and cells.

He slid into the booth where I was sitting and ordered a shot of whisky. He tossed it off, put the glass down and looked at me with his head tilted a little to one side and back.

"What's this guy got?" he said.

"A Tommy gun and about thirty-five grains of morphine."

"The morphine I can get rid of right away, but the Tommy gun may take a little time."

Two detectives walked in and leaned on the bar talking to the bartender. Jack jerked his head in their direction. "The law. Let's take a walk."

I followed him out of the bar. He walked through the door sliding sideways. "I'm taking you to someone who will want the morphine," he said. "You want to forget this address."

We went down to the bottom level of the Independent Subway. Jack's voice, talking to his invisible audience, went on and on. He had a knack of throwing his voice directly into your consciousness. No external noise drowned him out. "Give me a thirty-eight every time. Just flick back the hammer and let her go. I'll drop anyone at five hundred feet. Don't care what you say. My brother has two .30 caliber machine guns stashed in Iowa."

We got off the subway and began to walk on snow-covered sidewalks between tenements.

"The guy owed me for a long time, see? I knew he had it but he wouldn't pay, so I waited for him when he finished work. I had a roll of nickels. No one can hang anything on you for carrying U.S. currency. Told me he was broke. I cracked his jaw and took my money off him. Two of his friends standing there, but they kept out of it. I'd've switched a blade on them."

We were walking up tenement stairs. The stairs were made of worn black metal. We stopped in front of a narrow, metal-covered door, and Jack gave an elaborate knock inclining his head to the floor like a safe-cracker. The door was opened by a large, flabby, middle-aged queer, with tattooing on his forearms and even on the backs of his hands.

"This is Joey," Jack said, and Joey said, "Hello there."

Jack pulled a five-dollar bill from his pocket and gave it to Joey. "Get us a quart of Schenley's, will you, Joey?"

Joey put on an overcoat and went out.

In many tenement apartments the front door opens directly into the kitchen. This was such an apartment and we were in the kitchen.

After Joey went out I noticed another man who was standing there looking at me. Waves of hostility and suspicion flowed out from his large brown eyes like some sort of television broadcast. The effect was almost like a physical impact. The man was small and very thin, his neck loose in the collar of his shirt. His complexion faded from brown to a mottled yellow, and pancake make-up had been heavily applied in an attempt to conceal a skin eruption. His mouth was drawn down at the corners in a grimace of petulant annoyance.

"Who's this?" he said. His name, I learned later, was Herman.

"Friend of mine. He's got some morphine he wants to get rid of."

Herman shrugged and turned out his hands. "I don't think I want to bother, really."

"Okay," Jack said, "we'll sell it to someone else. Come on, Bill."

We went into the front room. There was a small radio, a china Buddha with a votive candle in front of it, pieces of bric-a-brac. A man was lying on a studio couch. He sat up as we entered the room and smiled pleasantly showing discolored, brownish teeth. It was a Southern voice with the accent of east Texas.

Jack said, "Roy, this is a friend of mine. He has some morphine he wants to sell."

The man sat up straighter and swung his legs off the couch. His jaw fell slackly, giving his face a vacant look. The skin of his face was smooth and brown. The cheekbones were high and he looked Oriental. His ears stuck out at right angles from his asymmetrical skull. The eyes were brown and they had a peculiar brilliance, as though points of light were shining behind them. The light in the room glinted on the points of light in his eyes like an opal.

"How much do you have?" he asked me.

"Seventy-five one-half grain syrettes."

"The regular price is two dollars a grain," he said, "but syrettes go for a little less. People want tablets. Those syrettes have too much water and you have to squeeze the stuff out and cook it down." He paused and his face went blank. "I could go about one-fifty a grain," he said finally.

"I guess that will be okay," I said.

He asked how we could make contact and I gave him my phone number.

Joey came back with the whisky and we all had a drink. Herman stuck his head in from the kitchen and said to Jack, "Could I talk to you for a minute?"

I could hear them arguing about something. Then Jack came back and Herman stayed in the kitchen. We all had a few drinks and Jack began telling a story.

"My partner was going through the joint. The guy was sleeping, and I was standing over him with a three-foot length of pipe I found in the bathroom. The pipe had a faucet on the end of it, see? All of a sudden he comes up and jumps straight out of bed, running. I let him have it with the faucet end, and he goes on running right out into the other room, the blood spurting out of his head ten feet every time his heart beat." He made a pumping motion with his hand. "You could see the brain there and the blood coming out of it." Jack began to laugh uncontrollably. "My girl was waiting out in the car. She called me—ha-ha-ha!—she called me—ha-ha-ha!—a cold-blooded killer."

He laughed until his face was purple.

• • •

A few nights after meeting Roy and Herman, I used one of the syrettes, which was my first experience with junk. A syrette is like a toothpaste tube with a needle on the end. You push a pin down through the needle; the pin punctures the seal; and the syrette is ready to shoot.

Morphine hits the backs of the legs first, then the back of the neck, a spreading wave of relaxation slackening the muscles away from the bones so that you seem to float without outlines like lying in warm salt water. As this relaxing wave spread through my tissues, I experienced a strong feeling of fear. I had the feeling that some horrible image was just beyond the field of vision, moving, as I turned my head, so that I never quite saw it. I felt nauseous; I lay down and closed my eyes. A series of pictures passed, like watching a movie: A huge, neon-lighted coctail bar that got larger and larger until streets, traffic, and street repairs were included in it; a waitress carrying a skull on a tray; stars in the clear sky. The physical impact of the fear of death; the shutting off of breath; the stopping of blood.

I dozed off and woke up with a start of fear. Next morning I vomited and felt sick until noon.

Roy called that night.

"About what we were discussing the other night," he said. "I could go about four dollars per box and take five boxes now. Are you busy? I'll come over to your place. We'll come to some kind of agreement."

A few minutes later he knocked at the door. He had on a Glen plaid suit and a dark, coffee-colored shirt. We said hello. He looked around blankly and said, "If you don't mind, I'll take one of those now."

I opened the box. He took out a syrette and injected it into his leg. He pulled up his pants briskly and took out twenty dollars. I put five boxes on the kitchen table.

"I think I'll take them out of the boxes," he said. "Too bulky."

He began putting the syrettes in his coat pockets. "I don't think they'll perforate this way," he said. "Listen, I'll call you again in a day or so after I get rid of these and have some more money." He was adjusting his hat over his asymmetrical skull. "I'll see you."

Next day he was back. He shot another syrette and pulled out forty dollars. I laid out ten boxes and kept two.

"These are for me," I said.

He looked at me, surprised. "You use it?"

"Now and then."

"It's bad stuff," he said, shaking his head. "The worst thing that can happen to a man. We all think we can control it at first. Sometimes we don't want to control it." He laughed. "I'll take all you can get at this price."

Next day he was back. He asked if I didn't want to change my mind about selling the two boxes. I said no. He bought two syrettes for a dollar each, shot them both, and left. He said he had signed on for a two-month trip.

• • •

During the next month I used up the eight syrettes I had not sold. The fear I had experienced after using the first syrette was not noticeable after the third; but still, from time to time, after taking a shot I would wake up with a start of fear. After six weeks or so I gave Roy a ring, not expecting him to be back from his trip, but then I heard his voice on the phone.

I said, "Say, do you have any to sell? Of the material I sold you before?"

There was a pause.

"Ye-es," he said, "I can let you have six, but the price will have to be three dollars per. You understand I don't have many."

"Okay," I said. "You know the way. Bring it on over."

It was twelve one-half grain tablets in a thin glass tube. I paid him eighteen dollars and he apologized again for the retail rate.

Next day he bought two grains back.

"It's mighty hard to get now at any price," he said, looking for a vein in his leg. He finally hit a vein and shot the liquid in with an air bubble. "If air bubbles could kill you, there wouldn't be a junkie alive."

Later that day Roy pointed out to me a drugstore where they sold needles without any questions—very few drugstores will sell them without a prescription. He showed me how to make a collar out of paper to fit the needle to an eyedropper. An eyedropper is easier to use than a regular hypo, especially for giving yourself vein shots.

Several days later Roy sent me to see a doctor with a story about kidney stones, to hit him for a morphine prescription. The doctor's wife slammed the door in my face, but Roy finally got past her and made the doctor for a ten-grain script.

The doctor's office was in junk territory on 102nd, off Broadway. He was a doddering old man and could not resist the junkies who filled his office and were, in fact, his only patients. It seemed to give him a feeling of importance to look out and see an office full of people. I guess he had reached a point where he could change the appearance of things to suit his needs and when he looked out there he saw a distinguished and diversified clientele, probably well-dressed in 1910 style, instead of a bunch of ratty-looking junkies come to hit him for a morphine script.

Roy shipped out at two- or three-week intervals. His trips were Army Transport and generally short. When he was in town we generally split a few scripts. The old croaker on 102nd finally lost his mind altogether and no drugstore would fill his scripts, but Roy located an Italian doctor out in the Bronx who would write.

I was taking a shot from time to time, but I was a long way from having a habit. At this time I moved into an apartment on the Lower East Side. It was a tenement apartment with the front door opening into the kitchen.

• • •

I began dropping into the Angle Bar every night and saw quite a bit of Herman. I managed to overcome his original bad impression of me, and soon I was buying his drinks and meals, and he was hitting me for "smash" (change) at regular intervals. Herman did not have a habit at this time. In fact, he seldom got a habit unless someone else paid for it. But he was always high on something—weed, benzedrine, or knocked out of his mind on "goof balls." He showed up at the Angle every night with a big slob called Whitey. There were four Whiteys in the Angle set, which made for confusion. This Whitey combined the sensitivity of a neurotic with a psychopath's readiness for violence. He was convinced that nobody liked him, a fact that seemed to cause him a great deal of worry.

One Tuesday night Roy and I were standing at the end of the Angle bar. Subway Mike was there, and Frankie Dolan. Dolan was an Irish boy with a cast in one eye. He specialized in crummy scores, beating up defenseless drunks, and holding out on his confederates. "I got no honor," he would say. "I'm a rat." And he would giggle.

Subway Mike had a large, pale face and long teeth. He looked like some specialized kind of underground animal that preys on the animals of the surface. He was a skillful lush-worker, but he had no front. Any cop would do a double-take at the sight of him, and he was well known to the subway squad. So Mike spent at least half of his time on the Island doing "five-twenty-nine" for jostling.

This night Herman was knocked out on "nembies" and his head kept falling down onto the bar. Whitey was stomping up and down the length of the bar trying to promote some free drinks. The boys at the bar sat rigid and tense, clutching their drinks, quickly pocketing their change. I heard Whitey say to the bartender, "Keep this for me, will you?" and he passed his large clasp knife across the bar. The boys sat there silent and gloomy under the fluorescent lights. They were all afraid of Whitey, all except Roy. Roy sipped his beer grimly. His eyes shone with their peculiar phosphorescence. His long asymmetrical body was draped against the bar. He didn't look at Whitey, but at the opposite wall where the booths were located. Once he said to me, "He's no more drunk than I am. He's just thirsty."

Whitey was standing in the middle of the bar, his fists doubled up, tears streaming down his face. "I'm no good," he said. "I'm no good. Can't anyone understand I don't know what I'm doing?"

The boys tried to get as far away from him as possible without attracting his attention.

Subway Slim, Mike's occasional partner, came in and ordered a beer. He was tall and bony, and his ugly face had a curiously inanimate look, as if made out of wood. Whitey slapped him on the back and I heard Slim say, "For Christ's sake, Whitey." There was more interchange I didn't hear. Somewhere along the line Whitey must have got his knife back from the bartender. He got behind Slim and suddenly pushed his hand against Slim's back. Slim fell forward against the bar, groaning. I saw Whitey walk to the front of the bar and look around. He closed his knife and slipped it into his pocket.

Roy said, "Let's go."

Whitey had disappeared and the bar was empty except for Mike who was holding Slim up on one side. Frankie Dolan was on the other.

I heard next day from Frankie that Slim was okay. "The croaker at the hospital said the knife just missed a kidney."

Roy said, "The big slob. I can see a real muscle man, but a guy like that going around picking up dimes and quarters off the bar. I was ready for him. I was going to kick him in the belly first, then get one of those quart beer bottles from the case on the floor and break it over his sconce. With a big villain like that you've got to use strategy."

We were all barred from the Angle, which shortly afterwards changed its name to the Kent Grill.

One night I went to the Henry Street address to look up Jack. A tall, red-haired girl met me at the door.

"I'm Mary," she said. "Come in."

It seemed that Jack was in Washington on business.

"Come on into the front room," she said, pushing aside a red corduroy curtain. "I talk to landlords and bill collectors in the kitchen. We *live* in here."

I looked around. The bric-a-brac had gone. The place looked like a chop suey joint. There were black and red lacquered tables scattered around, black curtains covered the window. A colored wheel had been painted on the ceiling with little squares and triangles of different colors giving a mosaic effect.

"Jack did that," Mary said, pointing to the wheel. "You should have seen him. He stretched a board between two ladders and lay down on it. Paint kept dripping into his face. He gets a kick out of doing things like that. We get some frantic kicks out of that wheel when we're high. We lay on our backs and dig the wheel and pretty soon it begins to spin. The longer you watch it, the faster it spins."

This wheel had the nightmarish vulgarity of Aztec mosaics, the bloody, vulgar nightmare, the heart throbbing in the morning sun, the garish pinks and blues of souvenir ashtrays, postcards and calendars. The walls were painted black and there was a Chinese character in red lacquer on one wall.

"We don't know what it means," she said.

"Shirts thirty-one cents," I suggested.

She turned on me her blank, cold smile. She began talking about Jack. "I'm queer for Jack," she said. "He works at being a thief just like any job. Used to come home nights and hand me his gun. 'Stash that!' He likes to work around the house, painting and making furniture."

As she talked she moved around the room, throwing herself from one chair to another, crossing and uncrossing her legs, adjusting her slip, so as to give me a view of her anatomy in installments.

She went on to tell me how her days were numbered by a rare disease. "Only twenty-six cases on record. In a few years I won't be able to get around at all. You see, my system can't absorb calcium and the bones are slowly dissolving. My legs will have to be amputated eventually, then the arms."

There was something boneless about her, like a deep sea creature. Her eyes were cold fish-eyes that looked at you through a viscous medium she carried about with her. I could see those eyes in a shapeless, protoplasmic mass undulating over the dark sea floor.

"Benzedrine is a good kick," she said. "Three strips of the paper or about ten tablets. Or take two strips of benny and two goof balls. They get down there and have a fight. It's a good drive."

Three young hoodlums from Brooklyn drifted in, wooden-faced, hands-in-pockets, stylized as a ballet. They were looking for Jack. He had given them a short count in some deal. At least, that was the general idea. They conveyed their meaning less by words than by significant jerks of the head and by stalking around the apartment and leaning against the walls. At length, one of them walked to the door and jerked his head. They filed out.

"Would you like to get high?" Mary asked. "There may be a roach around here somewhere." She began rummaging around in drawers and ashtrays. "No, I guess not. Why don't we go uptown? I know several good connections we can probably catch about now."

A young man lurched in with some object wrapped in brown paper under one arm. "Ditch this on your way out," he said, putting it down on the table. He staggered into the bedroom on the other side of the kitchen. When we got outside I let the wrapping paper fall loose revealing the coin box of a pay toilet crudely jimmied open.

In Times Square we got into a taxi and began cruising up and down the side streets, Mary giving directions. Every now and then she would yell "Stop!" and jump out, her red hair streaming, and I would see her overhaul some character and start talking. "The connection was here about ten minutes ago. This character's holding, but he won't turn loose of any." Later: "The regular connection is gone for the night. He lives in the Bronx. But just stop here for a minute. I may find someone in Rich's." Finally: "No one seems to be anywhere. It's a bit late to score. Let's buy some benny tubes and go over to Denny's. They have some gone numbers on the box. We can order coffee and get high on benny."

Denny's was a spot near 52nd and Sixth where musicians came for fried chicken and coffee after one P. M. We sat down in a booth and ordered coffee. Mary cracked a benzedrine tube expertly, extracting the folded paper, and handed me three strips. "Roll it up into a pill and wash it down with coffee."

The paper gave off a sickening odor of menthol. Several people sitting nearby sniffed and smiled. I nearly gagged on the wad of paper, but finally got it down. Mary selected some gone numbers and beat on the table with the expression of a masturbating idiot.

I began talking very fast. My mouth was dry and my spit came out in round white balls—spitting cotton, it's called. We were walking around Times Square. Mary wanted to locate someone with a "piccolo" (victrola). I was full of expansive, benevolent feelings, and suddenly wanted to call on people I hadn't seen in months or even years, people I did not like and who did not like me. We made a number of unsuccessful attempts to locate the ideal piccolo-owning host. Somewhere along the line we picked up Peter and finally decided to go back to the Henry Street apartment where there was at least a radio.

Peter and Mary and I spent the next thirty hours in the apartment. From time to time we would make coffee and swallow more benzedrine. Mary was describing the techniques she used to get money from the "Johns" who formed her principal source of revenue.

"Always build a John up. If he has any sort of body at all, say, 'Oh, don't ever hurt me.' A John is different from a sucker. When you're with a sucker you're on the alert all the time. You give him nothing. A sucker is just to be taken. But a John is different. You give him what he pays for. When you're with him you enjoy yourself and you want him to enjoy himself, too.

"If you want to really bring a man down, light a cigarette in the middle of intercourse. Of course, I really don't like men at all sexually. What I really dig is chicks. I get a kick out of taking a proud chick and breaking her spirit, making her see she is just an animal. A chick is never beautiful after she's been broken. Say, this is sort of a fireside kick," she said, pointing to the radio which was the only light in the room. Her face contorted into an expression of monkey-like rage as she talked about men who accosted her on the street. "Sonofabitch!" she snarled. "They can tell when a woman isn't looking for a pickup. I used to cruise around with brass knuckles on under my gloves just waiting for one of those peasants to crack at me."

• • •

One day Herman told me about a kilo of first-class New Orleans' weed I could pick up for seventy dollars. Pushing weed looks good on paper, like fur farming or raising frogs. At seventy-five cents a stick, seventy sticks to the ounce, it sounded like money. I was convinced, and bought the weed.

Herman and I formed a partnership to push the weed. He located a Lesbian named Marian who lived in the Village and said she was a poetess. We kept the weed in Marian's apartment, turned her on for all she could use, and gave her a 50 per cent commission on the sales. She knew a lot of teaheads. Another Lesbian moved in with her, and every time I went to Marian's apartment, there was this huge red-haired Lizzie watching me with her cold fish-eyes full of stupid hate.

One day, the red-haired Lizzie opened the door and stood there, her face dead white and puffy with nembutal sleep. She shoved the package of weed at me. "Take this and get out," she said. She looked at us through heavily lidded eyes. "You bastards!"

I said, "Tell Marian thanks for everything."

She slammed the door. The noise evidently woke her up. She opened the door again and began screaming with hysterical rage. We could still hear her out on the street.

Herman contacted other teaheads. They all gave us static.

In practice, pushing weed is a headache. To begin with, weed is bulky. You need a full suitcase to realize any money. If the cops start kicking your door in, it's like being with a bale of alfalfa.

Teaheads are not like junkies. A junkie hands you the money, takes his junk and cuts. But teaheads don't do things that way. They expect the peddler to light them up and sit around talking for half an hour to sell two dollars' worth of weed. If you come right to the point, they say you are a "bring down." In fact, a peddler should not come right out and say he is a peddler. No, he just scores for a few good "cats" and "chicks" because he is viperish. Everyone knows that he himself is the connection, but it is bad form to say so. God knows why. To me, teaheads are unfathomable.

There are a lot of trade secrets in the tea business, and teaheads guard these supposed secrets with imbecilic slyness. For example, tea must be cured, or it is green and rasps the throat. But ask a teahead how to cure weed and he will give you a sly, stupid look and come on with some doubletalk. Perhaps weed does affect the brain with constant use, or maybe teaheads are naturally silly.

The tea I had was green so I put it in a double boiler and set the boiler in the oven until the tea got the greenish-brown look it should have. This is the secret of curing tea, or at least one way to do it.

Teaheads are gregarious, they are sensitive, and they are paranoiac. If you get to be known as a "drag" or a "bring down," you can't do business with them. I soon found out I couldn't get along with these characters and I was glad to find someone to take the tea off my hands at cost. I decided right then I would never push any more tea.

some comments on being a criminal

ROBERT ALLERTON

In the following interview, a confirmed criminal (Robert Allerton) explains the philosophy behind his way of life. The life of a "professional" criminal includes a commitment to crime similar to that which ordinary citizens have toward their occupations. In the case of the professional criminal, one of the occupational hazards to be faced is the possibility of a prison sentence if caught. Allerton puts it: "I'm willing to gamble away a third of my life in prison so long as I can live the way I want for the other two-thirds." This interview provides a revealing insight into the mind of the professional criminal—how he became a criminal, and why he remains one.[1]

My first question is this: If you were to describe yourself in one word, would the description invariably be "A criminal"?

Yes, definitely. That's what I am, I never think of myself in any other way.

And have you any intention of changing, of going straight or reforming?

Reprinted with permission of Hutchinson and Company (Publishers) Ltd. from The Courage of His Convictions *by Tony Parker and Robert Allerton (London, 1962), pp. 85–92, 105–10.*

[1]Other autobiographies of professional criminals include Benton (1936), Booth (1929), Genêt (1954), Hapgood (1904), and MacKenzie (1955).

None whatsoever. There's one thing, though, I'd like to make clear right at the start—and that is, I don't want to try and pass myself off as a "master criminal" or anything like that. I'm not. I've had successes and failures in life like everyone else, and I'm nothing out of the ordinary as far as criminals go. I don't consider myself cleverer than most, or even cleverer than the police, for example. Sometimes I have been, and quite obviously sometimes not. On the whole I'd say I was just the ordinary run of professional criminal, similar to—well, let's say to a bank clerk from Surbiton in the straight world. But having said that, still definitely "a criminal," yes.

And would you say your earnings were comparable with those of a Surbiton bank clerk?

I don't know what he'd earn—quite honestly, I don't know how much I've made in my time either, because I haven't kept accounts to show to the income tax. My earnings have usually been large sums of money spread over short periods of time—both in the getting and the spending. I've gone into a club, a gambling place, not once but many times, with two or three hundred quid in my pocket—and come out with exactly nothing. One time a girl took sixty quid out of my pocket and I never even noticed it'd gone until somebody told me months afterward she'd had it. And at other times I've had only about fourpence in the world. It's so irregular, you see, it's difficult to say just how much I have had from crime. I should say that if I worked it all out with pencil and paper, relying on my memory—which is faulty at the best of times—and then dividing the whole lot by ten or twelve for the number of years I've been at it seriously. . . well, it'd come out at about £2,000 or £2,500 a year, perhaps a little bit more. We'd better change that first idea to a bank *manager* from Surbiton, I suppose, hadn't we? Still, the point's the same: that sort of figure, which is as near as I can get on a calculation, is not a tremendously rich living from crime or anything else, is it? Especially when you take into account how quick I spend it when I've got it. All the same, I don't know of a straight job I could do that'd bring me in that yearly income.

Is there any particular form of crime, or criminal activity, which you wouldn't commit?

A year or two ago I used to think I'd never go in for drug trafficking, but now I'm not so sure about that. I've never actually done it yet, but as I get older I seem to be losing my inhibitions, I don't feel as strongly about it as I used to. There's only one thing I still feel I could never do, and that's poncing. To me it's the worst thing of the lot, I'd never stoop to it—or at least I hope I wouldn't. Maybe I'm old-fashioned, or sentimental about women or something—but I just can't stomach the idea of poncing at all. I've nothing but contempt, real, deep contempt, for ponces.

There's no other limit you'd set yourself?

No. I'll go as far as necessary, whatever it is.

What does that mean, exactly?

What it says. If it was ever necessary to kill somebody, well, I'd go up to and including that. I'd kill somebody in a fit of temper, I'm quite capable of that—or if they were trying to stop me getting something I'd really made up my mind to have. Or if they were holding me down, and there was so much at stake that I'd just got to get away. But I think most people have it in them to do murder at some time in their lives, under certain circumstances.

The thing which I find most difficult to understand about you is that you're apparently quite undeterred by your repeated prison sentences. You've now reached the stage, with your record, that when you're caught next time it's more than likely you'll get about eight years' preventive detention. I don't understand how you can be prepared to face that.

I'm not prepared. This is the thing which people like you can never grasp. I'm no more "prepared" to do eight years' P.D. than you're prepared to knock somebody down in your car tomorrow. I don't think too much about the one more than you do about the other. It's an ever-present risk but one doesn't dwell on it—do you see what I mean?

I've always got this thing in my mind, and so have most other criminals like me—"it won't be this time that I'll get caught." Prison only becomes the dominant thought when you're actually back in the prison cell—or no, to be realistic, perhaps a bit before that, when you're actually in the arms of a police officer, although even then you've still got some hope you might not end up in the nick.

Occasionally I get the vague idea that if men who'd been in prison were to go back and contemplate the prison wall from outside, just before they set out on a job, they mightn't do it. But it wouldn't work. You see, three days after you've come out of prison, however long the sentence, you've forgotten all about it. You've forgotten the caged-up feeling, the monotonous food, the smell of latrines, the piggishness of the screws, the soul-destroying torture of visiting-boxes with your friends having to shout a conversation with you through plate-glass—it's all gone, soon after you come out, and you do everything you can to make it go, too.

Then one day one of your mates comes along and says: "I've heard of a peter wants blowing, it's got two grand in it, you want to come in on it and make one?" So you knock down the amount by 50% because people exaggerate, and you think: "Well, at least I'll have a look at it, there's no harm in that."

So he takes you along to look at the set-up, you weigh it up and work it out, and you think: "Well, this is an absolute doddle, it can't miss; yes, of course I'll do it." So you say to your mate: "O.K., sure I'll come in, when do we start?" It doesn't even occur to you that there's even a chance you might get nicked, it all looks so easy. And where's your "prepared" gone then?

I don't want to do eight years, no—but if I have to I have to, and that's all there is to it. If you're a criminal, what's the alternative to the risk of going to prison? Coal-miners don't spend their time worrying about the risk they might get killed by a fall at the coal-face either. Prison's an occupational risk, that's all—and one I'm quite prepared to take. I'll willingly gamble away a third of my life in prison, so long as I can live the way I want for the other two-thirds. After all, it's my life, and that's how I feel about it. The alternative—the prospect of vegetating the rest of my life away in a steady job, catching the 8.13 to work in the morning, and the 5.50 back again at night, all for ten or fifteen quid a week—now that really does terrify me, far more than the thought of a few years in the nick.

You don't think, then, that there's anything wrong in not working for your living?

But I do work for my living. Most crime—unless it's the senseless, petty-thieving sort—is quite hard work, you know. Planning a job, working out all the details of the best way to do it—and then carrying it out, under a lot of nervous strain and tension—and having to run round afterwards, if it's goods, fencing the stuff, getting a good price for it, delivering it to the fence, and so on—all this needs a lot of thinking and effort and concentration. It certainly is "work," don't kid yourself about that.

But anyway this whole point's not all that simple. A lot of other people don't "work" for their living, in the way you mean—but nobody goes on at them like they do at criminals. Quite a large proportion of the "upper classes," for instance. You can see them any day round Piccadilly, Vigo Street, Savile Row—nattily dressed half-wits who've never done a stroke of work in their lives, popping in and out of Fortnum's or Scott's, spending all their time trying to get rid of the money their fathers and grandfathers and great-grandfathers left them. And usually it's that sort who get fiercest about people like me, saying we ought to be caned and whipped and flogged because we never do an honest day's work.

I can steal from people like that without the faintest compunction at all, in fact I'm delighted to do it. I remember once screwing the town house of the Duke of... well, I'd better not say who, because I didn't get caught for it. The inside of the house was the most beautiful place I've ever been in in my life—gorgeous curtains and furnishings, antique furniture, silver bowls and vases all over the place, exquisite miniatures on the walls—it was a fabulous place. My only regret was I hadn't got a furniture van so I could strip it from top to bottom. His Lordship I suppose was up in

Scotland shooting wild birds, or some other civilized hobby, and his house was just standing unused until he chose to come back and live in it again.

I remember after I'd come out I passed an old man in rags, standing on the street-corner scraping at a violin to try and earn himself a few coppers, and I thought: "You mug, why don't you go in there and at least get yourself a good sleep in one of his Lordship's unused beds for a night."

All the things that were in that house, all those beautiful possessions, the duke had got for himself without the faintest effort of any kind. Most of them had been handed down to him, and all he'd ever had to do to get the others was write out a cheque—and he probably didn't even do that for himself but had a flunkey to do it. Never in his whole life had he known what it was like to be short of anything. Well, I had, and I don't think it was wrong to steal enough from him to subsidize me for a bit.

And those people, when they have something nicked, they've got it all insured anyway, so they don't suffer. Sometimes they advertise for its return—you know, "Sentimental value" and all that. I'm sure I'd feel sentimental, too, about losing something worth a few hundred quid, only I'd be a bit more honest about it.

And the stuff I pinched from that particular house I appreciated, I did really. In fact, if it hadn't been too dangerous, I'd gladly have kept a lot of it to have around my own place, because it was so beautiful. But I never felt bad about taking it—why should I? I felt terrific. He'd got no cause for complaint, because it was taken, after all, by someone who could really appreciate its artistic merit, not one of those insensitive thugs who couldn't differentiate between Royal Worcester and a Woolworth's chamber-pot.

Oh, yes, and one more thing. A couple of years later I read in the papers how this particular duke was involved in a real sordid court case. The details that came out about his private life then made me wonder if he ever did really appreciate those lovely possessions he had. From what they dragged out he sounded a right stinking bastard. But if I'd been caught that time I screwed his place he'd have been all up in arms about me—and the Law would have taken his side too. He was respectable and I wasn't, that's the way it would have been put.

But you don't confine yourself, like Robin Hood, entirely to stealing from the aristocracy, Bob, so let's consider another point as well. How do you justify wages-snatches for instance?

Could we get one thing clear first? I'm not trying to "justify" anything. There's always two points of view on any subject, a wrong one and an even more wrong one. There's so much injustice in the world that we could start swapping one for another all the way along, like me turning round on you and saying: "You justify some of your respectable society to me—like a managing director of a company taking five thousand a year for himself, from the efforts of people working for him whom he pays five hundred a year"—and so on.

So I'm not justifying anything; I'm just telling you what my point of view on a thing is when you ask me, and my point of view's probably as illogical and wrong as anyone else's is likely to be. I'm not saying: "This is a hundred per cent right and everything else is wrong." I'll put my point of view, but you're entitled to disagree with it and so is anyone else—in fact I wouldn't expect you to do anything other than disagree, because you belong in so-called "straight" society.

Yes, O.K., Bob, but let's just stick to the point, shall we, and save the fireworks. What about wages-snatches?

Sure—but you can't blame me if you leave yourself wide open, can you? All right, wages-snatches. I'll try and take it from the beginning.

If can see a chance of earning myself—or making myself, if you prefer it—a few thousand quid all at one go, naturally I'll do it. It's only what people, millions of them, are trying to do on the football pools every week. You could say: "Yes, but they're trying to do it honestly"—to which I'd reply: "It depends on your definition of honest, because while they're trying to get themselves several thousand of someone else's money for the outlay of a few shillings and no work, I'm trying to get it by some careful thinking and plotting, some bloody hard effort, and the risk of my own liberty into the bargain."

So who's doing more to earn the money—me or the pools "investors," as they're called? (By the promoters, of course. It's the old con-man's trick of persuading a mug you're going to give him something for nothing, playing on people's natural avarice and greed.) The "investors" trust to luck to bring them a lot of money—well, I back on my own efforts.

But there's a difference. Pools winnings come out of what the "investors" hand over voluntarily, so those who lose have no complaint. Workers don't hand over their wages voluntarily for you to steal.

I'll say they don't. But look, don't try to break my heart. Who loses on a wages-snatch—the workers? Of course not. It's the company—and they can usually stand it. It's the same with banks—if I have a few thousand from a bank, theoretically it's their customers' money I've taken. But you never hear of a bank apportioning the losses round their customers, do you? "We're so sorry, Major Bloodworthy, somebody blew our safe last night and too ten thousand quid—and it was your ten thousand that was in there!" Mind you, I'm not saying they shouldn't; to me it's quite an attractive idea.

No, let's face it, most of these people are insured against robberies, so it's only the insurance companies who pay up.

• • •

Bob, to get back to you yourself now. . . was there ever a point in your life when you made a conscious decision to be a criminal?

No, I can't think of one. I remember when I was doing my first lot of bird, I was quite determined I wasn't even going to try and go straight when I got out. I made up my mind that as soon as I was out I was going to get on with the business of having more money for myself, whatever way I had to use to get it. And going out to work for ten or twelve pounds a week wasn't one of the methods I even thought about. But there wasn't any one particular day when I got up in the morning and said: "I'm going to be a criminal," like the kid who says: "I know what I'll do, I'll be a fireman"—nothing like that. I more or less got accustomed to the idea gradually as I grew up, as I've tried to explain in the life-story part.

What really made you a criminal? Do you know?

This is the point, isn't it, where I should lay back in my chair, put my feet up on the mantelpiece, and say: "I never had a chance!" But it just wouldn't be true. I don't say I've never had a chance, because I have, I've had plenty of chances if I'd wanted to take them. But I never did.

What made me a criminal?. . . I could reel off a whole lot of reasons, but they'd all only be part of the real answer. I'm always afraid of saying circumstances made me what I am, because I don't think they did entirely at all. Seeing my father, a straight man, getting only poverty all through his life for being straight. . . living in an environment where nearly everyone I knew was dishonest, where stealing was a necessity at some times, an adventure at others, but was always acceptable whatever the reason. . . wanting to impress other kids, getting a reputation for being a tearaway. . . seeing the terrifying dreariness of the lives of other people who were "straight". . . not being able to face working for a living because I hated the idea of work. . . .

Those were the circumstances, but they were only part of the answer. I still think I'd have been a criminal, whatever they'd been. For one thing, there's this tremendous hatred of authority which I've got, this compulsion, almost, to defy it. I was born with that, I'm sure. Or I could say it was because I'd always had a desire for adventure, for living dangerously. That was true when I was young, but it isn't true now, and I still go on. Now crime's just business, that's all.

There's so many facets, you see, aren't there, to what makes anyone what they are? I don't think there's one reason for me being a criminal, there's many, many of them. Some I know about, some I don't—but they all contribute to a greater or lesser degree. I might say: "If only I'd had this, that, or the other," or: "If this had happened, or that hadn't. . . ." My mother dying, for instance, when I was young: that's one example.... If I'd been thrashed less, or thrashed more...I just don't know. I've never found one answer that convinced me, myself, in my own mind—you know, nothing I could think of and suddenly say: "Yes, that's why I became a criminal." I've thought about it a lot for many years and if I did know the answer, the answer you want, and could present it to you like that on a plate—well, I'd be a remarkable man. It seems to me that I've always been a criminal and always will be.

But, you know, you're asking me a question that far better people than me can't even answer. Some of them get paid for sitting in Chairs at universities and trying to work out the answer to this one, don't they? People like Grunhut and Mannheim and Radzinowitz. "What makes criminals?" —they're working on it all the time, getting paid thousands a year to try and come up with the answer.

I've read a lot of books by those people, articles in the *Journal of Criminology* and so on—after all, crime's the most interesting subject in the world to me, naturally—and none of them know, do they, however hard they try? And they're good people, those people, terrific brains—some of the work they do is first rate. I'm not knocking them, I wish there were more like them, working things out, trying to get other people to think deeply about these things instead of screaming all the time for more beatings, more imprisonment, more punishment. I think that fundamentally they're good and on the right lines. Dr. T. P. Morris, he's another one—I've read things of his, heard him on the radio, he knows his stuff, he talks sense.

And, well, sometimes some of them get near some of the answers. But they don't know *the* answer, any more than Lombroso or Alexander Paterson did. They can tell you about conditions, environment, heredity, reactions to treatment of one kind or another—but they still can't tell you why under one set of circumstances some people go bent and others go straight.

Don't get me wrong, I'm all for them hammering away at it. But take any one of them, take—well, let's take Radzinowitz, for instance, he's about the top man now, I suppose, isn't he? I can't help feeling this, that all the time he's working in the dark, he's guessing. Because he's not a criminal himself, and so he can't know.

Hugh Klare, he's another one. That Howard League of his, I think it's an organization working on the right lines: the pursuit of knowledge, that's always a good thing, a fine thing, there are some marvellous people in the Howard League. Even old man Butler, setting up his what-does-he-call-them, his research units on every little aspect of the problem—he's trying too. But there's one thing I think they're all missing, all of them—how do they ever think they're really going to find out what makes criminals tick if they go on looking on criminals just as specimens to experiment on?

You know, you can learn a lot about butterflies by catching one, sticking it on a board with a pin, and looking at it through a microscope. You can study its wing-structure, its anatomy, how it breeds, how it flies, its whole mechanism—but you're still nowhere near knowing what it's like to *be* a butterfly, are you?

Why don't these people sometimes set aside altogether the rights and wrongs of the matter, and get a few criminals to work in with them on the thing of what it's actually like to be one? Those who've given up crime now and reformed, they're no good, they're dead butterflies, their mental processes have atrophied—they've got too far away from it, mentally I mean. But an ordinary criminal, a working criminal, it's my guess if they could only dig down deep enough to find it in him—he'd know just by instinct some of the answers the butterfly inspectors are missing.

To return to yourself now, this feeling you have about being a criminal fundamentally—would it be right to say that in your case not only do you feel this, but, on an even deeper level perhaps, you feel you don't belong in "respectable" society at all?

Yes, I think that's true. I do feel that now, very strongly. I don't want to mix at all with people who have what might be called "suburban pretensions" or respectability. They don't interest me: in fact, more than that, I don't like them, I actively dislike them. To me it's much more interesting to be with a group of criminals than a group of suburbanites, because there's nothing about those people at all. I know what they're like, once you've met one you've met them all, you can foretell everything about them right down to the smallest detail. How their homes are furnished—all in the same way: the telly in the corner, lace curtains, a plaster dog in the window, a wooden clock on the mantelpiece, photographs in chromium frames on the sideboard, two armchairs in uncut moquette, four dining-chairs, one of those hideous, glossy cocktail cabinets if they really want to impress...they're so stereotyped they're dead. And their talk...the man, if you can get down to it, he always "fancies" the woman next door but of course he never gets round to actually doing her. It's frightening, it's chronic. At least criminals have something interesting to talk about, their talk is deeper and more real, the life they lead goes at a much faster tempo and has got some excitement in it.

I think, if I'm going to try and be strictly honest about this whole thing, that I ought to say, too, that now and again, on some points, I don't feel I belong all that completely in my own strata of society either. I'm not trying to flatter myself and say I'm a cut above them or anything like that—but I do find sometimes, over certain things, that I don't belong.

I can remember before now on more than one occasion, for instance, going into a public library near where I was living, and looking over my shoulder a couple of times before I actually went in, just to make sure no one who knew me was standing about and seeing me do it. You get this in all walks of life, of course, but I must admit a lot of the people I know aren't exactly what you might call "with it" on some things. I mean, I know blokes who if you mentioned Leonardo da Vinci to them, their first question would be: "Whose mob's he with?" and if you were to tell them he was a painter, they'd say: "Well, how much does he make?"

But I think perhaps this isn't all that important anyway, because certain types don't go much on this art business, and I don't look down my nose at them for that. If I had to choose between an art-addict and a sound, reliable screwsman for company, of course I'd choose the screwmans every time. It's the same with a woman—so long as she's reliable, and preferably a good screw into the bargain, that's far more important than she should be clever or things like that.

theft as a way of life

"CHIC" CONWAY

Here, sociologist Edwin H. Sutherland transcribes the description by a professional thief ("Chic" Conway) of the characteristics of his profession which distinguish him from other criminals. These include technical skill, status, consensus, and organization. Professional thieves share certain features—abilities and skills—with other groups such as physicians and lawyers. However, many of these same characteristics set the professional thief apart from other criminals. Conway relates the background techniques and behavior patterns of his way of life.[1]

The professional thief is one who steals professionally. This means, first, that he makes a regular business of stealing. He devotes his entire working time and energy to larceny and may steal three hundred and sixty-five days a year. Second, every act is carefully planned. The selection of spots, securing of the property, making a get away, disposing of the stolen property, and fixing cases in which he may be pinched (arrested)

Reprinted from The Professional Thief by a Professional Thief *by Edwin H. Sutherland by permission of The University of Chicago Press. Copyright © 1937 by the University of Chicago Press. (Footnotes omitted.)*

[1]Similar accounts can be found in Hapgood (1904), Hamilton (1902), Martin (1952), and MacKenzie (1955).

are all carefully planned. Third, the professional thief has technical skills and methods which are different from those of other professional criminals. Manual skill is important in some of the rackets, but the most important thing in all the rackets is the ability to manipulate people. The thief depends on his approach, front, wits, and in many instances his talking ability. The professional burglar or stickup man (robber with a gun), on the other hand, uses violence or threat of violence even though he may on occasion use soothing language in order to quiet people. Fourth, the professional thief is generally migratory and may work in all the cities of the United States. He generally uses a particular city as headquarters, and when two professional thieves first meet, the question is always asked: "Where are you out of?"

In addition to these four characteristics, professional thieves have many things in common. They have acquaintances, congeniality, sympathy, understandings, agreements, rules, codes of behavior, and language in common.

The professional thief has nothing in common with the amateur thief or with the amateur in any other racket. The professional thief will be in sympathy with the amateur's attempt to steal something but will not be interested in him, for they have no acquaintances or ideas of stealing in common. He would talk with an amateur whom he might happen to meet in the can (police lockup) no longer than necessary to find out that he was an amateur. He might offer advice on how to beat the rap (charge), but this would be very rare, for, in addition to the fact that the amateur means nothing in his life, there is danger in telling the intricacies of the fix to someone who may be loquacious.

The professional thief has nothing in common with those who commit sex crimes or other emotional crimes and would not even be courteous to them if he should chance to meet them in the can.

Sympathy and congeniality with professional burglars and stickups is nearly as close as between thieves in one racket. They are all thieves, and the fact that one has a different racket does not alter this feeling. To professional burglars whom he knows on the street he will tender ideas and spots, not as a 10 percent man (on a commission basis) but purely out of a spirit of congeniality. He will render assistance to a professional burglar in fixing cases, securing bonds, or escaping from a jailhouse as readily as to thieves in his own rackets.

• • •

Codes of ethics are much more binding among thieves than among legitimate commercial firms. Should an outfit have a putup touch (opportunity for theft suggested by an outsider) for 10 percent, no other outfit would think of offering the putup man 15 percent for it, although no commercial house would hesitate to outbid a competitor in a case like this.

There are few fixed rules of ethics, but there are some common understandings among thieves. One of them is illustrated in the following incident. A man complained that he had been beaten to the con (in a confidence game) for $1,200, and many con men were picked up and shown to the victim. He failed to identify anyone until the coppers coached him to the effect that the only way he could get his money back was to identify someone. It is believed that the coppers suggested a certain mob to him, believing that this mob had plenty of money and would kick in $1,200 rather than fight it. It was the wrongest rap in the world, but they had to come in with $1,200 for the victim and $300 for the coppers to square the case. The thieves knew that another mob had got the money. In an instance of this kind the mob that got the money is expected to make good the money the other mob lays out, and it is very unusual for a mob to fail. So coppers are not a bit particular whom they hang a rap on, so long as they get credit for the case, for the thieves at times even up among themselves in this way.

It is understood that no thief must squawk (inform) on another. The instances where professional thieves have squawked are so rare that no serious consideration of this angle is necessary. Prisoners squawk for one purpose only—to relieve themselves of punishment. Professional thieves have no thought of receiving punishment while in the hands of the fix, and they have no incentive to squawk. Police officials, prosecutors, and others rarely question professional thieves. They have or else haven't got a rap for the prisoner. In either case there is no gain from questioning. If a thief should squawk, the other thieves would not descend to the same plane and squawk on him. They use much better methods. The worst penalty is to keep him broke. This is done by spreading the news that he has squawked, which makes it impossible for him to get into any mob. That is the greatest disgrace and the greatest hardship that can befall a thief.

• • •

The distinctions most sought after among thieves are money and proficiency in their chosen lines. These, as a rule, go together. Thieves have the greatest respect for one who can succeed in the most difficult situations, although they recognize that success and failure are largely a matter of luck. All the thieves, for instance, speak about Big Jake who has the reputation of being the only con who beat anyone while in prison. He was a trusty in Joliet and used to run errands outside the walls. One time he was sent to town on an errand for the deputy, and while there he beat some sucker on a confidence game for several thousand dollars. That one thing would have made his reputation for the rest of his life, if it had not been made already.

A thief is not a professional until he is proficient. When a thief is taken on for unimportant tasks by some mob, he is not regarded as a professional. He may develop into a professional in the course of time if he does these unimportant jobs well enough to lead the mob to give him more important jobs. If he does not succeed in the first tasks, he is dropped and gets no opportunity to fill in with any mob even for unimportant tasks. He may then become a beggar, a pimp, a steerer for some gambler, get into the heavy rackets, or try to grift single-handed. If a professional who has an established reputation takes on a new racket, he may not be efficient at it. That is about the only condition in which a professional would not be proficient. He would quickly drop the new racket for some other professional racket if he did not become proficient at it in a short time.

The disgraces dreaded by thieves are the opposite of the distinctions, namely, inefficiency and poverty. Inefficiency, likewise, not merely means low success in stealing but also includes violation of any of the rules or codes of professional thievery, such as squawking, or burning his partners.

• • •

Because the underworld is an exclusive society, it is necessary that the stranger be identified before he is admitted. The language of the underworld is both an evidence of this isolation of the underworld and also a means of identification. Criminal slang of three hundred years ago is still being used today by criminals, though much of it is completely unknown to the general public. This language is passed from one crook to another by speech and not by writing. A slang dictionary published in England about 1585 had a lot of the same words and expressions we have now, and also a lot of the same rackets, such as dropping the poke, moll-buzzing, crashing windows.

A professional thief can tell in two minutes' conversation with a stranger whether he is acquainted with the criminal underworld and in two minutes more what particular rackets he knows intimately. If a thief were in the can and another person were brought in, the first might ask, "Where were you nailed?" The second might say, "In the shed." It is possible that an amateur might know that "nailed" in that connection meant "arrested," but no amateur would use the word "shed" for railroad station. Not only does the word "shed" help to identify the other as a professional but also the fact that he was arrested there helps to show the rackets which he might have been playing, such as the con game, or the cannon. Additional questions will draw out the technical words used in particular rackets, for each racket has words referring to the objects and actions peculiar to it. The cannon, for instance, has many technical terms referring to the different pockets. The word "prat" originally meant "buttock" but has been used by thieves for several centuries to refer to the hip pocket. Probably few members of the general public have ever heard of the word. Similarly one of the operations in picking pockets is to "prat a man in," which means that one of the stalls backs into a prospect and pushes him around gently in order to get him in a proper position.

• • •

Professional stealing is not organized crime. There is no organized crime unless we are to call each mob, troupe, outfit, or combination which is grifting together an organization. They are organized in the sense of being together as a stock company but not in the sense the newspapers would have readers believe. "Rings" are confined to the legitimate business world, as the cement manufacturers of Wichita, Germantown, Dover, and Spokane are members of a national association. The thieves in Wichita, Germantown, Dover, and Spokane may know one another, but they are not members of a national association. There is organized beer and booze running, gambling and prostitution, in the sense that a syndicate controls several spots in one city or spots in adjoining cities. This is the only semblance of a "ring," and it is not in the field of crime, for these are not considered crime by the professional criminals, the police, the lawyers, or the courts.

maxie the goniff

DAVID DRESSLER (TRANSCRIBER)

Maxie the Goniff is a professional cannon (pickpocket). In this transcription by David Dressler, Maxie indicates some rationalizations, behavior patterns, and techniques of his profession. Particularly revealing is his discussion of the various techniques of the professional. Using the argot of the criminal ("hook," "stall," "straight hoist," and "left-breech hook") he describes how he makes a living.[1]

Maxie the Goniff is a professional. Practically all cannons are. He is not very bright. His body is slight and springy; his fingers are long, tapering, and nervous. His face resembles a parrot's, the beak long and hooked downward. His eyes are furtive. He decided over fifty years ago that picking "pokes" was a fine way of making a living. He apprenticed himself to a master, studied hard, graduated with honors, and went on his

Reprinted by permission of the author and his agent, James Brown Associates, Inc. from Parole Chief *by David Dressler.*

[1]For an excellent study of the pickpocket and his argot, see Maurer (1964).

own. He wouldn't tell me how old he was at the time we spoke, but my guess is that he was at least sixty-five....

Like most of his kind, Maxie has a long criminal record. He has been arrested seventy-one times in twenty-two states.

"Doesn't speak so well for you, Maxie," I goaded him....

He flushed angrily. "Every one of them pinches came after a whole season's work. In fifty years I done six years time. I'm living good—well, pretty good—for forty-four years and it cost me six years! You should have it so good!"

He claims that both his parents were alcoholics, that they put him out of the house when he was twelve, and that he has been on his own ever since. For a time he was a petty thief, then a shoplifter, and finally, while still a kid, he met a man who took him on as an apprentice dip and taught him the business.

Picking pockets *is* a business, Maxie insists. "You've got to figure a certain amount of risk in any business. Suppose I open a saloon. I'm taking a chance, no? I might go broke, I might have to pay too much protection—it's all business."

Like all commercial enterprises, Maxie's has its seasons. "Summers we work the resorts, like Coney Island and the buses and subways going to and from. Beaches are good too. Certain holidays is season for us. Before Easter and Christmas. There's lots of shopping. That's when I hit department stores. In the elevators or even on the floor."

When he has had a run of bad luck he will depart from his more accustomed beat and cover a church wedding. "You don't often find much dough on the guys, but brother! Are they easy to take! They don't expect a thief in a church."

Occasional gravy is a convention or parade. Maxie plays the crowds. He loves American Legion groups because "half the time they don't even know *the next morning* whether they've been hooked or just spent the dough!"....

Maxie takes pride in his technique. He has little use for the lone operator, although he admits there are some good ones. He considers they take too many risks....

He likes to work in a mob of two or four people. Say you're on a subway or elevator. "You pick your mark and try to figure where he keeps his wallet. It ain't hard to find out. You just jostle the sucker and move off. Right away he puts his hand where he's got the wallet to see if it's there. He tips you off.

"Of course, if he don't fall for that, you've got to *fan* him. You feel around, very easy, until you locate the poke.

"Then comes pratting. You prat the guy around. That means you push him around, edge him around, not hard, gentle, just enough to distract his attention. Also to get him into position—the position you want him in for the score."

The man who does the pushing is the "stall." When the victim is in position, the "duke" (hand) of one thief extracts the poke. This man is called, variously, a "hook," "tool," "wire," or "instrument." He is the most skillful member of the team. The victim's attention is directed to the stall as the hook takes the wallet. Maxie is a hook.

"Funny thing," he said, chuckling. "Some guys look for a poke in a hip pocket. They like to take it from there. I'd rather score out of the breast pocket. Why? because the sucker thinks he's cute, see?...He thinks if he carries it in the breast pocket it's tough to take. It is, but a good thief likes that kind of meat. I always do." (I doubt it. Professional cannons are awful liars. Chances are, Maxie, good businessman that he is, will always go for the easier score when possible.)

While taking from the inside pocket, the wire "shades" the duke—covers his hand so the victim won't see it, perhaps with a newspaper. "What I do," says Maxie, "is 'put a throw' in his face. I shade my duke with a paper and annoy the guy by flappin' it under his nose. That makes 'im mad. He's concentratin' on the throw while I'm 'takin' off the score."

"In a good crowd, on a hip job, the 'push grift' works. No shadin' the duke, nothin'. Everybody's pushing, so you push all you want, and the guy don't even see or feel your hand."

In digging for the wallet the "straight hoist" is commonly employed. The cannon puts the first two fingers, held stiffly, into the pocket. He stiffens his body, lifts up on his toes, and out comes the wallet.

The next step is "cleaning." "The stall distracts attention, say. Now the wire's got the poke. He has to get clean right away.... If the sucker 'blows' (discovers his loss) he's gonna figure right away it's the wire, because the wire was closest to him. So I pass the wallet on right away to one of my stalls—the one who will be first off the car or elevator. If the guy grabs me I'm clean. I beef like hell. If he goes for the stall, he drops the poke and he's clean. Or better yet, he plants it on some bystander and we take it back later."

Maxie is proudest of the fact that he is a specialist among specialists, "a left-breech hook." That's a man who can draw a score out of a left pants pocket. "There ain't many can do that. It's hard. Try it!"

I asked him how much he earned a year by grifting. He became very evasive, even apologetic. "Oh, I had my ups and downs. Why talk about it? You do all right, year in, year out, if you're good. Some years I run five, ten thousand. Other times not so good...."

"Where did your money go?..."

"Well, the horses got a lot of it. Craps. Cards. Women. And I had to eat too." He forgot to mention that he has a wife and two children who are dependent upon him for their support.

I have never known an affluent pickpocket. I don't believe they make as much as Maxie claims, and their money seems to go fast. They live riotously. Some are drug addicts at times in their lives. Many have wives and children. I've never known one who wasn't a confirmed gambler or who wasn't fresh out of money every time I inquired.

Maxie is hurt because cannons are generally regarded with contempt, even in the professional underworld. He doesn't like to admit that contempt is earned. But the average dip is penny ante. Moreover, he is weak-willed, often turns in a pal to save his own skin. Perhaps because he is a weakling, the pickpocket is often a stool pigeon.

Maxie insists there is honor among thieves in his game. "Sure, a guy rats now and then. That don't prove nothin'. You'll always find a few rats. But most of us stick together. We help each other. We put up fall dough for a guy in trouble."

"Did you ever rat, Maxie?"

"Like I say, we stick together. We put up fall dough."....

"Maxie," I asked, "if you had it to do over again, what would you be instead of a pickpocket?"

"What's wrong," he snapped, "with this racket?"

gang boy

ANONYMOUS

Many theories have been advanced to explain the origins of gang delinquency.[1] Here we have a first-person account of gang organization and behavior by a member of a gang, Hank. He discusses structure and membership, fights, crime, and cops—throwing light on group life in a gang composed almost exclusively of working-class youths.

Gang Organization and Behavior as Hank Sees Them

The papers talk about a gang like it's a club, with officers and regular members and all. There are groups like that, but for every one of them there's hundreds of the other kind.

Reprinted with permission of Columbia University Press from Readings in Criminology and Penology, *edited by David Dressler (New York, 1964), pp. 155–58, 161–62.*

[1] See Cohen (1955), Cloward and Ohlin (1960), and Miller (1958, pp. 5–19).

STRUCTURE AND MEMBERSHIP

My gang don't have a name. It's just the gang. A fellow wants to hang out with us, he belongs. Anybody from our part of town can belong. I couldn't tell you how many is in our gang because it don't work that way. Today we might have ten, next week twenty guys. That don't mean we don't have a certain number of more or less regulars, that you see 'most every night. And if you was to ask me if a certain guy belongs with us I could pretty well tell you. But we didn't vote him in. He just got in. And he can leave any time.

We don't have officers and we don't have dues, and we don't have regular meetings. We don't have no rules.

You know which side of town a guy comes from, and if he's from your side he can belong. Now, there's no offense in a guy's being from a different side of town. Some of them fellows come over to our side and we get along fine with them. But they wouldn't really be part of our gang.

You meet a guy and ask, "Where are you from?" The other guy says, "I'm from the north side." Another guy says the south side. Them are more or less the gangs—the side of town you come from.

But even on our side, there's thousands of fellows we wouldn't consider part of our gang. Our fellows are the ones you more or less have dealings with. If there's a party or something, you'd rather mention it to them than somebody else. You got to know them in school or from the neighborhood. They're your buddies.

There's some guys don't get in with us. He's got to be our kind, a good sport. I wouldn't want to go with a guy, if he seen a girl, if you go to her house, he'd have to use the roughest language. I wouldn't want to go around with a guy like that because, you go to a girl's house, and he starts that crap, and then they say, "So-and-so come over last night with so-and-so, and boy, I mean to say, they were using the rottenest language!" *They* were. And *you* didn't use that language.

It don't make any difference how much money a fellow has or hasn't got. Lots of guys from rich neighborhoods, you couldn't find better guys. But then there's got to be a couple of wise guys in there that thinks just because their folks has provided for them a better car, better than you could provide for yourself, well, they think they're it. Well, you got to consider who paid for the car. If you paid for it, you're entitled to a higher standing, because you bought it, it wasn't provided for you. If I have a $500 car and you have a $500 car, but I paid for mine and you didn't, I deserve to rate higher. I got more to boast about.

Now, a guy don't have to be a good fighter to belong, at least not so far as I'm concerned. I don't even care if he's a sissy, so long as he minds his own business. If trouble starts, he don't have to be a Joe Louis, but he can't run off. I myself, I like to go out with a guy that isn't going to run from it. Now, a lot of times you run into guys that aren't going to have nothing to do with that fight. That's the kind of guy I don't like to go out with. I wouldn't want him part of my gang, because if it's your fight, you don't want to chicken out.

A fellow like that, if he hangs around, you don't drop him, because we don't have rules about dropping guys. What'll happen is this. He'll come up and say, "Where are you going tonight? Let's go get drunk." And I'll say, "Nah! I don't feel like it now. I think I'll go to a show." And if he says, "Good! I'll go, too," then you go and pick up a paper and look through and say, "Aw, shit! There ain't a thing here I want to see. Oh, well, I guess I'll go home and go to bed. Well, I'll see you later." So he'll take off and you'll go to a show or a girl's house. Only you didn't want him around. He'll catch on sooner or later.

A guy can belong, no matter who he is, if he's a right guy. If there's a colored fellow, or a Puerto Rican, or an Italian, that don't make a bit of difference. I don't go for that stuff about only certain fellows can belong. Everybody's as good as the next one, so long as he does what's expected.

Nobody is the leader, the boss, in our gang. When we decide to do something, each time it's somebody, spur of the moment, that sets it up. He's the leader. Next time another guy says, "Let's do this and that." He's the leader.

Very seldom do we plan something in advance. We don't say, "Let's do this and that tomorrow." Usually we decide it a minute in advance. Oh, once in a while a guy will say, "Let's meet tomorrow night and go out and snatch some hubcaps." But usually you don't plan that far ahead.

I seen an article by one of them *experts*. He says every gang is supposed to have a president and a secretary. He says there's a social president and a fighting president. Well, I never ran into a club like that. He says there's one guy they call a war counselor. I never heard of it. But I guess that could happen in a gang that wanted to be known as the roughest gang around.

In name gangs, more or less, you have to be voted in. Some, you get in on how tough you are. Name gangs, like the Dirty Dozen, the Coffin Chasers, they're likely to get pretty tough. They're more than likely the rat-packers. One gang fights another. That happens very often. When these clubs go by a name, then one gang has got to be the underdog. And that one don't want to take that name.

ABOUT FIGHTS

Every now and then it's fun to have a fight. It's like going to a party. You enjoy going to a party and you enjoy a fight every now and then.

There's two types of gang fights. One is where somebody from a gang gets hurt by a guy from another outfit. So the two gangs arrange to meet and have it out. The other kind is where two name gangs always consider each other enemies. They're going to fight every time they meet, any place, any time.

I don't consider it one bit smart to go around looking for a fight. But if you've got to mix it up, you want to be the ones that are able to walk away when it's over.

• • •

THE GANG AND CRIME

Most of the stuff me and the gang get into is just fun, raising hell, or orneriness. You wouldn't call it crime. But I guess we've done things you could. There ain't a kid that hasn't stolen something—cigarettes or a can of beer or a comic. Hub caps.

I remember there was three Chevvies sitting out there on Marlin Boulevard once, where the aircraft plant is. Well, three of our gang had Chevvies. We all went down there one night and when we was through, good God! We had all them cars stripped down to bare metal. We took the engines, wheels, dashboard equipment, steering wheels, every goddamn thing but the shell. You should have seen them silly things sitting there after we left!

I might roll a drunk, maybe get in a robbery. Snatch me some hubcaps. But certain things I wouldn't do, gang or no gang. Shaking down fags—that's dirty business. I wouldn't peddle dope. And I wouldn't commit one of them sex offenses, messing with little girls. I've got absolutely no use for that and I wouldn't give the time of day to any bastard that would do a thing like that. There's a limit.

ABOUT COPS

I don't hate all cops. The cops that kids hate earn it. Figure it out. I'll bet there isn't but three out of every ten people in the country that hasn't been pinched at least once. Now, that's a lot of people. If there's one bad cop, there's a lot of people hating him. Cops should think of that.

There's some decent cops. Let you get away with stuff. Dixville isn't too bad that way, as long as you're not living in the bad part of town, where we live. That's where you get the lousy cops.

What I mean by a good cop is he don't look to be hauling you in right away. Say you're under age, you're drinking. A cop is supposed to run you in. A decent cop won't run you in just for drinking. A cop you could get along with would be one, who'd say, "Well, as long as you fellows are only drinking beer, go ahead." I'd rather see kids sitting around with a can of beer than I would with a marijuana cigarette!

I've got nothing against cops or judges or probation officers, so long as they're decent. I just don't like to be robbed.

organized crime and the cosa nostra

JOSEPH VALACHI (TESTIMONY)

Criminologist Donald Cressey's recent analysis of organized crime in the United States (1969) shows that it is highly organized and consists of a nationwide network of at least twenty-four regional organizations or "families." The system has usually been called "Cosa Nostra" or the Mafia.[1] Cressey reveals that this criminal cartel has a virtual monopoly on an increasing number of legitimate businesses, at one time owned a large part of Las Vegas, and has actually controlled numerous politicians on the national level. It has been said that organized crime is America's biggest business, grossing over $40,000,000,000 per year according to the Department of Justice. Yet, despite the magnitude of criminal operations and organization, little has been done by law enforcement to curtail these operations.

Failure to control organized crime in the United States is largely the result of failure to obtain the legal evidence necessary to convict its leaders, many of whose names are known even to the man on the street. A break in the veil of secrecy surrounding these massive operations finally came when Joseph Valachi offered to cooperate with the federal government to avoid the death penalty for his slaying of a fellow prisoner. Valachi's testimony exposed much of the structure and organization of Cosa Nostra. He named names and identified families of members in major cities. He discussed the mechanisms acting to protect the hierarchy of Cosa Nostra, including secrecy, insulation, respect, "the buffer," "the appointment," "sitdowns," "discipline," "the disappearance," and "permission."

The excerpts which follow present some difficulties. Extracting meaningful statements from conversational contexts (in this case congressional testimony and examination) is normally difficult, but their erratic quality is also due to Valachi's limited vocabulary, his use of criminal argot, and the inevitable interruptions by his interrogators. Because of their historical importance, we include these excerpts. Any collection of criminal testimony would be incomplete without at least

This excerpted Valachi testimony is from U.S. Congress-Senate, Organized Crime and Illicit Traffic in Narcotics, Hearings Before the Permanent Subcommittee on Investigations of the Committee on Government Operations, *88th Congress, 1st Session, 1963,* passim.

[1]For a description of how the rural Mafia of Sicily has become the bureaucratized Cosa Nostra, see Anderson (1965, pp. 302–10). See also, Lewis (1964).

a fleeting glimpse of this landmark in criminal revelation. Valachi's description of a Mafia initiation illustrates the "code of secrecy" of the Cosa Nostra. He explains the ceremony that made him a member of the brotherhood. He was taken to a house in upstate New York where some thirty to thirty-five men were gathered:

The Chairman. What was the purpose of that meeting?

Mr. Valachi. The purpose of that meeting was to "make us."

The Chairman. To "make us" means make you members?

Mr. Valachi. To make new members and to meet all of them.

The Chairman. To meet the others that were in that family?

Mr. Valachi. That is right, for the first time....

The Chairman. Now, what happened after you got there and how many were there with you, to become members, to be "made"?...

Mr. Valachi. When I came in, I don't remember if I was first, second, or third, but let me talk about the time I got into the room.

When I came in, I sat down and they were at the edge of the table, it was a long table, and there was a gun and a knife on the table.... I repeated some words they told me, but I couldn't explain what he meant. I could repeat the words, but they were in Italian.... He went on to explain that they lived by the gun and by the knife and you die by the gun and by the knife.

The Chairman. Did you have a full understanding of what that meant at the time?

Mr. Valachi. Yes, sir.

The Chairman. It meant that you were what?

Mr. Valachi. Well, expected to die by the gun and by the knife.

The Chairman. In other words, when you took that oath, you expected some day to die either by the gun or by the knife?

Mr. Valachi. That is right.

The Chairman. That is what you were dedicating yourself to?

Mr. Valachi. That is right.

The Chairman. For what purpose?

Mr. Valachi. Well, I guess the purpose, that is what the rules were, of Cosa Nostra.

The Chairman. We will get to the rules in a minute. What kind of a ceremony did you go through in taking that oath?

Mr. Valachi. Well, then he gave me a piece of paper, and I was to burn it.... In other words, I took a piece of paper, and the piece of paper is burning, and it is lighted and then in your hand, you say—well, again, they give you words in Italian but I knew what it meant.

The Chairman. In other words, while you were repeating the words, you were burning the paper?

Mr. Valachi. This is the way I burn if I expose this organization.

The Chairman. And that was symbolic of the fate that was to befall you if you betrayed the organization.

Mr. Valachi. That is right; until the piece of paper burned.

The Chairman. You would be burned to ashes?

Mr. Valachi. That is right. . . .

Senator Mundt. That is the highest oath you took. In other words, that was the most sacred in this organization.

Mr. Valachi. That is right.

Senator Mundt. That you would never tell this.

Mr. Valachi. That is right. . . .

The Chairman. All right, then you became there a full-fledged member.

Mr. Valachi. Yes, sir. . . .

The Chairman. Were any of the rules explained to you there, or were they explained to you later?

Mr. Valachi. Just two rules at this time.

The Chairman. Just two at that time?

Mr. Valachi. At this time.

The Chairman. What were they?

Mr. Valachi. One was the secret which I was just telling you about, and the other rule was, for instance, a wife, if you violate the law of another member's wife, or sister, or daughter, these two rules were told; in other words, you had no defense.

The Chairman. You have no defense?

Mr. Valachi. These two main rules. If you give away the secret or you violate—at this time that is all of the rules I was told.

The top ranks of the Cosa Nostra families seldom become involved in crimes in such a manner that would subject them to arrest. Their personal conduct is free of obvious misdeeds. Social associations are generally very restricted, and contact with actual lawbreakers is nonexistent. Of necessity, as the levels descend, the members get closer to operations and become increasingly vulnerable to police activity.

If they (the bosses) want to have somebody "knocked off," for instance, the top man will speak to somebody who will speak to somebody else and order it. Valachi testified that this pattern was exactly followed in his management of the murder of a certain Giannini on September 20, 1952:

Mr. Valachi. Around that time Tony Bender sent for me. I met him in Thompson Street, in a restaurant called Rocco's. I sat on a table and he told me that word came from Charley Lucky that Giannini is an informer. So I said, "There goes my couple of thousand that he owes me.". . . So he said, "Anyway, it is none of our affairs. It is their affairs." Meaning the people he was associating with.

About a month later, Tony sent for me again. This time we went down to the Gold Key Club, I met him.

He said, "They can't seem to find him."

Mr. Adlerman. Can't seem to find Giannini?

Mr. Valachi. Giannini. He said to me, "Gee, Joe, you are not thinking about the money?" I said, "They are going to start this business? Can't they find him? I will find him."

He said, "Well, I will have to talk to the old man about that," meaning Vito Genovese, of course.

So, the next night I met him and he told me that Vito Genovese liked the idea.

The Chairman. When you said you would find him, what did you mean by that?

Mr. Valachi. I would get him. If they can't find him means they can't find him to shoot him. So I said I will find him.

The Chairman. What does that mean in your terms?

Does that mean you were agreeing yourself to kill him?

Mr. Valachi. I volunteered because I figured now they are looking for excuses. Maybe somebody else will make a lead with him and blame me because he owes me money and accuse me for tipping him off. That is the reason why I answered that way. If they can't find him, I will find him.

The Chairman. What I am trying to determine, was that in effect, "I will take the contract, I will kill him"?

Mr. Valachi. Yes, Senator.

The Chairman. You were taking the contract, yourself?

Mr. Valachi. Right.

The Chairman. To kill him, find him and kill him?

Mr. Valachi. Right; and I had to get the OK.

The Chairman. You had to get the OK from the old man and the old man was Genovese?

Mr. Valachi. Right.

The top members of the Cosa Nostra, as a rule, do not mix or even do business with their immediate subordinates. They deal through a "buffer," a member, usually around the same age, who is carefully selected and highly trusted.

This underling acts as an aide, but he is no menial. He drives the boss when necessary, but he is not his chauffeur; he handles messages from the field, but he is not a messenger; he discusses problems with the boss, but he is not a counselor, and so on. The buffer's main duty is to stay between the boss and trouble. Valachi described how some Cosa Nostra members (soldiers) never even saw a boss:

The Chairman. Let me ask you this: Can a soldier just simply make an appointment and go up and see the boss, the top boss, any time he wants to?

Mr. Valachi. No, he can't.

The Chairman. Do many of the soldiers never see or know the boss personally?

Mr. Valachi. There are really many soldiers that never know the boss.

The Chairman. Soldiers that never know the boss?

Mr. Valachi. Yes.

The Chairman. Is it difficult, is it most unusual to ever get them to talk to the top boss?

Mr. Valachi. It is not unusual.

The Chairman. Some of them do?

Mr. Valachi. Soldiers are in there 10 years, probably, and never saw a boss.

Another inviolate rule of the Cosa Nostra is the requirement that there must be a strong sense of respect for leaders and traditions. This respect exceeds deference due any one leader, and goes beyond the mere protection of the boss. With relation to the individual, it seems to be achieved partly by position and partly by seniority, with stress on the former, although all things being reasonably equal, the older member has more prestige. Valachi spoke of the respect he had for Vito Genovese:

Mr. Valachi. [Concerning Vito Genovese]...At this time right now I am losing respect for him, see.

The Chairman. You are losing respect?

Mr. Valachi. Yes. I am losing respect.

The Chairman. Prior to that time?

Mr. Valachi. I had the highest, all through the 30 years.

The Chairman. Meaning you would do anything he told you to do?

Mr. Valachi. Yes, anything. I even stuttered when I talked to him.

The Chairman. Stuttered?

Mr. Valachi. At times. That is how much I thought of him. I must tell you the truth. You see, Senator, he is my compáre. He stood up for me when I got married.

In the Cosa Nostra families, all important matters go through channels. At the last stage it comes to one man—the buffer—and he takes it to the overlord. This procedure is strictly followed, but there have been times when a low-level superior was permitted to speak to the boss on business. This is unusual, and requires following a set method. The member concerned must obtain permission from his immediate boss. This request then goes through channels to the buffer, who presents it to the head. Valachi recalled the description given him of this procedure:

Mr. Valachi. ...We have the boss and then we have an underboss under the boss. Then we have the caporegima. He was explaining all this. Now, if a soldier wants to talk to a boss, he should not take the privilege for him to try to go direct to the boss. He must speak first to the caporegima, and the caporegima, if it is required and it is important enough, the caporegima will make an appointment for the soldier. He went out and explained the rules. This is what I called second government.

A "sitdown" (group meeting) develops when there is a threat to gangland peace because of a dispute between members of this subsociety. At one time, force—frequent and ruthless—was the ultimate pacifier. However, according to the chiefs of these clans, when open violence is used, "the only winners are the cops." If a question comes up, the syndicate's lesser leaders arrange to sit down and thrash it out. In most cases, the issue can be resolved at this level. If necessary it can go higher. Valachi spoke of his own infraction of discipline:

The Chairman. You were involved in one charge of hitting another member.?

Mr. Valachi. That is right....

The Chairman. Had you learned about that rule before you committed the offense?

Mr. Valachi. Yes, I knew it.

The Chairman. What is the defense to that?

Mr. Valachi. Well, the defense was that we had a business together and he was stealing....

The Chairman. Now, as a result of your accusing him of stealing from the business, the partnership, and as a result of your having hit him or struck him, did your organization or your family government take any action?

Mr. Valachi. Yes, sir; I was brought on the carpet.

The Chairman. What is that?

Mr. Valachi. I was brought on the carpet.

The Chairman. On the carpet?

Mr. Valachi. Yes, sir.

The Chairman. Tell us what occurred?

Mr. Valachi. The carpet is a table, and he was represented by his lieutenant, and I was represented by my lieutenant.

The Chairman. Is that what you call a trial now, in your group?

Mr. Valachi. This is a small trial.

All discipline meted out to members of Cosa Nostra, including murder, is done within the same house or family, by its own members. Thus, if a family member has violated the rules or refuses to abide by a superior's decision, he must be punished according to Cosa Nostra rules. This punishment varies from a warning, through cutting a member out of some lucrative endeavor, to murder. Keeping the killing within the family eliminates the development of vendettas, makes it easy to perform the task, and paves the way for the disappearance. Valachi related how the murder of Willie Moretti was handled:

Mr. Adlerman. Did he [Genovese] advocate or did he have anything to do to agitate the murder of Moretti?

Mr. Valachi. Yes, I would say around about 1949, in around that time, we, us, you see us boys in the village actually belonged with Vito Genovese. In other words, what I want to explain to you, if Vito Genovese had any trouble, he depended on Tony Bender and his crew, which is us. Second, Mike Miranda, and third, Richy Nowak. That was his stronghold. Willie Moretti had lots of men, about 40 or 50 men in Jersey, throughout Jersey. Some of them were members and some of them were not, but they still were with Willie Moretti. He was like independent, and he had his own little army, and we expressed it that way, the way we thought.

Rumors started getting around between us that Vito is sore, and there is no money, and the agitating about Willie losing his mind, with syphilitic, but remember that he also lost his mind some years before that, and it even came out on the Kefauver committee. Costello was asked about it, and Costello explained how they took care of Willie Moretti, at the time before. But now they are talking about hitting him. That is about 2 years before the talk like that was getting around, only in our regime, our group.

Mr. Adlerman. If I understand you correctly, he became talkative?

Mr. Valachi. Only to Tony Bender, and his close ones. In other words, it was between us. One time he was known to say, "What are we, men or mouse?" and in that line, you see, and well, it finally happened around 1951 that Willie Moretti was killed and they expressed it that he was a sick man, and once Vito even told us, and he said, "Lord have mercy on his soul," and he said he has lost his mind, and that is the way that life is. "If tomorrow I go wrong, I want you to hit me in the head, too," he said. You know, like he was making us understand that he was hit because he was not well. But naturally I formed my own conclusions.

Mr. Adlerman. Who do you think ordered the killing?

Mr. Valachi. Well, in that case, with Willie Moretti, as long as they made it official that he was sick, that you could say was by "commissione." It means they all agreed.

Mr. Adlerman. In other words, this was a rule that came from above?

Mr. Valachi. That is right.

Mr. Adlerman. And they all agreed that he should be killed?

Mr. Valachi. Yes, sir; for instance, the funeral itself came from it. He had lots and lots of automobiles, with flowers, and usually when a boss like Anastasia or even Moranzano, they were deserted, but Willie was not deserted, because it was sort of, as we put it, he was supposed to be a mercy killing because he was sick, and he was supposed to be talking, and he was going to go to radio, and all of that kind of talk got around.

Sometimes during a sitdown of the family members it is decided that murder is the only solution to the problem discussed. As mentioned, the homicide is assigned to the family to which the victim belongs. Within a short time, the man disappears. These murders are usually carried out by close "friends" of the victim—possibly actual blood relatives—completely trusted by the victim. Victims show no fear, no change from routine, prior to their disappearance. This technique has great advantages. There is no apparent violence, no sprawled body in a bullet-punctured car, and no inflamed press and public. The case is carried as a missing person, a disappearance. Valachi described the "disappearance" of his immediate boss:

Mr. Valachi. Well, he first told me about Tony Bender. At this time I saw about a week maybe, or 10 days, and I don't remember, Tony Bender disappeared, and he first told me.

The Chairman. He told you Tony Bender disappeared?

Mr. Valachi. Oh, no; it was in the papers, and on radio, and I am just telling you at this time he had disappeared.

The Chairman. I might ask you, has he ever been found?

Mr. Valachi. No; he never has been found.

The Chairman. Go ahead.

Mr. Valachi. Vito Genovese told me that it was the best thing that could have happened to Tony, because Tony couldn't take it "like you and I," and he is talking to me, and so I looked at him, like I snapped back with my head. I thought maybe he was going to tell me he was an informer or something.

The Chairman. What is that?

Mr. Valachi. I thought he was going to tell me he was an informer.

The Chairman. That Tony was an informer?

Mr. Valachi. That is what I thought, and I said, "What do you mean?"

And he said, "Well, you know he was a sick guy, and he won't be able to take it like you and I." Like he couldn't take time, to put it this way, time in prison, or long prison sentence, and so that is the best thing that could have happened.

The Chairman. The best thing to happen was for him to disappear. That is what Genovese thought and he said to you?

Mr. Valachi. Yes, sir.

The Chairman. Does that "disappear" mean that that is about the end of him?

Mr. Valachi. It meant that in our language, that he had ordered his death.

The Chairman. That he had ordered his death.

Mr. Valachi. Yes, sir.

The Chairman. That Genovese had ordered his death?

Mr. Valachi. Yes, sir.

Members of the Cosa Nostra are required to obtain permission to enter any illegal enterprise—commit a stickup or burglary, dispose of stolen property, or even borrow from a shylock. The explanation given is that only undertakings in keeping with family policy will be allowed. Valachi spoke of the position taken by the Cosa Nostra families on narcotics:

Mr. Adlerman. Mr. Valachi, there had been considerable dealing in narcotics among the members of the five families, or the Cosa Nostra?

Mr. Valachi. Yes, sir.

Mr. Adlerman. And it reached a point where the heat of the narcotics prosecutions, and the investigations and the publicity, caused a rule to be laid down by Frank Costello while he was boss of one of the families?

Mr. Valachi. Yes, sir; in 1948.

Mr. Adlerman. What was the rule that he laid down?

Mr. Valachi. No narcotics. You are in serious trouble if you were arrested for narcotics. You had to prove to them—you have another trial after having a trial with the Government.

Mr. Adlerman. You would have a trial by the Cosa Nostra or the family. Now, this related to Frank Costello's rule, and that was what is now the Genovese family, at that time, the Luciano or Costello family.

Mr. Valachi. In 1948; yes, sir.

Mr. Adlerman. Now, did this apply to the other families at that time?

Mr. Valachi. No, it did not.

Mr. Adlerman. Now, did there come a time when the other families laid down the rule?

Mr. Valachi. After Anastasia died in 1957, all families were notified—no narcotics.

Mr. Adlerman. Who laid down that rule?

Mr. Valachi. That was a rule that was discussed by the bosses themselves.

Mr. Adlerman. Was that the consigliere and the bosses themselves made that rule?

Mr. Valachi. That is right; that covered all families.

While in jail, Valachi wrote a manuscript describing his life in crime as a member of the "secret society." However, the U.S. Department of Justice has not allowed this document to be released. Until his death on April 4, 1971, Valachi remained in prison under maximum security conditions for his own protection rather than society's.[2]

---

[2]For the most recent study of the importance of the Valachi revelations, the reader is referred to Mass (1968).

policy: the eternal dream

ANONYMOUS

Gambling is one of the most lucrative "businesses" engaged in by organized crime today. Despite many journalistic accounts of organized crime, however, we know very little about its operations.[1] One reason for this is that these criminals rarely meet law enforcement officials. Secondly, persons involved in organized crime usually live by a strict code of silence. In this selection, recorded by James D. Horan, a former member of a mob reveals what he knows about how the policy racket works in Harlem.[2]

Before I describe my role in the policy racket, I had better explain exactly how the racket works and why it is entrenched so deeply in our society.

First of all, it is the financial fiber of the underworld. It funnels its vast profits into more vicious rackets, like narcotics, and helps support the legitimate enterprises run by racketeers who operate through fronts. For example, trucking companies run by garment-center racketeers undoubtedly have absorbed profits of the policy racket, but no one will ever prove it. "Money has no marks," as the racket guys say.

More important, policy is so vicious because most citizens merely shrug when they hear about it.

"That nickel and dime game?" they say. "So let them play. It's harmless."

I am shocked at such ignorance. It is true that nickels and dimes are wagered, even pennies, but such plays are in the minority; a large number of plays in Harlem are from one to five dollars. I have seen, not once but hundreds of times, families wagering their entire relief checks on a series of plays.

In Harlem, where poverty is widespread, policy is a way of life; it will

[1] An exception, of course, is the previous selection by Joseph Valachi.

[2] Additional literature examining gambling and organized crime can be found in Landesco (1968), Lindesmith (1941, pp. 76–83), Zola (1963, pp. 353–61), and McCall (1964, pp. 51–66).

never be crushed. Each time a number is played a dream is born; perhaps this is *the* time. If it strikes, the player dreams he'll be riding in a pink Cadillac before nightfall. His wife will be dripping mink, and he'll be wearing the finest Buddy Lee (hat) that money can buy.

To the porter in an office building who is making sixty dollars a week or the cleaning lady creaking with rheumatism, policy is a part of their existence. They would no more give it up than stop breathing.

There are all sorts of legends and rumors, but it is generally believed that Casper Holstein and Madam St. Clair brought the numbers racket from the West Indies in the twenties. I don't believe that; I think it was introduced to Manhattan long before then, and that Casper and Madam St. Clair popularized it and made it into a business. Before they came along it was a haphazard thing; Casper had the foresight to pull the collectors together and made them into one combination.

After Dutch Schultz had enough of bootlegging, he turned to the policy racket. He did it on a big scale; he had enough gunmen and strong-arm men to muscle into Harlem and take over. He also had political protection and enough crooked cops on the pad to build a vast empire.

One of the men he muscled was Henry Morro, another early and legendary figure in the New York policy racket. All except the veteran cops and assistant district attorneys have forgotten Morro, but he helped organize New York before the Dutchman sent him word to get out or be killed.

Henry had sense; he retired gracefully and took his money and went back to the West Indies to live like a prince.

Casper Holstein never regained his influence after his kidnaping in 1928. He tried several times to make a comeback, but was either raided or jailed. In 1941 he died penniless and almost forgotten. He was saved from Potter's Field by a man he had once befriended.

The reason why Casper never made a comeback is that control of the racket had shifted from West Harlem to East Harlem, the headquarters of Trigger Mike Coppola, the real boss of East Harlem. You will recall that it was Mike who was jailed as a material witness in the beating murder of Republican Party worker, Scottoriggio. It is believed, but no one has ever proved, that Mike is the boss of the policy mob in East Harlem. I haven't any proof and certainly the police or the D.A. haven't, but there is no doubt in the policy underworld that Mike's lieutenants boss the operation.

Coppola is a fine example of remote-control operation in the rackets today. He's seldom in East Harlem. Since the Scottoriggio murder he lives mostly in Florida, haven for the majority of the nation's big racketeers. But it's significant that he returned one day in 1957 and was nabbed on the same block where three of the mob's big banks were located.

The structure of the policy mob is similar to that of any American big business. There are presidents, vice-presidents, boards of directors, comptrollers and large clerical staffs, and so on. The banks are run as efficiently as the bank where you deposit your money.

In Harlem the racket represents not only the eternal dream but also a big industry which hires a large part of the population. Hundreds of men and women—even children—work for the mob in West Harlem. In East Harlem there is a small army of bookkeepers, clerks and messengers.

Until recently the racket ran openly on the street in West Harlem. Before opening time at certain numbers drops—places where bets are made or dropped off by runners—there would be lines of men and women, mostly on relief, waiting to play the first number. Hundreds of stores, with sun-dry chocolates or dusty hams in the windows, were rented and used as the drops.

But across Fifth Avenue on the East Side, the racket is guarded by security measures which would do credit to the Pentagon. The ordinary child in the street bouncing a ball, the housewife reading a newspaper on the porch, are on the lookout for strangers.

From early morning until late at night these lookouts are on the alert. In the East 116th Street block, news of a stranger's arrival is flashed to strategic points in a matter of minutes. As you will see...

• • •

Policy flourishes in two sections of New York: Harlem and Brooklyn. From these sections the ring does a business estimated at $100,000,000 a year. This is no wild newspaper estimate; these are the figures of the police and the District Attorney, based on a study of the thousands of slips found in the East Harlem raids last year.

The game itself is probably the simplest form of gambling yet invented. If you want to play, all you do is select three digits—say 547—and bet anything from a penny (although the lowest total bet must be a dime) to $100. The winning number is based on a complicated formula geared to the money bet that day on various races at the nearest race track. The pay-off is huge—600 to 1.

Even bets on a single number—called "single action"—pay off 8 to 1. You specify where a number will turn up in the winning combination. Seven, say, to come in last, as in 547.

The reasons why the game is so widely played are the vast odds and the ease with which you can play a number. All you have to do is ring the elevator button; nine out of ten times the elevator operator is your local runner. Buy a pound of butter and play a number. There are few stores in Harlem which do not take numbers. Walk downstairs for a breath of air—the kid on the steps will take your number to the runner who makes his stand at the corner.

The make-up of the racket is like this: Low men on the totem pole are the runners and collectors. The runners may be people like store clerks or manicurists, and they take all their numbers to a collector, who may service a fleet of runners. Outside of Harlem, collectors usually hold other jobs, such as elevator operators in a garment-center dress house. Runners and collectors are paid in various ways—some get a straight salary; others, a percentage of the day's take and a part of their customers' hits.

If a runner or collector is arrested, the mob sends down a lawyer and bails him out in a matter of hours. If he is fined they pay it. If he goes to jail they send his wife a weekly rate. When he comes out he gets a bonus and gets back his beat.

Most of the time he doesn't even go to court after the first arraignment. The mob is constantly organizing the winos for "stand-ins"; that is, the mob sends a man to represent himself as the defendant. The "stand-in" is paid either for going to jail or for just appearing.

Collectors take their money to the top man on the ladder, who is the comptroller. He organizes the small army of runners and collectors and pays them off out of his cut, which is usually around 35 percent of the day's take. He also pays off the free-lancers, such as pickup men, porters and lookouts.

There are also other regular employees of the East Side mob. Most important of these are the moneymen. They handle the money and the "ribbons"—the adding machine tapes which record the day's total play. The "ribbon car" makes two round trips a day between East and West Harlem. The first is to collect the day's work for the banks to total, and the last trip is to take back the ribbon and pick up the money due the mob after the hits and the comptroller have been paid off.

The banks are the secret hideouts on the East Side where all the slips—written on matchbooks, napkins, menus, shopping bags, whatever—are copied off with office precision and tabulated. Here the ribbon is made up. Here, too, are the bookkeepers and clerks, who get regular salaries, are guaranteed their fines, and whose families are provided for if they are nabbed in a raid.

Since runners and collectors give no receipts, the original betting slips are held at the banks for a week in case some player beefs that his winning number was overlooked. It's a tribute to the efficiency of the operation that hardly a slip fails to return to the beefer stamped "No Overlook."

In the bookmaking racket the telephone is vital. In the policy racket the adding machine is. The comptroller must know during the day how much has been bet on a certain number. If there is a run on a particular number—a number which has figured in a tragedy may be grabbed by the policy players and may sweep through Harlem like wild fire—the banks must be alerted. The smaller independent operator may want to "lay off" part of the bet with some other banker. He has to know the big play for one good reason—he has to have 600 times as much in his kitty if that number hits.

Some banks are operated independently of the mob; they are usually run by two or three men who may have bought into an established bank. Sometimes these men are runners who saved their coin for a rainy day and who use their relatives for employees, or perhaps such an independent is a collector who came into an insurance claim or who himself hit the numbers. These independents must also have connections with the bigger racketeers so that they will be able to lay off bets when the money is running heavily on one number. The independents, of course, never—but never—cut into the mob's territory. There are several still unsolved murders to testify to what happened when someone tried to muscle in.

A banker's life, on the surface, is pleasant; he usually lounges in a bar or restaurant near his bank so he can keep an eye on it and also on the estimated number of players during the day. Actually, his is a tense business. At least three of the big bankers I worked for had businessman's ulcers.

Security measures for the mob's setup, as I said, are admirable in East Harlem. In West Harlem they are more crude. The watchers on the stoops usually raise a rolled paper when a suspicious stranger appears, or what is believed to be a PD on the prowl. This signal is caught by another watcher further down the block, who will signal to someone else, until finally word is passed to the collector. If the danger is valid, the collector gives the word to his boys, who hustle the players out of the store or the hallway.

"No play—no play—the cops are on the block."

But the mob seldom has to worry about the cop on the beat. I know there are many honest patrolmen in Harlem, but they know I speak the truth when I say that the majority are on the take.

I have seen many come into our drop and brazenly accept their five- or ten-dollar bills. Corruption among cops is widespread. If a cop is honest, pressure is put on him by his fellow officers to accept money; once he takes it, he is smeared with the same brush.

For years I have heard of a mysterious "Mr. Big downtown"—meaning police headquarters downtown—who is supposed to be the main protector of the mob, but if he exists he is known to only a favored few of the syndicate. In my personal opinion, someone higher up must be on the pad. It would be naïve to suppose that an operation estimated even by top police brass as doing an illegal $100,000,000-a-year business could operate and flourish without the connivance of some high officials.

Another phase of the racket is "cut numbers." These are numbers which hit with such regularity that the mob has to lower the odds. The new odds are printed by the mob and distributed throughout Harlem.

For example, when I was in the racket, 957 hit several times and fortunes were given out to the winners. So the mob from East Harlem sent over boxes of cards lowering the odds to 300 to 1 on 957. On that card, which I still have as a policy memento, the odds had been lowered to 400 to 1 on 325, 495, 898, 519, 125, 100, 214, 101, 123, 319, 500.

• • •

The headquarters for the West Harlem policy mob was in a makeshift, ostensibly vacant store on West 116th Street. There was a guard on the outside, who nodded to Richie, and another who opened the street door.

Inside were several tough-looking hoods sitting around a stove. To the left was a candy counter with bits of licorice and gum that must have been there since the store was built. Behind the counter was a big, good-looking man in a dark blue overcoat and snap-brimmed hat, who was watching a man sorting numbers just taken from a paper bag. He was the most powerful man I had ever seen.

He looked up as Richie approached him.

"Big Bo, I want you to meet Andy. He just came out yesterday."

Bo reached out and took my hand. "Hiya, Andy. Let's go in back where we can talk."

We followed him into the small rear room, where he waved us to a chair.

"Richie's been telling me about you," he said as he lit a Corona Corona. "He thinks you could do us some good."

"Andy's got a lot of heart," Richie said.

"So I heard from some of the boys. We need another man on the Avenue to keep it clean. I can take you on for a C-note a week."

"Do I have to carry a heat?"

He shook his head. "Too dangerous when you're on the street. But there'll be one here if you want it."

"What about the cops?"

"What about them?"

"Will they pick me up?"

Bo laughed. "If they do, just tell them you're one of Bo's boys. We take care of them."

"When do I start?"

"The first number today. Come on and meet some of the boys."

We returned to the front of the store, and Bo introduced me to the collectors, runners and the lookouts who were waiting to start the day's work. I knew most of them either from the Four Queens or from prison. They were small-time, and although they looked tough I wasn't impressed with Bo's setup.

Outside I said as much to Richie. He nodded.

"Bo's the comptroller. The East Side is the boss. You'll meet one of their guys tonight."

"But who's the head man?"

"A guy named Fat Tony. That's all I know. He's supposed to be fronting for Trigger Mike, but who knows?"

"Have you had to use the muscle yet?"

"Only once. A guy from downtown said he had the okay. We checked with the East Side, and they said get rid of him. We got him in an alley and worked him over." He looked behind him. "I wanted you to get a look at the setup, Andy, before I talked with you about my idea."

"What idea?"

"Bo may look powerful, but he's a big hunk of nothing. He walked in when another guy had a hit and went broke. The East Side backed him and he expanded. In a few months he'll be ripe to take over."

"What do you expect him to do? Just roll over?"

"By the time we're ready he won't make a peep. Personally, I think he's fed up. His doctor put him on a milk diet because of ulcers, and his wife wants to live in Florida."

"Can he afford to?"

Richie whistled. "Man, he's got money that he hasn't unfolded yet. You know that guy's got six TV sets in his house!" I could feel the edge of excitement creeping into his voice. "Andy, there's big dough in this racket!"

I was beginning to think so.

i turned on 200 fellow students

"RIC"

In this unusual testimony, "Ric" describes becoming a pusher of marijuana ("pot") while attending college. A "pot" user for a considerable period of time, "Ric" describes the terrific market for marijuana and the lucrative business he joined after selling his first three ounces. This rather hip account details techniques of marijuana use, as well as the type of "high" experienced from its use.[1]

This isn't a confession. It's more like letting you in so maybe there'll be a slight chance you won't walk around spilling all that typical misinformation I hear and read wherever I go. For instance, after the big midwinter bust in Detroit, some professor came on the late news and gave his sixty-second serious-dangers-of-narcotics speech, which he picked up from a 1937 ad. After four years of college I can tell. You're flying blind, middle-class-land, and it's fear and Plymouth Rock hardheadedness that makes you tear down Maypoles. Not much of a change since Sixteen-twenty. Anyway I'll lay off the message. Don't get scared so soon—let me entertain you.

I'm a pusher. I should say I was a pusher. ATTENTION SYSTEM: I am no longer. Just in case you're interested, I quit because it became a hassle. Too much business—I developed this real capitalist outlook. Sitting in my room with the door locked making stacks of my money. I caught myself and got out. Like Hesse's Siddhartha. He went to the river. I just went straight. Good boy me, diploma in hand ready to step into my slot—but that's another story.

I pushed in my senior year at the University of Michigan, starting I remember after I quit this incredibly boring job showing early-morning educational movies. We were sick of buying lousy grass at exorbitant prices around Ann Arbor, so over Thanksgiving we all chipped in and bought a

[1]Further autobiographical accounts include Krassner (1965, pp. 1–2). Leary (1966, 93ff.), and Leary (1969, 221ff.). For scholarly accounts, see Becker (1953, pp. 235–43), Goode (1969), and Solomon (1966).

pound in New York through one of our business associates who lived there and knew a fairly reliable contact. It cost four of us about thirty-five dollars apiece and after weighing it on these great homemade blind-justice-type scales we each wound up with four honest ounces. Then the idea hit—we could sell a couple, make back our investment, and still have buckets to smoke ourselves. So, we cut the stuff up—this is a technique we eventually got down to a real science—and packaged the ounces in baggies. Now we had to find a market. At the time, see, we were just looking for a few friends who might want a decent deal, and we'd come out with free grass. So I phoned up a chick I knew who smoked quite a bit and asked her to look around. About a half hour later she called back with an order for three ounces. We were in business. Our pound went within two days and people were lined up begging for more. What could we do? You have to understand that this is a pretty common way for pushers to get started. They're not these crummy, slinky, little junkies you read about turning school kids on to pot and dirty pictures. It's the puritan ethic, people, the capitalist way—make a buck. Sure, simple supply and demand—like loan companies and bootleg liquor—hell, like used-car lots and Gimbel's basement. Nobody's a nonprofit organization. One of my partners is an economics major. He filled us in on the real story: just business as usual in the true American tradition.

Before I started pushing I was a long-haired sometime-student Ann Arbor fringe member, cashing my monthly check from upper-suburbia home, and after I started I was just the same—only I was independently wealthy, my parents could save their money for Miami Beach. I mean I didn't make a fortune—just enough for records and repairs on my car and of course reinvestment. After our first success we decided the market could easily bear a kilo at a time—which is two-point-two pounds (thirty-five ounces) and costs usually around two hundred and fifty dollars—naturally the more you buy the cheaper it is. We got hold of a Detroit contact through an amazing kid—a Wanderer dropout who knew everybody and everything that was happening, especially the younger hippies and old-time hard-core heads. See, each of us eventually developed his own clientele, from the Wanderer's friends to fraternity straight people just getting into the thing. Anyway, we began in full swing after Christmas with a trip into Detroit for two kilos. I didn't go along and I didn't ask questions so I can't tell you much about it. Except that it was bad sugar-cured grass that dried up to nowhere near four and a half pounds, but got sold eventually for a not-too-disappointing profit. Fact is, the New Yorker and the Wanderer had to put up the cash, so they took charge of the whole bit. During that time all I got was free grass and lots of customer inquiries. Then rumor filtered in about a big bust, snow started pouring down, and Midwest winter doldrums hit us. Everybody was still jumpy about the fifty-six heads they hauled in in Detroit—we locked up all the grass, pipes and paper in a sympathetic sorority house and sat uptight. This was very safe but I remember one one slushy night we drove all over Ann Arbor looking for the silly chick who had the stuff in her room while customers complained and we pined for a pleasant high. In short the situation got a bit grim, and the New Yorker decided now was a good time to make it down South—with Wanderer, who grabbed a ride just out of the clutches of the local narcos.

A few days before they left we gathered up some money and drove into Detroit so that I could be introduced to our contact and start a regular transaction while the others were in Florida. We drove through a few streets of Jesus Saves churches and parked next to a typical grey row of Victorian monstrosities turned into student apartments. Looked pretty much like the rest of Detroit, I guess. We knocked on an upstairs door of one of these places and a skinny chick answered. I was nervous the contact would close up because he didn't know me, but the chick said he was sick anyway and wasn't selling. We argued for a while about telephone arrangements that had been made and the hassle to drive here in rush hour, but she held her ground and stared us down. After a few minutes we left, pissed off. The whole place smelled like chicken soup. See, big pushers are real too.

Well, now we were in sort of bad shape—not even a joint to smoke ourselves. We killed time drinking cough syrup for about a week, and then one day our fraternity partner got a great surprise package from the capital city—an almost full kilo of beautiful grass in a plain brown wrapper. Maybe a little risky but it did get through addressed to Zelda Zero or something. And we were back in business. This was just before the University of Michigan's two-day spring break at the beginning of March and we wondered if anybody would be around to buy. We opened up sales with a few discreet phone calls after spending half a night cutting and weighing and smoking (for testing purposes) and by suppertime the next day we were clean. Not even a pipeful left between us. Our enterprise was really rolling. It gave us enough money to fly East for the vacation—half fare of course. I mean we weren't lighting our cigarettes with dollar bills. In fact, after every sale I got tighter and tighter, like J. Paul Getty. I told you that's why I quit.

Time in college is measured between vacations, so I called the two months after Christmas until spring break our building-up period, and after that, from March till we went home at the end of April, our solid establishment time. We started pushing with comfortable regularity. We got a motto: Buy low, Sell Highs—sort of cute. The important thing was we made a name for ourselves in town. Sometimes it got a little out of hand. One night my straight room-mate brought back incredibly blown-up reports of our business from a sorority house I didn't even know existed. Our big boast was that we never promised, we delivered. There were endless stories circulating about the kilo of Acapulco Gold (supposedly good grass) somebody's gonna get for seventy dollars, but these same characters always showed up for a few ounces whenever we sold, complaining about our prices and our small amounts. Next week, forever mañana he'd be in the Gold—just doing us a favor for the time being. Also we were strategic. Like G.M. stockpiling for the big year, we'd hold up on our sales until we were sure that the market was empty and then we'd open up shop to lines of ten-dollar bills.

We alternated buying between Detroit and New York, and although New York City was more chancy, because of the distance, the grass was infinitely better and a lot closer to the real weight—never more than an ounce or two off. Detroit was dishonest through and through. One time sticks in my mind. The contact—he'd gotten over his flu I guess—called us later in March with a great deal on good grass. And he was anxious to get rid of it. All three of us drove in the next afternoon bulging with money and went up to his crummy room. He had a friend along, a dark greasy guy with his two-year-old daughter, who cried the whole goddam time. There's a technique to buying; first you bullshit, sit around and talk about business, busts, play the guitar, look at his psychedelic pictures. Everybody's real friendly and phony. Nervous. Then you say, "Well, we'd like a kilo." They go, "Yeah, sure, fine"—give you some wine. You wander around a little bit more and finally you ask what's the price. You look at their eyes which start to sneak all over the place.

"Two ninety," they say.

"What? Two ninety! Come on, we never pay more than two and a half. That's the standard rate."

And you hassle. So after we've made it clear, they give us a line about the guy who owns the stuff wants two ninety. It's not their fault, but the greasy guy goes, "I'll put up twenty bucks." This guy won't call marijuana any of the regular names like grass or pot—he's gotta call it "weed" and "boo" (I was waiting for "maryjane"). And the contact says, "Sure, I'll put up another twenty and we'll take, lemme see"—he figures it out too fast—"one seventh of the kilo." But what the hell, we wanted the grass. It was a prime time to push in Ann Arbor. Wanderer had left New York by then, leaving us without a contact there. And the little kid's crying was really bringing us down. So of course we gave in. They took the money and disappeared for a half hour. I figure they went to the greasy guy's place where they had it stored—probably around the corner—laughed for a half hour, and came back. It's not hard to figure. They poured out this damp pile of seeds and stems, "It's good weed, man." Yeah, it looked like the Sequoia National Forest. Then they took a coffee jar and measured out their one-seventh—five "cans" (he wouldn't call it ounces), packing it in so they got at least six. And that was it. Friendly good-byes all around. We were still hopeful on the way home that we'd get anyway around thirty ounces. It looked like quite a bit sitting in its week-old *National Enquirer* wrapper. We rushed in and put it on the scales: a bare twenty-five "cans." We got burned. It meant in sales a hundred and twenty-five dollars short. That hurt. And we felt bad that all our customers were going to get a mighty weak amount for their parents' money. What do you expect? Dishonesty breeds dishonesty. For instance, later on we got a real kilo from New York and sold whopping real ounces—almost. A pusher is not without a conscience. One consolation is that we heard those two got busted big later on. Which I guess I wouldn't wish on anybody.

Obviously we stopped buying from Detroit then and there and the rest of the year was relatively normal. Quiet, steady pushing to our quiet, steadily complaining, no-face, no-name clientele. It's funny. On my rare trips to campus and classes from my almost upper-suburban instantelectric apartment just down the road, the only people I ever recognized among the thirty thousand were my customers. But it's not like the local merchant who tips his hat to his clients as he walks to church. There wasn't even the slightest bit of recognition shown between us. Not a glance. Strictly business—a different world entirely when I was a pusher than when I was a student. And not a chance the twain ever met.

Anyway the snow finally melted in Ann Arbor and the temperature soared to sixty during the last few weeks and I took to sunning myself. I explained it all in the beginning. I closed the store, got stoned, and relaxed on my roof—spent all my money on nothing and went back to being poor. Believe me, businessman, it's just as good.

Now, let me explain. I've sort of mentioned a lot of terms I figure you should be conversant with after all those *Time* and *Saturday Evening Post* stories about the worthless addicted New Generation, but I'll fill you in anyway from my side of the fence.

Grass—marijuana—is a minor psychedelic weed, grows almost everywhere. You always hear about police burning a vacant lot full of it in some big city. And when we get it from the big suppliers it's either in a pile of loose stems, seeds and leaves, or compressed into different size blocks. Our job is to cut it and clean it and package it for sales. We chop it up first on a grater then push it through a strainer until it's fine. Seeds can be mashed between two bricks and mixed in, but the stems are a problem. If we were going to sell only top-rate pot we'd take out all the seeds and stems, and market just the finely ground leaves, but that would cut our profit a few hundred percent. The trick is not to cut the stuff too fine because the customer would much rather buy a fuller bag of crap than a thinner bag of really beautiful stuff. We measure ounces by eye—that is if we get an honest deal and there are around thirty-five ounces in the kilo, we split the stuff into thirty-five piles and pour them into little manila envelopes. Most often though, we get burned to some extent, so we have to create arbitrary ounces—anywhere from a half to almost a full ounce, and sometimes we've really been taken, like the time I told you we got two kilos of grass that was cured in sugar (an expedient to dry it) and still damp. It looked big and weighed a lot, but in less than a week it dried up and shrank away to some fluffy, gluey, worthless waste in the bottom of a shopping bag. In such cases we're forced to beef it up with green tea, which makes your throat into raw meat after a couple joints, but otherwise not even an old-time hard-core smoker can tell the difference. See, we figure on a three-hundred-percent return on our investment. An ounce sells for twenty-five dollars. That means we pay no more than eight bucks for the same amount—no matter how thin it is. Smaller quantities are even more dishonest. A nickel bag—five dollars' worth—should be a fifth of an ounce but we always get at least seven nickels to one ounce, or three dimes—ten dollars' worth each. If you stretch it you can make forty or even fifty dollars on one ounce by selling it in nickels and dimes. I can never understand the guy who comes in every other day for a skimpy nickel instead of saving a while and getting a whole ounce at half the price. I mean it's not like he's hooked on it. Customers are funny. Some hassle for an hour before they buy and some don't even open the envelope. We always give them the same blurb: "It's good grass, man, and it cost us a fortune—you're getting a good deal." They usually pay.

You wouldn't believe the cross-section of people coming in to buy. It's impossible to type our customers—they're not all long-haired dropouts by any means. You figure: there are thirty-one thousand students at the university plus a couple thousand hangers-on and a few hundred high-school hippies—all potential customers. And we four businessmen had our finger on the whole action. My clientele revolved around one intellectual sorority and their non-student very hippie friends. I also took care of a lot of people just getting into the thing. See, our business wasn't just sales, we were our own promotion men. We turned newcomers on by the living room full—even the straightest, strictest Wasp chick would come out after an evening of logical argument and pipes of grass convinced and stoned. And back for more soon. My fraternity partner turned on half his house overnight and when I saw these ultraconservative kids a few weeks later their hair was already starting to grow. What an influence. The frat-head's customers also were two or three other fraternities and sororities, mostly beginners who didn't argue about price and quality, but smoked in huge quantities—because they were beginners it took them a lot to get high. Every once in a while we'd run into a real case—someone who just couldn't get high. So we'd empty out a closet, give him a huge pipeful, a couple packs of matches, and stick him in. The closet would fill up with smoke and after an hour of breathing pure grass instead of air he'd stumble out completely stoned. Success. People know when they're high. It's when they stop asking how they should feel—and start smiling. We turned on one very orderly crabby type straight man with about a nickel bag (enough for about five heads to get stoned on) and he sat there grinning like an idiot, listening to an incredible Ravi Shankar rãga, just saying very quietly, "Yeah. That's nice."

New Yorker's clientele was quite different. They were the real smokers, mostly from one arty-type section of town that has withstood the modern cement-cube apartments, and from the M.U.G.—the Michigan Union Grill—where the high-schoolers and the more showy hippies hang all day. Half of them are students, if that many, and they'd usually follow Wanderer for grass back to New Yorker's apartment, which was strategically placed between their psychedelic pads and the Union.

There were thousands of these people—invariably long-haired, young, messed-up and pleasant. There were so many, in fact, that our fourth partner, the Econ-head, dealt almost exclusively to the excess and took over the whole bag when New Yorker left. These were the real heads, into a lot of different drugs, stoned a good portion of the time, dead against the system—looking outside the U.S. for their futures—wanting to be left alone by Middleamerica, but dependent on parents' money or else totally broke. Bored too, not at all productive from a straight-person's point of view. But there's something—hard to pin down—between heads that there isn't between people outside. A sort of understanding, and acceptance, an easiness at first meeting like you already know them, very little arguing or bad humor. A group smoking can be loud and laughing but never destructive like a bunch of drinkers. Listening to records is big—all different kinds, from The Blues Magoos to Debussy. Being quiet is big too, and simply sitting. With patience enough for everybody else and an ocean of peace. You sit and stare and just can't figure why They're out to bust you. I could be sent down for ten years if I got caught pushing one crummy nickel, and I've had some close calls.

One time going through customs at Kennedy Airport some very nosy officer found an old hash pipe I'd never even used in my trunk. I gave him a quick line about sentimental value and an old Arab in Tangiers, but he didn't buy it. The pipe was nothing—what concerned me was the matchbox full of acid and opium in my pocket. They got a shopping cart, loaded my luggage on it, and pointed to this little scary-looking room—three of them with their hungry goddam eyes glued to me. So I nodded and very nonchalantly stuck a cigarette butt in my mouth, pulled out the matchbox, lit the cigarette and casually tossed the box in a garbage can. They searched every inch of me and my belongings and I just smiled. Clean. Legal. I got it all from a grade-B French-secret-agent flick. Thank God for the mass media.

You see then how an underworld is created. Every one of us is Wanted—by the local police, the state police, the F.B.I., the C.I.A., the F.D.A.—you name it, and so we go below ground. Wait, now, don't get the idea we're always slinking around in alleys and talking code over the phone. Hell, if you're that uptight it stops being enjoyable—it's just not worth it. We're still functioning members of society, intelligent and reasoning—but we've got a subculture below the surface where it's really happening. We know what dope is in town and what isn't and how much it costs and who might be a narco and what's going on in City Hall and the whole Midwest abortion scene—to help poor careless chicks. We know about Lieutenant Staudenmeier, the local heavy who runs around "busting" people and confiscating pornographic movies. He'd love to see a University of Michigan like it used to be—Mary Poppins playing at all the theatres and for kicks a screaming Saturday-night pantie raid. He's not much of a threat. Neither is the university. As a matter of fact, they have an eyes-closed policy about the whole thing. It's all politics—they just switched presidents and don't need any adverse publicity. But one professor, I remember, a guy named Pollard, came out in the student newspaper with this exposé on the campus scene: he told everybody there were only about two hundred smokers and twenty acid-heads. Christ, I know I've had more than that just in my living room this year, but I won't complain—it's reassuring to see how far off the system is.

Sure you can say our whole bag is a game maybe but it's a group—and I won't accept the crap about being completely independent. Everybody needs an empathetic ear. Security man. Simple and basic. The same reason the A.M.A. or the John Birch Society sticks together. The difference is we don't push our point.

And if you're wondering what I mean when I say drugs, stay close. I'm talking about every mind-bender we can get our hands on—every psychedelic, hallucinogen, consciousness-expanding, brain-changing tablet, capsule, liquid, powder, vegetable that's ever been smuggled into this country or sold at the corner drugstore. It sounds sort of like a soma holiday and everybody's scared to death of a Brave New World but—two things: just look around for a few minutes. Have you ever eaten a frozen chicken pie? Or a fifteen-cent hamburger? Or filled out forms for a big university? Or, man, just seen a computer—an electronic brain? And next, listen: don't criticize till you try. Aldous Huxley himself took mescaline.

Okay—the drugs: Marijuana's probably the mildest. It makes you high. I can't describe it any better than that. Hashish, the unripe pollen from the marijuana plant, has similar effects but usually a lot stronger. One joint of good hash is easily enough to turn on two people for a solid high. It comes in little brittle cubes that you break up and smoke or else it's already in powder form. Sometimes it's cut (mixed) with opium. It's got a beautiful sweet smell and taste, but a brutal price tag—around here it goes for a hundred to a hundred and fifty dollars an ounce. Supposed to be magic I guess. Anyway, very exotic. We pushed a whole ounce broken into tiny cubes at twenty-five per and never got a complaint. Ah, the sophisticated Midwest.

And amyl nitrite vials—poppers—are always good to snort while you're stoned. They're legal—for heart conditions or asthma and they speed up your blood so it's like your head is an atom-bomb test. Wild. They only last for a minute or so, which is good, and one is enough for quite a few people.

The new kick is banana peels but I've smoked them and they run a pretty distant second to grass. And they taste just like you'd expect burning banana peels to taste. I can live without it. And there's always the old standby—glue sniffing. It gives you an odd echoey-type high but it's very dangerous and you inevitably wind up stuck together from the leaky bag. Then there are the downs—the codeine or fake codeine cough syrups. You can buy them at quite a few drugstores in Ann Arbor, but now they're starting to get wary of the same wild-eyed hippies coming in every five minutes with a bad cough. One of the syrups has a very longname synthetic codeine in it and it's not bad but another is chock-full of the real stuff—it's an amazing experience. You drink a bottle, which is a bit hard to get down, and then wait for your body to go away. You're lying, eyes closed, making pretty, silent hallucinations, listening only to very soft instrumental pieces—Fauré, Saint-Saëns, Brahms, Sibelius—at total peace in a dream; that's the closest we get to the junkie's world.

At the other extreme are the forwards—Dexedrine, Methedrine—speed that dries out your mouth, opens your eyes, and glues you on the ceiling. I used to take them for studying all night or fast term-paper production and I hated the comedown shakes and nausea—it was a necessary evil for scholastic success. I never realized how many people took the stuff for a high, either by popping (swallowing) capsules, or sniffing crystals or mainlining pure Methedrine. A Meth-head is easy to spot—he's always licking his lips because he's dry and his eyes are always opening wide like he can't see well enough. And he chain-smokes and eats candy bars and catches serum hepatitis from the needle. The one point in speed's favor is the energy you get, but I don't trust the creativity of it. I've seen it dissipated too many times—dancing to one song all night, talking for six straight hours about nothing. You can see I don't much like it.

But that's nothing compared to the horror drug—belladonna. You can get it in patent medicines for asthma—they're legal and available. And let me warn you: you might not come back. One night six of us swallowed a heaping teaspoonful mixed with water—it's thick green and unbearably bitter. The rest of the evening was just a horrible nightmare of sounds and moving and nagging nausea, exhaustion and restlessness at the same time. We lost our motor facilities like drunkards and the Econ-head couldn't make intelligible sounds and when he did it was only a string of disconnected words. I lay on my bed and had a long conversation with nobody, and I'd shake my head and say, Wait, there isn't anybody here. And they'd all answer, "Right!" Real. Absolutely concrete. I figure we took O.D.'s (overdoses). It expanded our pupils so I couldn't have read the "E" on an eye chart. And it didn't go away until late the next day. I know people who say they've had quarter and half teaspoonfuls and a relatively pleasant time. I don't believe it.

And, last of all, L.S.D. You've all heard about it. It sells for between a half-cent to as much as two cents a microgram and you usually take anywhere from two hundred and fifty to a thousand mikes a trip. It's hard to get in large quantities at a good price so we never pushed any, which is a shame because it sells like wildfire. There are similar compounds—psilocybin, mescaline, peyote—but acid is far stronger, one of the few new experiences you'll ever have—a true consciousness-expander—man, a revelation. I'll try to tell you what it's like: It was just at sunset in a Swiss skiing village on the top of a mountain and some chick and I walked up the road floating in fog so we couldn't see one inch except tiny water pearls in her hair. Muffled. Dead like seashells on our ears. And a million miles away clicking skis coming down the slope like velvet, creamy soft, you can't believe it. Then all of a sudden two people appeared in front of us. Talking. Faded. And gone. Shhhhhhhhhhhhhhh then BANG, we looked back and it's crystal-clear sunset snow and a dark green forest in one second. Pinpoint skiers going home. And we turn around, OH wow. The whole sky is purple and the valley is filled from side to side with clouds so you could walk across and the sun is exactly between two peaks, pure red, and we stood and laughed because it was fiction to be so beautiful and not a way in the world to say it.

And that's the real story.

But that was in Switzerland a long time ago. Here: Picture a quiet night in conservative little Ann Arbor. The library is full of studiers. The bars and the movies are doing a light business. The law-abiding burghers are home reading the latest *National Review*. But somewhere, behind everybody's back, there are all these people smoking and tripping and flying—experiments in seeing tonight, maybe—we worked it out—almost two thousand people eyes open and hands out for any mind change—a funny kind of courage—they're illegal and all set to blow up everything inside, for simple reasons, like—"Just look," they'd say. That's all. Very smug together, and you people start looking. More and more. Around campus I see so many smiling stumblers now where not even a year ago there were just three-piece suits and circle pins. One time a bunch of us high on acid went into the local straight ice-cream parlor to buy fantastic colored cones. The guy wouldn't take our money. He said, "Save it. Stay stoned."

the tarnished shield

EX-DEPUTY SHERIFF (TESTIMONY)

Here, an ex-police officer and deputy sheriff relates his surprise at discovering—only shortly after becoming an officer—that law enforcement is different from what he had expected. Finding that fellow officers were accepting bribes, he too began to accept them.[1] This selection describes his involvement in payoffs protecting large gambling establishments from police raids.[2] (All names used here are false.)

My first job there was a bartender at Pete's bar near city hall on Washington Avenue, Miami Beach, Fla. After about two months I went to work as a patrolman for the Miami Beach Police Department. I went on the payroll about November 1946 for the police department.

Some time after joining this police department, I learned for the first time that law enforcement didn't always operate the way I thought it did. I found that on my beat it was a regular practice for the hotels and bars to pay regular weekly amounts to the night squad-car officers to overlook staying open after hours, selling liquor after hours, etc. The squad-car officers then would give a portion of their weekly receipts for this purpose to the night officer on the beat. I believe that the squad-car boys on my beat were getting at least $300 to $400 a week. Of this amount, the two officers of this squad car were giving me varying amounts up to a maximum of about $50 a week as my share.

. . .

My receipts from the two men in the squad car did not last very long for the reason that I was transferred from my first beat which covered from

Reprinted testimony from U.S. Congress-Senate, Hearings Before a Special Committee to Investigate Organized Crime in Interstate Commerce, *81st Congress, 2nd Session, 1950, pp. 459–65*

[1] The speaker estimates that while a police officer he received a total of $15,000 as his share of graft payments described here.

[2] For further investigations of police malpractice, the reader is referred to Skolnick (1966), and Stoddard (1968, pp. 201–13).

Twenty-seventh Street and Collins Avenue North to Forty-fourth Street and over to Indian Creek Drive. My second and last beat was on Collins Avenue from Sixty-ninth Street to Seventy-fifth Street on Miami Beach.

While on this second beat at one time "the heat" was on, and such large and well-known gambling establishments as Sunny Isles Casino, the Island Club, and others in Miami Beach or nearby were closed. During this period I discovered that a floating crap game was operating on my beat. I reported this to my superior, Acting Lt. Joseph Johnson. He told me to "smarten up, take what I was given and forget it." This game was on the second floor over an Italian restaurant about a hundred feet off Collins Avenue on Seventy-fourth Street when I discovered and reported it. The Jewish boys who were running the game and whose names I do not now remember gave me $50 to overlook their operation which did not last but about a week. The morning after they moved the game, Johnson and I raided the place and confiscated all the gambling equipment which had not yet been moved. This was one large crap table.

I recall also that when I was attending rookie school at Miami Beach Police Department that I discovered that the McArthur Hotel on Fifth Street, Miami Beach, contained prostitutes, bums of various sorts and marijuana addicts. I discovered this because, while I was a bartender, I had met in the bar a frequent customer named Irene Vermillion who spent large sums of money, and I was curious as to how she happened to have so much money. While a rookie, I looked up her record and found she had a long list of arrests for prostitution and narcotics, too, if I remember correctly. Thereafter, she invited me to visit her at the McArthur Hotel where she lived. I did and very shortly after my arrival she produced a supply of marijuana cigarettes and offered me one.

I reported this incident to my rookie instructor, Sgt. "Ramjet" Wolfe. Nothing happened. No raid was made and no one was arrested on the report I made to Wolfe. I later learned that Wolfe was supposed to have some sort of connection at this hotel and knew what had been going on even before I told him. Some of the other boys on the force indicated to me that Wolfe was afraid of me after my report to him on what I knew about this hotel.

On another occasion while I was on my first beat, the Park Avenue Restaurant was robbed. I obtained the name of a good suspect and his address. I reported this to Superintendent of Detectives Fulverson and asked permission to work on the case in plain clothes for a few days. He refused to let me do this but asked for the name and address of the suspect. I gave the name of this suspect, Louis Curry, to Fulverson. I later learned that the detectives had picked up Curry and later escorted him to the railroad station so he could leave town. This was around Christmas 1946.

I learned that it was said to be an established practice among the beach detectives to pick up persons wanted in other cities or for failure to register their criminal records at the Miami Beach Police Department and to "shake-down" these persons for as much as they could. The "shake-downs" sometimes amounted to thousands of dollars, and it was said after the "shake-down" or payoff the detectives would then assist their victims to leave town. This was done with the victims never being brought in for booking at the police station.

While I was still on the Miami Beach police force, a friend of mine and former sports promoter, Jack Carruthers, who was also a close friend of Dade County Sheriff Tommy Trelstad, tried to talk me into seeking a deputy's job in the sheriff's office. He took me to meet Tommy Trelstad in his office. Later, through Bob Handler, who was at that time Trelstad's chief criminal deputy, I was offered a deputy's job. I turned it down but later accepted the offer when my temporary appointment to the police force was canceled in an economy move by Miami Beach.

I had to wait about a month and a half after being cut off by the Miami Beach Police Department before going to work for the sheriff. This was in order for the sheriff's reelection to be assured.

During this wait I worked for Burdines Department Store in Miami.

I reported for duty at the sheriff's office around June 1948. My first assignment was that of night jailer from 12 midnight to 8 a.m. This assignment lasted about six months and entailed making a transcript record of bookings of prisoners brought in during the day, posting on the ledger, dispatching cars, handling complaints, etc. At the end of this period, I was assigned to a day shift, doing about the same thing. My first outside assignment came while serving on the day shift. The sheriff's office was seeking to make a raid on Dave Meyer's horse book in the Aviation Building at Northwest Twenty-seventh Avenue, Miami. I was assigned to this job with Deputies Tom Oake and Carl Myland because I was not known. The raid was successful and Meyer was convicted.

My next chance to do outside work for the sheriff's office was on Labor Day in September 1949. I was assigned to work with other deputies in a raid on gambling at the Latin American Club at 128 Northeast First Avenue in the city of Miami. We arrested Gardiner. Shortly after this raid, I was transferred to the criminal division to do outside work under Robert Gage who by then was serving as chief criminal deputy.

• • •

About a month after my transfer to the criminal division, I received a telephone call from Ben Lattimer, who is associated with Jack Christopher, and related by marriage. Ben said, "Someone important" wanted to meet me. I met Ben that night and he took me to the vicinity of a drug store on Southwest S Street near First or Second Avenue in Miami, where he introduced me to Jack Christopher, who was waiting in a car.

Christopher told me that he had heard of me from other sources and was going to do everything he could to get me on the gambling squad in the sheriff's office. I told Christopher that I didn't want to sell the sheriff down the river or see him hurt in any way. Christopher said, "Don't worry about it, as no one is going to hurt the sheriff."

Soon after meeting Christopher, I was called by Tom Brown, attorney for the S & G Gambling Syndicate on Miami Beach. At Brown's request, I went to his office. This was on a Saturday afternoon. Brown told me that he had been observing me and thought I was a pretty smart boy. He said that attempts were going to be made to get me placed on the sheriff's gambling squad and that he wanted me to become in the sheriff's office what Joe Sutter was to them in the Miami Beach Police Department.

Brown then said he wanted me to meet the "headman," and then made a phone call. In about a minute or so after the call, Henry Rienker came in. I didn't know Rienker and had never seen him before. Tom Brown introduced me to Henry Rienker and then went to his outer office. Rienker and I then had a private conversation in Attorney Tom Brown's private office.

Rienker remarked that I had helped a friend of his to accomplish something and therefore he, Rienker, felt that I was a capable man. . . . He, too, said he was going to try to have me put on the gambling squad. He instructed me to be careful in my actions and to "be as smart as Joe Sutter is." He said, "Not one gambler gives Joe anything because we take good care of him." Joe Sutter is an officer of the Miami Beach Police Department. Rienker told me that whatever I had taken up to then in graft from gamblers was all right, but said that from now on, "We don't want you to take anything from anybody—only when we give it to you."

When I was leaving Brown's office after the talk with Henry Rienker, Tom Brown said to me that if I listened to them, meaning Rienker and him, that I'd "be a very smart boy and have a lot to gain."

Up to the meeting with Rienker and Tom Brown, actually I had received very little in the way of graft payments. Some of the other deputies had given me small "cuts" on an occasion or two.

Several weeks after meeting with Rienker and Tom Brown, I was telephoned at my home on a Sunday morning by Ben Lattimer, who said that a meeting was being held immediately at the beach and that they wanted me to be present. I met Lattimer and went with him to Henry Rienker's house at 4415 Post Avenue, Miami Beach. Present at the meeting were Henry Rienker, Jack Christopher, George Sommer, and me. It was made clear at this meeting that there was a dispute among the gamblers as to whom they wanted put in charge of the sheriff's gambling squad, and it was also clear that these men expected whoever was in charge of the gambling squad to take orders from them. These men indicated that another faction of gamblers were holding out for Deputy Robert Pirrotta but they wanted me to be on the gambling squad. I later learned from Pirrotta that the gamblers who wanted him to head the squad were Jimmy Brandon, Joseph Yakoubian, and Eddie Buckner. They wanted Pirrotta teamed with Deputy James Philips, a brother-in-law of Sheriff Trelstad.

At this meeting at Rienker's house, Rienker, Christopher, and Sommer again said to me about the same thing which Rienker and Tom Brown had told me previously in Tom Brown's office. This was that I should "keep clean" and not take any graft from anyone or do anything that would compromise me. They said they were still maneuvering to get me on the gambling squad and that if I followed instructions they would make up to me whatever I lost in pay-offs in the meantime.

They then discussed who should work with me on the gambling squad and asked for suggestions from me. I didn't have any preferences and said so. At this point, Sommer spoke up that no matter what happened or who was appointed "you are the man we want to deal with."

I don't know exactly why Sommer attended this meeting, but from what he said it seemed that he represented Tallahassee or Jacksonville interests. He made several references to these places but mentioned no names. He also remarked that setting up the fix in Dade County was pretty easy. He said he had had to take care of a couple of hundred people. He didn't say where he had done this.

Shortly after this meeting, Pirrotta and Philips were appointed to be the deputy sheriffs in charge of gambling. This appointment was made by the sheriff. I should add that at this particular time there had been no deputies assigned especially to gambling.

Pirrotta and Philips had not been the two-man gambling squad very long before orders were given them to raid some gambling place, the name of which I don't know but which is located in northwest Miami. The place appeared to have been tipped off in advance of the raid and the raid was therefore a failure.

Tommy Trelstad was very much upset about the failure of this raid and the fact that Pirrota or Philips must have tipped off the place. He called a meeting of all the deputies in the criminal division at which time he made reference to "certain deputies" making their own deals with the gamblers. He called on the deputies to be honest. At the end of the meeting, he called Robert Swanson and me aside and appointed us at that time as the new gambling squad to work under Chief Criminal Deputy Robert Gage.

Later Jack Christopher, in talking with me about the failure of Pirrotta and Philips to make a successful raid, told me that this had made him very angry. Christopher said "When I want a raid made, I want it done!" Christopher said that definitely either Pirrotta or Philips had telephoned the place and tipped it off prior to the raid.

Very shortly after Sheriff Trelstad appointed Swanson and me to handle gambling, I was called either by Christopher or someone calling for him and told to meet Christopher that night at the parking lot at the rear of the Island Club, a gambling casino then operating up the beach from Miami Beach. When I arrived, I found Christopher and Henry Rienker together waiting for me. This meeting was very close to Christmas in 1949.

Both Rienker and Christopher said they were happy over my appointment and indicated indirectly that they had been responsible for my getting the appointment. One or the other said, "It took a little time and a little work but we finally accomplished it." Swanson was not with me at this meeting or any subsequent ones. Both Rienker and Christopher had doubts about whether Swanson could be trusted or controlled and speculated on how they could bring about a switch that would replace Swanson with someone of their own choosing. I told them I felt that I could control Swanson.

Although Philips had been removed from the gambling squad, he continued to collect the payoff money from Rienker and Christopher for the deputies up to about the last of January 1950. He would bring this money in cash and would distribute it on the nineteenth floor of the sheriff's department to Deputies Robert Pirrotta, Wayne Seymour, Robert Swanson, and me and was, of course, taking his share. The payoffs ranged from $75 to $100 each week. All of us, of course, know where this money was coming from and why.

Some of the deputies began complaining that Philips did not seem to be making any headway in collections from these gamblers, Rienker and Christopher. They felt we were not being paid in proportion to what we were expected to do for the gamblers, such as staying away from their places and closing up others. Philips, himself, was not too happy in his rule of collector or " bag man," and agreed that I should begin making the collections from Rienker and Christopher. I then became the collector and functioned in this role from about the last of January to the latter part of March or the first of April 1950.

Usually I would meet Christopher and sometimes Christopher and Rienker together about once a week at night in the parking lot behind the Island Club. Sometimes Christopher would call me in advance and say to meet him around Forty-first Street and Alton Road on Miami Beach which is not far from his home. At each of these meetings, I would be given sums up to $800 in cash to be distributed among the deputies in the criminal division of Sheriff Trelstad's office. This money was being paid for protection of certain Miami Beach and other beachside gambling activities and was specifically on behalf of the S. & G. Syndicate, the Sunny Isles Casino, and bolita.

The only gambling not on the beach included in the payoff was bolita. It was my understanding from Christopher that the money was being paid in the following proportions: When I was receiving $800 a week, $300 was from S. & G., $300 was from Sunny Isle Casino, and $200 was from bolita.

The Island Club, in which Christopher had an interest, was not contributing anything to the payoff although it was clearly understood that the Island Club was one of the places we shouldn't bother. Christopher argued with me that since he'd gone to all the trouble to organize a smoothly working centralized payoff and was himself doing the collecting from the gamblers and the paying to me, that he should not have to pay anything on behalf of his Island Club.

It was clearly understood between Rienker, Christopher, and myself that the payoff was to insure that the sheriff's office would not molest the gambling operations of the Sunny Isles Casino, the Island Club, the S. & G. Syndicate, and bolita. They agreed that for the sake of appearances and statistics that occasionally these several operations would have to be subjected to a "token raid" but insisted that in all instances of such a raid, they must be tipped off in advance. I agreed for the deputies that we would do that.

Every time I collected from Christopher and Rienker, I would split the money, always given to me in cash, between Deputy Sheriffs Wayne Seymour, Robert Swanson, James Philips, Robert Pirrotta, and M. J. Buddie. Deputy Dave Keenan was not included in this payoff arrangement as he was functioning under another arrangement with Jack Christopher. Christopher gave Keenan the down payment on his car and $100 a month. Christopher paid Keenan directly and when he was out of town, Bob Fair, also known as Bob Russo and other names and who is a partner or possibly a subordinate of Jack Christopher, would make the payments to Keenan. Once during last season, this payoff to Keenan was left with Donny Fillinger who runs Mammy's Restaurant on Miami Beach. I should add that the Card Club which has gambling was located in the same building as Mammy's. That was one of the places that Christopher frequented quite a bit and he insisted that we never molest it.

I would bring the cash paid to me by Rienker and Christopher to the nineteenth floor of the sheriff's office and would pay the deputies whom I have named their equal share by meeting them one at a time in the washroom, locking the door and handing them their share.

The payoffs from Rienker and Christopher as handled by us all worked rather smoothly expect for the amounts I was promised from bolita. Sometimes it appeared that Christopher could not make contact with Richard Hallett, former chief of police for South Miami, who was collecting the bolita payoff money from the operators. On a few such occasions, I met Hallett myself for direct payment for protection of the bolita operations. Also, the payments from bolita varied quite a bit. At the outset, I was promised by Christopher that the deputies would receive altogether from bolita $600 to $800 a month, but never actually got that much but about once.

One time when Christopher had been unable to contact Hallett, I contacted him in a back room at the Te Pee Club, a gambling casino which has operated openly in the city of West Miami, at which time Hallett gave me $400. We always had trouble getting this money and the deputies were complaining. At one time, Deputy Philips said he thought we ought to close all the bolita operators down because of this. So Deputy M. J. Buddie and I went straight to Hallett and saw him in his trailer in South Miami. Hallett, who is really an employee of Eddie Buckner, said he couldn't pay the $2,500 we demanded of him as the amount he was in arrears. He explained his inability to pay by telling us, "Well, I can't help it if certain people want swimming pools." I knew that Chief Criminal Deputy Robert Gage had just had swimming pool installed at his house, but I asked Hallett what he meant and he answered, "You work for somebody don't you? You take orders from somebody. I can't help it if he demands a swimming pool." Therefore, Hallett gave us nothing.

Christopher would at times tell me to pass along instructions to the other deputies not to raid or otherwise molest certain places. Other than the places I have already mentioned, I recall at one time that he wanted us to stay completely away from Surfside, a community just north of Miami Beach.

Regarding staying away from Surfside, Dave Abbot, who was in control of the Surfside gambling apparently, told me that between August and September he had paid over to Jack Christopher approximately $2,500, which Christopher told him he had to pay to the sheriff's deputies, including me. We never received any of this money. Christopher denied to me that Abbot was telling the truth but I believe he was. Abbot also told me that he controlled Chief of Police Leggett of Surfside.

Another place Christopher didn't want bothered was his place on Northwest Twenty-seventh Avenue in Miami at about Twenty-eighth Street where the Uneeda Vending Co. was operated on the ground floor and on the second floor were many telephones, etc., which were used by Christopher and his associates. We followed his instructions and never bothered these places, although we knew illegal gambling operations were being carried on in them.

I did not know all of the places in which Christopher had an interest. Occasionally we would raid a place and Christopher would immediately contact me and demand to know why the raid had been made. I would tell him the truth that we had been instructed by Chief Criminal Deputy Robert Gage to make the raid. Christopher would then be very angry and say Gage "was being taken care of" and that he couldn't understand why he directed the raid to be made.

Many times various of the deputies, including me, would seize money from various gamblers or bolita employees, when we raided or arrested, but we would not at time report in this money, or all of it, as seized. This was particularly easy to do when bolita runners were picked up as they would have several envelopes in their possession with varying sums of money in them, which they had just picked up, and most likely the runner would not know how much was in the envelopes. So out of any $300 in an envelope it was easy to extract half or more of it. Whatever we got this way we would split among the deputies I have named before. Also Robert Gage would get his share and I have at times given Gage a part of such seized moneys myself, and he, of course, knew where the others and I had gotten it.

annie the cop fighter

ANONYMOUS

This account by an alcoholic traces the stages by which she became a problem drinker. As a confirmed alcoholic, "Annie" frequently met the law on drunk and disorderly conduct charges—representing one of the thousands of petty offenders who occupy the attention of the courts today.[1]

I started to drink in 1913, when the women sat in the back rooms. We had a good time in those back rooms. I had two little boys at the time, but my family didn't worry me, because one drunk always led to another. Of course there were days in between when I was sober because I was broke. But mostly I was drunk. So my husband left me and took the two boys; one was six and one was nine. They were going off to school in those days, and it didn't worry me a bit. I loved the liquor and I loved the crowd that I hung out with. As far as my family was concerned, I lost everything of love and respect and everything else.

Believe me, this is no made up story. This is a true story from my own

Reprinted with permission of Alcoholic World Services, Inc. from Alcoholics Anonymous, *2nd edition (New York, 1955), pp. 514–22.*

[1]Additional literature includes the following: Deutscher (1954, pp. 592–95), Peterson and Maxwell (1958, pp. 308–16), and Pittman and Gordon (1958). Autobiographical accounts by former alcoholics include Riddell (1955), and Willis (1956).

life. When my husband left me, I had to be on my own. I never worked before, but I had to get out and get a job if I wanted to drink. So I got a pretty tough job. I wasn't any chicken. I was a woman of thirty-one when I had my first drink. I got a job as cleaner after mechanics in buildings. I would have done anything to get the money for drink. Any place I threw my hat was home-sweet-home to me. It could be a basement or a cellar or a back yard. I fell plenty low, but if I tell it maybe it will help some gal or some guy so they don't have to get down that low.

Finally one day, as usual, drunk, I was standing on a corner waiting for a streetcar, and a guy comes over to me and he says, "Lady, you're on the wrong side." And I says, "Mind your own business!" And as I looked up, it was a feller in uniform! So we had a few words, and he pushed me, and I wasn't going to let anybody get the best of me, and I shoved him back, and we had a little tussle there, and finally I had two buttons off his overcoat, and he says, "I'm takin' you in!" And I says, "Do as you damn please!" I was a tough piece of furniture in those days; if the Almighty God had come down I'd have done the same thing to Him. So I landed in the 67th Street station house on the east side, and I stayed there all night long. The next day I had to appear, and I was finger printed for molesting a policeman's uniform. So I got five days in the House of Detention. It didn't bother me whatsoever. The only thing I was worrying about was how was the gang making out without me. I thought I was missed all over! But they made out all right.

So I got out, and then I had to grab myself another job again, so what did I get into but hotel work! That was during the Prohibition days, and the bottles were flying all over the place. When I went to work on the floor, my first idea was to look in the guests' closets where the bottles were. I was all right going in, but I was cockeyed drunk coming out. And I'd have the help drunk with me. One time I got so drunk I blacked out and fell asleep in the guest's bed. I had the nerve to go back on the job the next morning—I didn't know what happened the day before—and the housekeeper was right there with her little note and my check. "Your service no longer required." And I had the nerve to ask, "Why?" I was told, all right. Well, in those days you could get jobs any time. It wasn't like today. If they had ever looked for references from me I think I'd never have got a job, because I never stayed in one.

I never hit hospitals, and I don't know why because I was fit for hospitals many a time. All the time I saw queer things crawling up the wall in my bedroom. In 1918, I got pinched again for the same thing. I turned out to be a cop fighter; I thought I could beat the whole force. I landed in the same court, had the same judge, and he asked me was I ever arrested before. I says, "No, your Honor!" Just as brazen as can be. And all he done was give me that sneering look, and he says, "For lying in court," he says, "you're not getting away with five days this trip!" I had gone under an assumed name, and I had forgot that I was finger printed, and I thought, being away for two years, he wouldn't know who I was! Playing so innocent! But I got thirty days then, five days off for good behavior, over on the Island.

Another time I was in court on the same old charge of Drunk and Disorderly. "Thirty days," says the Judge. And I was that mad and disgusting that I reared right up and spit clean in the judge's eye. It was a distance of at least five feet, too! You should have seen him leap. "Another thirty days," he says, "for spittin' in the eye of the Court." "Nuts to you," says I, but I had to serve the whole sixty days just the same.

I was worrying about my liquor and I was worrying about the crowd I hung out with. As far as my family was concerned, they never entered my mind. So I did my twenty-five days on the Island, and all I could do was look through the bars across the East River and see First Avenue and the joints that I hung out in.

When I got out of the workhouse that time I got a domestic job, and it was right up my alley because I got paid every day, and paid by the hour. In my day the women only got twenty-five cents an hour, but the liquor was cheap, and that would be all there was to it—maybe. I had blackouts, and many a night I don't know how I ever got home. I always did say, well, thank God I'm in one piece. But where I had been I would never know.

I had been away from home for fifteen years, and one day I was walking up First Avenue and I met my beloved husband. He called to me and he said, "Where are you going?" I was running like blue blazes to a speakeasy to get a drink, and I didn't know what to say, so I said, "I'm goin' up to the Five and Ten to get hairnets." I wanted to beat it, but he says, "Wait a minute." So I did, and we had a few words, and he looked me over, and he says, "You smoke, too, don't you?" He didn't know what all I was into; he should have known the rest! I said, "Listen here, you! This is my body and soul, and I can do as I please about it! I have been on my own for all these years, and I can still do as I please!" He didn't get angry over it, and then finally he popped the question to me: "Would you like a drink?" Whooh! There's what I was running for! And I says, "Sure, I would." So we went into a speakeasy up along the line and we had quite a few drinks, and we talked things over and I went back home with him.

But believe me, when I went back home it was too much of a decent life for me to lead. I didn't want that decent, clean life. I wanted to be what I was, a drunk. So I spent more time over on First Avenue than I did at home. Of course when I went back home, my two boys were raised, which I will give my husband the credit for. He raised them as gentlemen. The oldest boy was married, and the youngest boy was going to Delehanty's—to become a policeman! Brother! Well, it was all right. I had to take it and accept it. But every time I thought of that uniform, it killed me! After he had been in the force one year he got married. I was invited to that wedding with his father. But I invited myself to the old gin mill over on First Avenue again, and celebrated his wedding with my crowd that I hung out with. That's the kind of a mother I was.

I went back home again anyway. I was always forgiven, somehow or other. But I wasn't back home very long before it was the same old roundabout—back again to the friends and the blazes with the family. When the doors opened up for the women to sit at the bars, I thought that was the terriblest thing—for a woman to sit at the bar! Well, it didn't take me a long while until I got myself initiated to the bar. I was thrown off those stools so often that, believe me, it wasn't funny.

I had everybody's answers. I butted in to everybody's conversation. If a guy would fall asleep and leave his change on the bar, I was handy to help myself. He couldn't sleep and spend his money, so what was I waiting for? And I'd hang around like an old jackass until I got loaded. Brother, was I black and blue! I was kicked and I was banged and pulled by the hair. I'm surprised today that I'm not lame or something like that, the way I was knocked and kicked.

Then I got so low that I hung out with the guys and gals that were on the Bowery. I was loused up too. My whole clothes on my body were full of lice. How low can a woman get!

I got in tow with a gal named Irene, and we used to drink. When we had good money, we'd drink the best, but when we had only a little bit, beer was good enough. So one day in 1946, I happened to go into our hangout again as usual, and I asked Irene what she was drinking. She says, "Anna, to tell you the truth, I can't take the first drink. I'm havin' coke." (She nearly knocked me dead!) I says, "Saints above! What happened to you?" She says, "I can't take the first drink." "Well," I says, "nuts to you. I'm havin' mine!" "But," she says, "I'm gonna get you yet!" I says, "Over me dead body!"

She got into A.A. in March of 1946, and in May of that year, Mother's Day was on the 12th. The day before that I was having a good time in a gin mill again, and I don't know whatever come over me, but I asked some of the younger folks that could dial the phone to call Irene. I don't remember doing it. This was all told to me after. The next day was Mother's Day, and like everyone else I wanted to be such a wonderful mother that I had to buy a gardenia for my coat. I went up to this same gin mill to celebrate Mother's Day. I sat on the stool drinking, and pretty soon in comes my friend.

"Oh!" I says, "Hello, Irene!" She says, "Hello my eye! You got me lookin' all over the town for you! You made a date with me yesterday!"

I says, "*I?*" She says, "Not you, but the crowd in here had the ears rung off me with the telephone. They said that you wanted to meet me tonight and you wanted me to take you where I go on Sunday nights." "Hmmmm," I says, "That's news to me. Have a drink?" "No," she says, "I can't take the first drink. There's a cab there waitin' for me to take you down to A.A."

So down to the old 41st Street Club House I landed. In those days they used to have three meetings a week—Sunday, Tuesday, and Thursday. So I went down to that A.A. meeting that night. They took me to the beginners' meeting. I don't know what was said, but I do remember that when the meeting was over, when the door of the 41st Street Club House opened, I sobered up that very night after thirty-two years of knocking liquor around. I drank coke there that night, and I went back and forth to the meetings for eight months.

I was sober for eight months, physically, but not mentally. I never mingled with a soul in the meetings. I never shook hands or said hello to my neighbor sitting alongside of me. I never stopped for coffee. I just ran in and ran out. In the meanwhile I got married the second time. I picked a swell partner, another drunk like myself. I would come home from the meetings and tell him all about these stories, about these women hitting all the jails so often and all the hospitals so often, and he says, "You old so-and-so, you should've been there yourself!" That's what I got for an answer. But it didn't bother me.

Then one night a little argument started. I think I was waiting to start something. It was a foolish thing, over pig's knuckles, believe it or not. I was waiting for that pig's knuckles argument. He told me he was gonna have the gang up to eat up my sauerkraut and pig's knuckles for Saturday night, and I said, "You will in a pig's eye!" And I went out and got a fine load on. I only drank for two days, but I carried enough for a year in those two days.

I got off that two-day drunk through the A.A.'s. The nosey A.A.'s caught up with me somehow or other. They went to the place where I worked. The woman there was very interested in alcoholics. She said to me, "You're drinking." I says, "How do you know?" She said, "Come on in—sit down awhile and rest yourself." She says, "Charlie called up." I says, "That son-of-a-gun! He's got me so advertised that this damn organization knows my whole business! Nobody stepped over my territory before in my life! Now I gotta get into a thing like this and they know it all!" "Don't get excited," she says. "They're comin' up to see you tonight." I nearly dropped dead.

They came up all right. And I humbled myself. I felt so guilty. I don't know what A.A. does to you, but you never can drink the same again. So they suggested to me to go up to a farm in Connecticut, nothing but wide open spaces in the Berkshire Hills. It was a beautiful place. I stayed up there two days, and I came back a new woman.

Today I have a lot to be thankful for. A.A. has taught me the way of life. It has given me back my respect. It has given me back the love of everybody I know. It has taught me to show gratitude, which I never did before. It has taught me to be humble when I have to be humble.

I am what you call a lucky woman. I live alone now. I have a television which my boys have treated me to, and now I have a telephone too! I do love to go to A.A. meetings, and I meet with everybody, the old and the new. I'm a twenty-four hour person. I live on that twenty-four hour plan. I am five years and seven months without a drink, but I could go out tonight, but for the grace of God, and get drunk. There's another thing I must remember, that once an alcoholic always an alcoholic. I don't mind the name of alcoholic, because I was called a son-of-a-this and a son-of-a-that, and alcoholic is a good enough name for me. So I'm very, very happy. To newcomers I say, go to meetings, and God take care of each and every one of you!

hustler!

HENRY WILLIAMSON

Thief, racketeer, junkie, hold-up man, and mugger, Henry Williamson provides a stirring account of his success at pool hustling. In his own colorful language he relates how "hustling" provided him with a major source of income.[1]

Then I got me a little something else to make money, 'cause I had quit workin' at Chapman Brothers. The guy in the poolroom gave me a job rackin' pool. I already knew how to shoot, but not too good. I actually learned to shoot at this time. As I learned to shoot, the guy in the poolroom would let me shoot guys. If I lost I didn't have to pay for the game. When the poolroom closed, that's when we got down to the business of learnin' to shoot ourselves. That's when the guys workin' there had their chance. We'd

[1]For an interesting sociological description of hustlers, see Polsky (1964, pp. 3–15).

shoot among ourselves, 'cause the tricks[2] wasn't comin' in. Sometimes we'd shoot all night.

Now I wasn't goin' home in the evening. Me and Jesse was shootin' at that time, and improvin' our game. This was the guy I used in order to trick peoples to bet on one of us.

If things were slow in the poolroom, we would shoot amongst ourselves. See, there's always somebody in the poolroom that wants to bet. If he thought I was better'n Jesse, he'd bet on me. In order to make sure that we would get a sucker, we would start arguin' amongst ourselves over the money we had bet. This would convince peoples that we weren't friends. Now if a sucker was bettin' a small portion of money on Jesse, I would let him win until this guy's bet got larger. If I couldn't beat Jesse out, he would throw off[3] just enough to make the game look right, and let me win. You'd be surprised at the suckers in the poolroom that want to bet on a game like that.

During the time I was learnin' how to shoot, there was one incident I won't forget! Me and Jesse had burglarized a home, and in the burglary we had got a .22 automatic. So, to make some money, we sold it to one of the guys who worked in the poolroom. About two or three weeks later this guy we had sold the gun to got into a fight with a customer in the poolroom. This was an off-the-cuff customer. He didn't come in at regular hours, but came in at night when there wasn't suppose to be no customers. I don't know the full details of what went down in order to start the fight, but it was over a bet. Anyway, durin' the fight this guy pulled the gun that we had sold him, shot this guy twice, and shot hisself once in the foot. I knew he didn't kill the guy because he ran out, and the guy that shot him just laid up on the pool table and went to sleep. The police got him later on, and I was really shook up, 'cause I was afraid he would tell the police where he got the gun. But he went to jail without tellin', and later on everything went back to normal.

Workin' in the poolroom didn't stop any of my other activities. If I wanted to go home, I did. If I wanted to make some money, I went out on the streets and made it. But I always came back to the poolroom, 'cause that was something I really loved. It was always a challenge to me to be better than the next guy if possible.

Now after you become good at shootin' pool you can't stay at one place, 'cause it becomes very hard to get a game and make any money to amount to anything. You got to keep movin' from one place to another in order to make money shootin' pool. After we had got good, me and Jesse branched out to different poolrooms, 'cause it had become damn near impossible to

[2]Suckers.
[3]Not play as hard.

get a game with any money in it where we were. See, when you go into different poolrooms it's easy to get tricks until you're known.

There's one thing about tricks shootin' pool. Huh! You got to let 'em beat you. If you go in a poolroom and beat a trick two or three times straight, he won't shoot you no more. You cannot wrench a trick! You got to lay there with him! You got to lose money! Not if you want to hook him, that is! If you don't want to hook him, you might as well shoot the mother fucker for a dollar a game. You don't care nothin' about it. You might never see him no more! Go on beat him!

Now I could come in the poolroom and make a bet, and everyone'd bet on it! They knew I could shoot, but they didn't know how I'd shoot because if a sucker made a big enough bet I was not goin' a win!

Say me and you are shootin' pool. If a guy made a big enough bet with you I'm not goin' a beat you if I see more money in it for me. Maybe I'm bettin' you a couple dollars, and a guy will bet ten on you. I'm not goin' a make that game if we can get together and split that ten! But if you're a square and don't want to come in, I got to beat you! If I give you the eye that I'm goin' a shoot slow, you better come on in and win this game! If you don't, I'll beat you, and you won't win this ten dollars. If you win, I'm goin' a lose two dollars to you, but you're goin' a make it up to me, and we'll beat this guy for his money! If you don't want to play, I'm goin' a beat you if I can, and if I don't think I can beat you, then I'm not goin' a be shootin' no more than one or two games noway! I'm not goin' a lose no more than four dollars if I can't beat a man.

I'd always start off as a trick in a new poolroom if I was goin' a make any money. Let's say it's a Saturday night. Now among colored peoples Saturday night's the big night, and the majority of people have money. So me and Jesse would take the money we had hustled for that day with the intention of runnin' it up to as much as we could. I would let him go into the poolroom first. Then I would come in as "Trick Willey."[4] Anybody come in half drunk with money in his hand is considered a trick. I'd come in talkin' loud and have my money where every stud can see it! There's always guys layin' 'round a poolroom waitin' for tricks! Now sometimes I'd catch a trick, and sometimes I'd wind up bein' a trick. You see, Jesse's there to shoot with me if I can't get a bet, and to bet on the game if I do get a bet. Maybe he would bet against me or with me accordin' to how the game is goin'.

Now you don't bet durin' a game. Very few bet durin' a game. Most peoples wait and size up what's goin' to happen to see how good me and the guy I'm shootin' can shoot.

Now I could always tell how good the guy can shoot by the way the

[4] Trick Willey—any trick. The same kind of term of reference as G. I. Joe.

peoples would bet. See, every poolroom has its shark that peoples believe in. When peoples bet, I know what I'm shootin'. If a guy's a shark don't mean he's goin' a shoot like no shark. At first he's goin' a feel me out, and I'm goin' a feel him out. Since the guy thinks I'm drunk, this makes me have an advantage over him. To really get the point across to him I'd take a few drinks from the bottle I got in my back pocket.

If I see that the guy's goin' a let me win, go on and win, and if he wants to win, I let him. But as he win, I keep tellin' him that my game gets better as I shoot. If the guy's winnin', I let him win for four or five times, and I keep tryin' to raise the bet. If he don't raise the bet, I quits him.

Durin' this time if I'm losin', my boy's bettin' against me. If the guy raises the bet, I shoot better, and when it gets to where I want it, I give my boy the signal to bet with me. I'm goin' a shoot in order that I can beat him, but in a very small amount. You'd be surprised how good both of us could shoot once the bet went up! I'd make money the greater majority of times, 'cause if I saw where I couldn't take down anything, I would quit. I wasn't no die-hard!

• • •

After I got out wasn't nothin' to do, so I started doin' what I always have been doin'. . .wrong! I was sellin' safety stickers and shootin' pool in the evening. It was pretty good money comin' in, and I had me a couple of tricks lined up. At this time there was about three or four brothers that had a grocery store on Fifty-first and Dearborn, and three or four others. But the main one was on Fifty-first and Dearborn. They had a brother-in-law or some kinda kin runnin' it. This guy's name was Otis. He loved to shoot pool! Believe it or not he couldn't shoot worth a damn, but he loved to shoot. Liked bank.[5] He was shootin' three or four other guys who came in. Now he's bettin' this man's money in the grocery store. Runnin' him broke!

I was shootin' in Sam's then. That's between State and Dearborn. This man who owned the poolroom knew I could shoot pool! So he put me on.

He said, "Why don't you shoot this fool? He can't shoot no pool! You shoot a pretty fast stick. He can't do nothin'!"

I said, "The man ain't goin' a lose no money!"

"Look here! The man'll lose twenty-six or twenty-seven dollars a day! Shoot him! He's friendly with all the man's money anyway!"

So I tried the guy out. We shot eight-ball. I let him beat me. The guy's game is bank. I knew I could beat him when he shoot eight-ball! I knew it! I let him beat me in about two or three games and I quit him. We shot for half-a-dollar and a dollar. He's right back there the next evening. Now

[5]Bank—like straight pool except each ball has to be banked off a cushion before it goes into a pocket.

I had been shootin' for some time. I was shootin' over ace, and I was shootin' the Home of the Champs,[6] and I was winnin' that way! So I knew how to bait a trick in. And I shot him again that night. He'd beat me three or four games of eight-ball and I'd tie him a couple of games. And I let him leave with his winnings for three or four nights. If I didn't have the money the pool man would give it to me, 'cause he goin' a win too when I start winnin'. He wanted me to bait him in right. I do! We started shootin' for two dollars. He went back to his original game which he know the best. It's bank. And I know I can beat him 'cause my best game of pool is bank! That's my only game that I shot for money. I shot eight-ball, and rotation a little. Rotation is a luck game until a professional shoot it.

Anyway we started shootin' bank. I still let him beat me a couple of games. And then I tightened up on him . . . which the pool man expected me to do! And I beat him out of three or four dollars, then five or six, and then seven or eight! But Sam told me the man would lose twenty-six or twenty-seven dollars a day! I wanted to weigh myself into him![7] See, you can let a guy beat you three or four games and he'll swear before damnation that he can beat you from then on! But if you beat him four or five games straight he's scared of you! You got to lean yourself off!

Now I was takin' all these bets on the side and still losin', so he knew he could beat me! Within himself he knew it! But I knew he couldn't! When he got out to bank, he's shootin' my game! I'm never goin' a suggest my game first! Anything he want to shoot! I was pretty fair at anything.

So as I said, finally we got down to my game, which he think is his game but is really mine! Bank! I think the first day I tightened up on the guy I beat him out of thirty-some dollars! Now the pool man, the man who owns the poolroom, really makes the money! Then he was bettin' on the side, 'cause he knew I could beat this guy. If I'd give him the eye to go on and bet I was goin' a beat the sucker! The pool man knew I could shoot!

Now when you start out you let the guy win two games and you win one. When you tighten up, you let him win one and you win two. When you really tighten up you let him win one and you win three. At this point he's not too far losin', but the pool man is steady gettin' the money! On a trick you can't really never tighten up! Any time you beat him you got to make sure it's only by two balls or one . . . and always play him safe so that he's shootin' on the last ball two or three times. But you got him so he can't do nothin' with it! What he goin' a do with it? All he can do is shoot it somewhere where you can make it next time! The really hard thing about it is tryin' not to make shots, and makin' him believe that you actually tryin' to make it!

[6] Home of the Champs—pool hall noted as hangout for "sharks."

[7] To "hook" him.

I didn't bet this guy no hell of a lot of money! I only had one game where I bet a hell of a lot of money on. But I beat this guy out of twenty-six or twenty-seven dollars two or three times. He was a good money loser, 'cause every time I'd come in there I'd find him layin' there waitin' for me! 'Cause the guy actually believed in himself, although I was beatin' him goin' and comin'. I never came out a loser. I was at least ten or fifteen dollars ahead, and he still thought he could beat me! I let him think that! Now this guy was livin' in the neighborhood and peoples steady talkin' about how good I could shoot, so I had to let him come close every time! That's the most difficult money I ever won in my life! I got to beat him, but not by too great a margin! I got to let him shoot on the last ball a whole lot of times. Now there were other guys in there who knew he was a trick and wanted to bet him, and would give him some balls off! I was givin' him some balls off too, but their game was not as hard[8] as mine!

[8]Good.

reflections of a tramp

GEORGE ORWELL

In this selection from one of his earlier books, the well-known English writer George Orwell (Eric A. Blair) discusses the ways of a tramp's life. Since he himself was subject to possible arrest for vagrancy, Orwell can, with authority, reveal the many perils of the life of a tramp.[1]

I want to set down some general remarks about tramps. When one comes to think of it, tramps are a queer product and worth thinking over. It is queer that a tribe of men, tens of thousands in number, should be marching up and down England like so many Wandering Jews. But though the case obviously wants considering, one cannot even start to consider it

[1]Interesting sociological studies of this phenomenon include Anderson (1923), and Dees (1948). See also Chambliss (1964, pp. 67–77).

until one has got rid of certain prejudices. These prejudices are rooted in the idea that every tramp, *ipso facto,* is a blackguard. In childhood we have been taught that tramps are blackguards, and consequently there exists in our minds a sort of ideal or typical tramp—a repulsive, rather dangerous creature, who would die rather than work or wash, and wants nothing but to beg, drink and rob hen-houses. This tramp-monster is no truer to life than the sinister Chinaman of the magazine stories, but he is very hard to get rid of. The very word "tramp" evokes his image. And the belief in him obscures the real questions of vagrancy.

To take a fundamental question about vagrancy: Why do tramps exist at all? It is a curious thing, but very few people know what makes a tramp take to the road. And, because of the belief in the tramp-monster, the most fantastic reasons are suggested. It is said, for instance, that tramps tramp to avoid work, to beg more easily, to seek opportunities for crime, even—least probable of reasons—because they like tramping. I have even read in a book of criminology that the tramp is an atavism, a throwback to the nomadic stage of humanity. And meanwhile the quite obvious cause of vagrancy is staring one in the face. Of course a tramp is not a nomadic atavism—one might as well say that a commercial traveller is an atavism. A tramp tramps, not because he likes it, but for the same reason as a car keeps to the left; because there happens to be a law compelling him to do so. A destitute man, if he is not supported by the parish, can only get relief at the casual wards, and as each casual ward will only admit him for one night, he is automatically kept moving. He is a vagrant because, in the state of the law, it is that or starve. But people have been brought up to believe in the tramp-monster, and so they prefer to think that there must be some more or less villainous motive for tramping.

As a matter of fact, very little of the tramp-monster will survive inquiry. Take the generally accepted idea that tramps are dangerous characters. Quite apart from experience, one can say *a priori* that very few tramps are dangerous, because if they were dangerous they would be treated accordingly. A casual ward will often admit a hundred tramps in one night, and these are handled by a staff of at most three porters. A hundred ruffians could not be controlled by three unarmed men. Indeed, when one sees how tramps let themselves be bullied by the workhouse officials, it is obvious that they are the most docile, broken-spirited creatures imaginable. Or take the idea that all tramps are drunkards—an idea ridiculous on the face of it. No doubt many tramps would drink if they got the chance, but in the nature of things they cannot get the chance. At this moment a pale watery stuff called beer is sevenpence a pint in England. To be drunk on it would cost at least half a crown, and a man who can command half a crown at all often is not a tramp. The idea that tramps are impudent social parasites ("sturdy beggars") is not absolutely unfounded, but it is only true in a few percent of the cases. Deliberate, cynical parasitism, such as one reads of in Jack London's books on American tramping, is not in the English character. The English are a conscience-ridden race, with a strong sense of the sinfulness of poverty. One cannot imagine the average Englishman deliberately turning parasite, and this national character does not necessarily change because a man is thrown out of work. Indeed, if one remembers that a tramp is only an Englishman out of work, forced by law to live as a vagabond, then the tramp-monster vanishes. I am not saying, of course, that most tramps are ideal characters; I am only saying that they are ordinary human beings, and that if they are worse than other people it is the result and not the cause of their way of life.

It follows that the "Serve them damned well right" attitude that is normally taken towards tramps is no fairer than it would be towards cripples or invalids. When one has realised that, one begins to put oneself in a tramp's place and understand what his life is like. It is an extraordinarily futile, acutely unpleasant life. I have described the casual ward—the routine of a tramp's day—but there are three especial evils that need insisting upon. The first is hunger, which is the almost general fate of tramps. The casual ward gives them a ration which is probably not even meant to be sufficient, and anything beyond this must be got by begging—that is, by breaking the law. The result is that nearly every tramp is rotted by malnutrition; for proof of which one need only look at the men lining up outside any casual ward. The second great evil of a tramp's life—it seems much smaller at first sight, but it is a good second—is that he is entirely cut off from contact with women. This point needs elaborating.

Tramps are cut off from women, in the first place, because there are very few women at their level of society. One might imagine that among destitute people the sexes would be as equally balanced as elsewhere. But it is not so; in fact, one can almost say that below a certain level society is entirely male. The following figures, published by the L.C.C. from a night census taken on February 13th, 1931, will show the relative numbers of destitute men and destitute women:

Spending the night in the streets, 60 men, 18 women.

In shelters and homes not licensed as common lodging houses, 1,057 men, 137 women.

In the crypt of St. Martin's-in-the-Fields Church, 88 men, 12 women.

In L.C.C. casual wards and hostels, 674 men, 15 women.

It will be seen from these figures that at the charity-level men outnumber women by something like ten to one. The cause is presumably that unemployment affects women less than men; also that any presentable woman can, in the last resort, attach herself to some man. The result, for a tramp, is that he is condemned to perpetual celibacy. For of course it goes without saying that if a tramp finds no women at his own level, those above—even a very little above—are as far out of his reach as the moon. The reasons are not worth discussing, but there is no doubt that women never, or hardly ever, condescend to men who are much poorer than themselves. A tramp, therefore, is a celibate from the moment when he takes to the road. He is absolutely without hope of getting a wife, a mistress, or any kind of woman except—very rarely, when he can raise a few shillings—a prostitute.

It is obvious what the results of this must be: homosexuality, for instance, and occasional rape cases. But deeper than these there is the degradation worked in a man who knows that he is not even considered fit for marriage. The sexual impulse, not to put it any higher, is a fundamental impulse, and starvation of it can be almost as demoralising as physical hunger. The evil of poverty is not so much that it makes a man suffer as that it rots him physically and spiritually. And there can be no doubt that sexual starvation contributes to this rotting process. Cut off from the whole race of women, a tramp feels himself degraded to the rank of a cripple or a lunatic. No humiliation could do more damage to a man's self-respect.

The other great evil of a tramp's life is enforced idleness. By our vagrancy laws things are so arranged that when he is not walking the road he is sitting in a cell; or, in the intervals, lying on the ground waiting for the casual ward to open. It is obvious that this is a dismal, demoralising way of life, especially for an uneducated man.

Besides these one could enumerate scores of minor evils—to name only one, discomfort, which is inseparable from life on the road; it is worth remembering that the average tramp has no clothes but what he stands up in, wears boots that are ill-fitting, and does not sit in a chair for months together. But the important point is that a tramp's sufferings are entirely useless. He lives a fantastically disagreeable life, and lives it to no purpose whatever. One could not, in fact, invent a more futile routine than walking from prison to prison, spending perhaps eighteen hours a day in the cell and on the road. There must be at the least several tens of thousands of tramps in England. Each day they expend innumerable footpounds of energy—enough to plough thousands of acres, build miles of road, put up dozens of houses—in mere, useless walking. Each day they waste between them possibly ten years of time in staring at cell walls. They cost the country at least a pound a week a man, and give nothing in return for it. They go round and round, on an endless boring game of general post, which is of no use, and is not even meant to be of any use to any person whatever. The law keeps this process going, and we have got so accustomed to it that we are not surprised. But it is very silly.

Granting the futility of a tramp's life, the question is whether anything could be done to improve it. Obviously it would be possible, for instance, to make the casual wards a little more habitable, and this is actually being done in some cases. During the last year some of the casual wards have been improved—beyond recognition, if the accounts are true—and there is talk of doing the same to all of them. But this does not go to the heart of the problem. The problem is how to turn the tramp from a bored, half alive vagrant into a self-respecting human being. A mere increase of comfort cannot do this. Even if the casual wards became positively luxurious (they never will), a tramp's life would still be wasted. He would still be a pauper, cut off from marriage and home life, and a dead loss to the community. What is needed is to depauperise him, and this can only be done by finding him work—not work for the sake of working, but work of which he can enjoy the benefit. At present, in the great majority of casual wards, tramps do no work whatever. At one time they were made to break stones for their food, but this was stopped when they had broken enough stone for years ahead and put the stone-breakers out of work. Nowadays they are kept idle, because there is seemingly nothing for them to do. Yet there is a fairly obvious way of making them useful, namely this: Each workhouse could run a small farm, or at least a kitchen garden, and every able-bodied tramp who presented himself could be made to do a sound day's work. The produce of the farm or garden could be used for feeding the tramps, and at the worst it would be better than the filthy diet of bread and margarine and tea. Of course the casual wards could never be quite self-supporting, but they could go a long ways towards it, and the rates would probably benefit in the long run. It must be remembered that under the present system tramps are as dead a loss to the country as they could possibly be, for they not only do no work, but they live on a diet that is bound to undermine their health; the system, therefore, loses lives as well as money. A scheme which fed them decently, and made them produce at least a part of their own food, would be worth trying.

It may be objected that a farm or even a garden could not be run with casual labour. But there is no real reason why tramps should only stay a day at each casual ward; they might stay a month or even a year, if there were work for them to do. The constant circulation of tramps is something quite artificial. At present a tramp is an expense to the rates, and the object of each workhouse is therefore to push him on to the next; hence the rule that he can stay only one night. If he returns within a month he is penalised by being confined for a week, and, as this is much the same as being in prison, naturally he keeps moving. But if he represented labour to the workhouse, and the workhouse represented sound food to him, it would be another matter. The workhouses would develop into partially self-supporting institutions, and the tramps, settling down here or there according as they were needed, would cease to be tramps. They would be doing something comparatively useful, getting decent food, and living a settled life. By degrees, if the scheme worked well, they might even cease to be regarded as paupers, and be able to marry and take a respectable place in society.

This is only a rough idea, and there are some obvious objections to it. Nevertheless, it does suggest a way of improving the status of tramps without piling new burdens on the rates. And the solution must, in any case, be something of this kind. For the question is, what to do with men who are underfed and idle; and the answer—to make them grow their own food—imposes itself automatically.

streetwalker

ANONYMOUS

A London prostitute wrote the following piece on the life of a streetwalker. Through her description we see the loneliness of her profession, the routine and boredom of her daily life, and her alienation from conventional society. She also discusses the people ("johns" or clients) who make her profession possible.[1]

One in the morning, and in spite of the lamps Piccadilly is very grey. Most of the sightseers and partygoers have gone home, and the long street is once again in the possession of the night people—the outcasts and the eccentrics, the profit seekers and the escapers, the buyers and the bought.

Across the road I can see the looming darkness of trees, overhung by a heavy autumn sky billowed with rain. The grass is another darkness, subtly different in texture, distinguishable only to eyes used to the night and with time to spare. Few people look into the shadows or step onto the darkness, though. They keep determinedly to the paths civilized by electricity, walking a little faster through unlit alleys and the black, open spaces of the park, as if they would prefer to run.

In my profession, however, there is time to learn the warp and weft of leaf and grass blade, if one cares so to spend it. And nightfall itself holds

Reprinted with permission of The Bodley Head, Ltd. from Streetwalker, *author anonymous (London, 1959), pp. 3–12.*

[1]Other autobiographical accounts by prostitutes can be found in Benuto (1967), Harris and Freeman (1967), Mol (1967), McManus (1967), Rubin (1961), and Su-Ling (1967). For relevant sociological studies, see Jackman and others (1963, pp. 150–61), Bryan (1966, pp. 441–50), and the studies cited earlier in conjunction with the Polly Adler selection.

few terrors, because the dangers of the job are much more immediate and tangible, and the lesser fear gives way to the greater caution.

I always stand here, where Half Moon Street and Piccadilly meet, and every brick of this shop front, every fault in its paintwork, every crack in the pavement is familiar to me. There is a certain safety and advantage in this familarity, too: I know the quickest route to take if I spot the police, the best angle of light from the street-lamp for my face and figure, the most comfortable section of wall to lean on when the minutes drag. Besides, they expect to find me somewhere near this corner if they come back for more, and a good many of them do.

This is a slack night and spare time must be carefully used. Introspection is obviously to be avoided, but the streets themselves have many things to teach. Learning how to survive in London's grey wilderness and among its people is no easy course, though getting to know the heart of the city and its physical geography, the patterns of its squares and byways, is absorbing.

And so one whiles away the hours until habit and the clock on the car showroom say that it is time to go, time to abandon the street, to plunge into the pulsing jungle of basement club, spieler,*or backroom café, or simply into a warm cab, and then home. Preferably, of course, the time is too busy with money-making to need any other filling.

Twenty yards away, down to my right, Big Barbara is chatting a geezer, though the stream of polished professional patter she is directing at him warrants a less terse description. Barbara is an old hand, with the articulation and the grand manner of a duchess. She swoops on her prey, hand outstretched, smiling with autocratic charm. Taking an arm, she walks him swiftly up and down, outlining her plans and capabilities, hinting at bizarre possibilities and never mentioning money; she might be describing a charity bazaar, and, as it would take a strong man to avoid subscribing in that case, so it takes iron nerve to refuse her actual suggestion. Even more will power is needed to leave her flat with any cash. I wish I knew how she did it—there she goes now, fifty if she's a day, hobbling the only visible sheep to shear him in the befrilled luxury of her pink and mauve bedroom.

To be a successful prostitute, you've got to have at least one of three things: either outstandingly good looks and figure—and many of us are really beautiful; or the personality and individuality to make a man look at you twice, and then come back again and again; or the ability to talk or scare your clients, once you've got them back in your flat, into paying more than the original sum stipulated for extra attentions, or less ordinary functions—you must persuade them into something new, or roll them, steal from them.

If you possess all these assets, you have no business being connected with

*Gambling den.

commercial sex at all. Your place in the world is assured, if it is money and power that you want. If you have two of these qualifications, your best bet is to be a telephone number on an agency list, a hostess in a top-rank club, or the mistress of wealthy men. Most of us, however, are endowed with only one of these qualities, and quite a large number have none at all.

A girl in this most unfortunate position should really consider going home to her parents, or marrying the first reasonable man who comes her way, to whom she will probably make a passable wife. She certainly shouldn't waste her time on the streets, because, unless you can earn ten pounds a night without much difficulty, it isn't worth it. The toll is much too heavy.

If I fit into any category I suppose it is the second. I'm certainly not beautiful to look at and I'm twenty-two, which, while being by no means old, is still four or five important years more than some. My figure isn't bad, and I've got the smallest waist in Piccadilly after midnight, but that isn't enough to qualify in the first section.

As far as the financial wizardry is concerned, I'm useless. I've never learned to haggle, and I don't think I shall ever be able to do so now. I prefer to put a price-tag on myself, so to speak, before leaving the street, and then take that amount without asking for more. I'm no good at rolling, either, not because I believe it to be morally wrong, for it seems no crime to take from a man who is buying this particular commodity, but because I'm too clumsy. I simply haven't got the courage to be caught tripping over the doormat on my way out with someone's wallet.

Willy, the contraceptive man, is coming in the distance. He must be at least sixty-five, and nobody can remember how long he has been plying this particular trade. He used to be an undertaker, selling this commodity as an extremely profitable sideline, but his firm retired him because his health wasn't good enough for coffin-bearing. However, he makes enough money out of us to keep himself in Wills Whiffs, and to support his wife, an old car, and two Pekinese dogs. I think he'd miss us if he gave it up, anyway. He likes to have a chat in passing, whether his wares are needed or not, and it breaks the monotony to see his sprightly, birdlike figure approaching.

"All right, Jay?" he calls as he passes.

"Yes, thanks. None tonight."

He smiles brightly and passes on up the street, an integral part of the night, the cuckoo who calls the hours for us.

It is remarkable how much of a routine this business of being on the streets can develop into. I go to the same club every night, leave it at a quarter to twelve, wander down Shaftesbury Avenue, across Piccadilly Circus, up Regent Street as far as Air Street, which cuts through to Picadilly itself, and then dawdle along to Half Moon Street, which I reach at about five to midnight.

I stand just inside Half Moon Street until one o'clock, when the crowd has thinned to the buyers and us, the sellers, and when Willy puts in his first appearance, and then move round to Piccadilly to really get to work. At four, as a rule, I make my way back to Soho for a meal before going home.

There is a routine of approach, performance, and farewell, too. Even the smallest action—the call to a cab, the switching on of a light, the pocketing of money, is duplicated time and time again. The same small-talk, the same phrases are repeated, with only slight variations for the differing types of client, who behave with equally monotonous uniformity, within their type.

I've always thought the "Hello, darling! How about a nice time?" sort of approach rather crude. "How about a nice short time?" strikes me as downright bad taste, and as inviting as a slap round the face. What one might call the "filthy picture" one is a little more acceptable: "Why don't you come home with me and look at my photos, books, sketches?" does at least suggest an interesting meal, or one with a piquant sauce to it.

Naturally, it is sensible to promise rather more than one intends to give, especially since one gives the minimum. It is not a good idea to state any definite length of time, because although most men like to leave as soon as they've had what they came for, quite a few are determined to get every penny of what they consider to be their money's worth, or even more, which can be most unpleasant.

If the giving of some sort of time limit seems unavoidable, I find it best to say, "Oh, about half an hour!" with the sort of smile which suggests I might stretch a point, just for them. Actually, it is quite possible to leave Piccadilly, take a cab for the five minutes' drive back to your gaff, or flat—for no flat should be out of five minutes' travelling reach to be practical—get the performance over, and be back on your corner, all within twenty minutes. I know, because I've done it often.

When I first went on the game, it seemed to me that I was meeting a gallery of widely various and interesting people. Turning from bank manager to sailor, from poet to business magnate, playboy to thief held a definite excitement because of the outward trappings of their trades and ways of life. But as the weeks went by, army uniform and Savile Row suit became united as one anonymous garment, hanging over the back of my chair; complexions, features, hair lost their individuality and one face became all faces, one body all bodies, so that even crippled and distorted limbs were not much more distasteful than the flabby, sagging flesh of the old, and the muscular straightness of the young men not much better. Occupation and class lost significance, becoming no more than a rough guide to financial status and a useful subject for small-talk during the moments when conversation was called for.

Not, of course, that I stopped showing interest in clients as individuals—merely, I feign this interest now, and the imitation passes as genuine, so there is no loss on either side. But much more important than what a man does, I have learned, is what he wants from me, how he is going to try to get it, and how little he will be satisfied with.

Since clothes and speech are no certain guide to character or inclination, when a total stranger comes up to me in the street, assessment of his true self and his potentiality has to be largely instinctive. A man who is rude may be naturally aggressive, or he may be disguising shyness in this way. Timidity may be simply what it seems, or it may be a nervous approach to some perverted act long craved for, the outward sign of some inner, contorted desire whose very existence and strength is frightening enough, but whose execution and fulfilment is even more terrifying, though at the same time intensely exciting.

A man who behaves normally and naturally is unlikely to provide any unpleasantness. A man who haggles about price and conditions, who wants fine details as to exactly what he is going to get, is best left alone, unless it is a very slack night, as is the one with salaciousness over-brightening his eyes, or with hands quick to fumble at you in the open street. And the drunkard, too, is to be avoided, as is the tough, the obviously insane, and the frequently met practical joker.

Once at the gaff, the hurried, the efficient, and the businesslike are obviously favourites. Those who refuse to part with their money in advance must be got rid of, as must be those whose peculiarities did not reveal themselves at first meeting. The timid must be reassured of their safety or flattered into feeling that they are the men they want to be. The Don Juans, with prowess to display and achievements to be retailed, must be suffered with patience; the Galahads who, with immense condescension, allow you contact with their persons, counting you lucky to have been favoured and expecting due appreciation for the honour, must also be supported.

Personally, I find what one might term the "post-act" reformers the hardest to bear as, sated, they condemn the means by which they achieved satiation—prostitution and its instrument, yourself, abjuring you to give it up before it's too late, a nice girl like you.

In many if not most cases an encounter such as this slips quickly from a man's mind, and out of consideration or sheer hurry he leaves without delay. Then there are those—and not as many of them as might be expected—who, when they have made use of your physical and agreed-upon services in their various ways, are driven away quickly by disgust at what they have done: for paying for that which should always be a gift or taken by force, for running the risk of passing disease on to wives and sweethearts, for using what another man had probably only half an hour before and what hundreds have used in a twelvemonth.

A fairly large proportion come to us not only for physical relief, but for mental as well, and for sympathy, because of marital or economic troubles, and these are apt to linger. At such times, all one's humanitarian instincts must be fought back if one is not to waste valuable time to give them the comfort they seek. Some, of course, are so nauseating in their self-pity that it is easy to steel oneself against them. Others, though, are genuinely at their wits' end and desperate for help and solace, and few of us are cruel enough to refuse it in these cases.

I think that the release of talking about an unhappy home situation may well have saved many a marriage, and possibly even lives, when nerves have been strained to breaking point. It is well known that it is easier to unburden serious trouble onto a total stranger whose face you need never recall. Easier still to tell a girl whose time you have bought, whom nothing will surprise, and who is in no position to despise you, whatever you've done or want to do.

Others among the malingerers who incite pity are the vast army of lonely, unloved, and unwanted men who come to us seeking an oasis in their loneliness, fooling themselves out of desperation that the friendliness they have bought is genuine, feeling at home in the warm pink glow of a shaded lamp and fire and feminine company, relaxing, replenishing themselves, treating one for as long as they are allowed to as their own, shyly or urgently clinging, and loth to break the spell, to leave their short moment of content, so that in the end one has to be brutal, to remind them of what they are and where they are, and that their time is up.

Really infuriating are those who demand your attention and time until the last pennyworth of their due has been extracted, either because they are mean by nature, or because they are at once intelligent and sadistic enough to know that you long to be rid of their company and of your intense irritation at their continuing presence. These latter derive immense satisfaction from the sight of your annoyance, while the former derive equal pleasure from each moment they get "free." Both need firm handling.

on being a homosexual

KENNETH MARLOWE

Kenneth Marlowe, once a female impersonator and later a male madam, comments on his feelings about being a homosexual. Marlowe notes the fact that homosexuals constitute a minority group in America—a minority group which is denied its rights. He also points up the hypocrisy of the large number of married men who use the services of his male hustlers.[1]

Very often clients didn't want the boys too good-looking. Not ugly, but not *too* pretty. Pretty boys are often too conceited, generally dull in bed, and too commercial looking. Clients weren't interested in down-on-their-luck would-be actors. Muscle men weren't too exciting or successful because all they would do was lay back and show their muscles and, most of the time, with very little equipment. They made up in muscle what they lacked elsewhere. Although men would say they wanted this type they called back to complain, afterwards, because they were dull bed partners.

I found the best hustlers were average looking, wholesome types, not nellie —more boyish, and not too experienced-looking.

The really good ones made the customers feel they were only doing it out of temporary necessity and weren't *really* professionals.

Several of my boys were married men, bisexuals; some were college students, office workers and some were just hustlers who worked at nothing else.

Not all of the boys did *everything* and that occasionally created a problem. Some did all things and didn't care whom they were with, but a few of the boys limited themselves as to that in which they would participate. I was soon to learn a couple of lessons from them.

Most hustlers aren't like female whores because unlike women, they'll cheat. They'll go with one man for free, charge another, and go free with still another.

Reprinted with permission of Sherbourne Press from Mr. Madam: Confessions of a Male Madam *by Kenneth Marlowe (Los Angeles, Calif., 1964), pp. 211–15.*

[1]Sociological literature on homosexuality includes Leznoff and Westley (1956, pp. 257–63), Reiss (1961, pp. 102–20), and Humphreys (1970).

Most of the boys are like people from *normal* life. But they're of a type—*oversexed.* They cheat themselves. If they couldn't sell enough sex each day, they'll give it away. So long as they get enough each day is all that matters to them.

In any group there are certain types. Most straight people think all homosexuals are alike. Even among homosexuals there are the same classifications of types of people as there are among heterosexuals. And there are gay people in *every* walk of life.

Just because you know a boy in the office is gay, it doesn't mean he's done all the things I've done in my life, or would do. Many would never do *any* of the things I've done. Most heterosexuals know *some* homosexuals even though they don't recognize them as such.

Some homosexuals cover up their "problem" very effectively and you'd *never* spot them. And some don't care whether or not you know they're gay. Many things in life are done in secret and *suspicions are not facts!*

There are female prostitutes but that doesn't make every woman a prostitute. There are a lot of gay boys but they're not *all* hustlers and drag queens. Many homosexuals go to gay bars who wouldn't *think* of hustling a trick. And if they do or do not *isn't really important.* Whose business *is* it besides their own?

In my private life most of my friendships are with heterosexuals and they do not fear or shun me.

Many a wife is married to a homosexual and doesn't know it. And sometimes neither does *he!* Most men have done something homosexual in their lives. But *few* will admit the fact until they've accepted their homosexuality.

Kinsey put the rate of homosexual incidence quite high. And all the critics howled "Foul!" But if the rate isn't as high as that why did so many married men with children come seeking my "call boys"?

Of course, as soon as women have the ring in men's noses, they let go of the waistline, the sweet tone, and the lovely appearance fades. They're so involved with family, and children, friends and obligations, they treat their husbands like just another thing that has to be handled through their day. They should study the geisha girl, and perhaps their husbands would stay home more nights.

I've had so many married men tell me they can't stand looking at their wives that I wish I'd kept count. But men felt they weren't cheating on their wives when they're with my boys, or another man. The psychology of our American adult morality says it is "wrong" only if he has his sex with another woman, prostitute or otherwise. When he's with the boys he's not cheating. But *he sure as hell is getting his satisfaction!*

Beware of those who talk too strongly against homosexuals or the women who yell too loudly—you should check out *their* husbands—because they must have something in their own lives to hide. They are usually associated close enough with the subject or they're too frightened, or too uneducated to know what to do about it, in their own lives.

The public is still carried along on such ancient myths that it's pathetic. Generally, homosexuals *don't* rape three year olds—boys or girls, nor do they kill people, nor do they give off a disease by being in the same room with *normal* people. Most publicized rape cases have been proven to be committed by heterosexuals. Homosexuals aren't lepers, you know. We're people.

There are no stereotypes among homosexuals just as there are none in any other area of sex. But realizing the human factor, it's understandable that the public thinks "homosexuals" seduce children.

When I waltzed down the street or sat in a movie theatre, tricked up and down the Y halls or anywhere else, *I didn't force any man to bed.* He came of his own free will. I was just available.

A *real* "straight" heterosexual wouldn't *see* me standing there on the corner or, if he did, would ignore me. Men never climb into the feathers with you unless they *want* to do so. *It is impossible to entice any adult individual into a homosexual act unless he consents.*

Being around homosexuals doesn't affect heterosexual men *if* they are *sure of themselves.* Homosexuals don't concern themselves with men who are obviously not interested.

The only men I ever found afraid of homosexuals were those who *were* unsure of themselves, who were afraid of their own state of masculinity, and feared they might *lose* it.

Borderline cases are the *haters.* They do the most yelling about and against overt homosexuals.

Heterosexuals who have to get their *kicks* by going out to "beat up queers" are the ones who are *kidding themselves.* They talk about it boldly because they have to "prove" *they* aren't homosexuals.

Homosexuals are a minority group who are denied their human rights!

The public, usually with the aid of front page newspaper publicity, confuses and links mentally deficients who commit sex crimes with all homosexuals. *Most* homosexuals are *not* sex criminals except in the eyes of the law because laws are antiquatedly against morals, which should be intelligently relegated back to the province of religion and medicine.

American police departments make a big show of "wiping out" the homosexual element in their cities because it gives them great amounts of publicity and certainly makes them *look busy* to the Public Eye. And crime is often left unsolved because they're so busy with the morals of men who don't bother *other men who are not responsive.*

Vice squad officers are another breed. They certainly are "interested" in their work! Too many of them are *enjoying* the sexual favors of their entrapments *before* they get around to make the arrests. You'll never, however, find *those* statistics available. Nobody seems to have kept them!

One of our largest west coast cities does a huge business in homosexual entrapment. Annually, the city reaps enough from aggressive Vice Squad entrapments to enrich the coffers by half a million dollars in fines. And that's big business. It pays a lot of salaries. And the whole dirty method should be shocking. It is. But the only shocking the city promotes is convincing the citizenry a lot of homosexuals are dangerous. They neglect to inform them that these same homosexuals are very profitably used.

When entrapped, each homosexual pays an average fine of $300. . .for inviting someone for a "cup of coffee." Or accepting an encouraging come-on, only to find bitter results rather than emotional pleasure.

If homosexuals ever organized, banding together for mutual protection and rights, like other minorities, they could exist without bondage as long as they publicly behaved themselves as thinking adults.

i gypped insurance companies for $1,000,000

DAVID SCHIFFER

This unusual selection describes how the author made $1,000,000 through a phony insurance claim racket. Faking accidents and then collecting from insurance companies, Schiffer developed a lucrative racket. In this account, a master swindler reveals the techniques he used, including phony X-rays, "floppers," and "divers."

My racket was gypping insurance companies. I got them for a million dollars. Last December I stood up in front of a judge in a New York court and traded the million for four-to-eight in Sing Sing, but it took detectives and fraud investigators fifteen years to tumble to my racket. They knew I was working, but they never knew how. I drove them nuts.

I faked accidents on New York streets. I hired "floppers" and "divers" to make out they had been hit by cars, and then I collected from the

Reprinted with permission of the publisher from Colliers Magazine 123 *(February 5, 1949), pp. 13, 42–43.*

insurance companies. I sold doctors and lawyers a bill of goods. I fooled insurance investigators. I made the cops work for me. With nothing but a library of phony X-rays I beat every insurance company on the street.

It wasn't easy. I had to study broken bones until I was an expert. I could read X-rays. I knew insurance law, so I posed as a legitimate insurance adjuster and fooled my best friends. I even posed as a lawyer and fooled judges in their own courtrooms. Not bad for a guy who never got past the fourth grade in school.

I discovered this insurance racket in the Building of the Forty Thieves in downtown New York. This is a building where a lot of lawyers have offices and a lot of guys hang out looking to make a buck. I met Harry S—— in this building and he taught me the pattern.

At first we were chasing ambulances. I would run into him sometimes when he was going out on a case. He was a con man who originated in Jersey somewhere and he looked like more of a judge than anything else. He was older than me. I wasn't twenty-eight yet. I am forty-four now.

All this was businesslike. We used to get tipped off by city hospitals on accidents, but the competition was tough. There were other guys in the same business. We were able to shake some of them down by using phony cops to chase them, but the lawyers started to get into the racket and that ruined it for us.

S—— knew about fraudulent insurance claims and he taught me what he knew. About 1933 we branched into fake-accident claims. A Bowery bum got us started.

One day I was standing on a street corner with S——, and a car making a turn hit a derelict. The car stopped. The bum got up, brushed his pants, and went away. I took the license-plate number of the car and reported a hit-and-run case in order to get the accident on record. I then turned the case over to an attorney who knew what it was all about but didn't want me to explain fully as he figured it was a racket. The attorney agreed to work for a one-third cut of the settlement.

I then called police headquarters and told them, "This is Walsh, Badge Number such-and-such," and the fellow on the other end said, "How do you feel today?" I said, "Okay," and gave him the license number and asked him what the owner's name was. He was very helpful and got me the information. I then called the car owner on the phone, saying I represented the social service at Bellevue Hospital.

I told him we had a bill for medical treatment and asked for the name of his insurance carrier, which he gave me. I ventured on jokingly that the fellow has developed a dread disease due to this accident and that I hoped he carried enough insurance. He admitted he carried a twenty-to-forty-thousand-dollar policy and he volunteered the name of his insurance broker.

A summons was served for $25,000, and a physical examination was arranged at the attorney's office. My partner dressed as the bum for the act and displayed an X-ray showing a fracture of the shoulder. I had not known about this X-ray side line before.

Three weeks after the examination my partner and I called an adjuster we knew in this particular company and asked him to see what figure he could put on this particular case, if any. Later in the day he gave us a figure of $4,000.

We waited a little while and then called this adjuster again and told him we needed another $500 to settle the case, which brought the figure up to $4,500. We then told the attorney that we had to bribe the adjuster with $1,000, which we kept. Later we gave the adjuster $200 to keep him happy, and the lawyer, who was working on one-third and thought we really gave the adjuster $1,000, came in for a piece. He never knew we chiseled him and split $3,100.

Now that I had seen the way my partner's pattern worked, I became very much interested. At this time my partner was losing his money on horses and in dice games and was forever borrowing money from me to support his habit. I quit him and went on my own. He has no police record. He was never caught. But he is on the rocks today.

I saw immediately that I would need a file of X-rays to build up my pattern of operation. My first step was to go to the Municipal Lodging House, which had bums and derelicts. I spoke to a bum with a cast on his arm and asked him how old the injury was, where the break was, how he got it, and if there was any lawsuit pending. I then took him into my car, saying I was a student from some medical school and was making a study of fresh fractures. If he would comply with my request and have X-rays taken at a doctor's office in the Bronx I would give him two bottles of whisky and $5 for himself.

Ten minutes after the X-ray was taken the doctor convinced me this bum was telling the truth that it was a fresh injury. I then made a deal with the doctor for a dozen plates with two views of this fracture, and gave him $75 for these X-rays.

Later I got X-rays of other fractures, but these first X-rays were all alike except each plate had different initials and there was no doctor's name on them to trip me up. They usually put a patient's initials on X-rays for purposes of identification. One plate had the initials "D.C.L." on it and I used it under such names as David C. Levy, Daniel C. Levine and others. This fooled the insurance investigators, who were always checking to see if a claimant had a previous accident with them.

I now set about getting people to work for me who could pretend they got hurt in the fake accidents as the victim. They were called "floppers" and "divers." A flopper is a person who knows how to fake getting hit by a car making a turn at an intersection. This person dashes out to cross the street as the car comes around the corner at low speed. He puts his hands on the front fender and flips over backward and lays in the street groaning.

It is very hard to get good actors. Some floppers were very good actors, but others would only wince here and there. Floppers could work at any time of day, but not divers. Divers were best at night.

A diver is a person who takes a car going straight down the street, maybe thirty miles an hour. This party stands several feet off the curb and as the car approaches he runs out and sort of crouches while he slams his hand against the door, making a very loud noise. He then falls into the street. The car stops, and from there on the routine is the same as it is with a flopper.

I collected $1,750 on my first case. I found a truck driver who would play ball. He told me the stops on his route and I introduced the party to be injured to the driver. I then selected a street corner that had no drugstore. I did not want them picking him up and carrying him into a drugstore instead of sending him to the hospital, which was very important as I had to have official records when I got ready to make my claim.

Before the "accident" took place it was necessary to set up a fake address for the "injured." I soon found this was the most important link if my case was going to stand up. This job took several days.

If possible I preferred to deal with prostitutes who operated in apartment houses, since they moved around a lot and were hard to keep track of. However, I also knew many other people I could go to who would say the injured lived there if an insurance investigator came around. I would give them $10 or $15 to say this.

I would give the injured a name like Joe Marino and the next day I would go to the superintendent of the building and ask him what apartment Marino lives in. The superintendent would say no, there was no Marino there. I would then say, "Oh, he lives upstairs with John Jones," and the superintendent would give me the number of the apartment that Jones lived in.

A day later my lieutenant would go to the superintendent and ask him again what apartment Marino lived in. The superintendent would still not remember Marino so my lieutenant would say, "He is the fellow that broke his elbow in that big accident. He lives with John Jones." Now the idea was planted in the superintendent's brain, and when the insurance investigator finally got around to checking the address the superintendent would tell him, "Sure, Marino lives here. He's the guy who broke his elbow in that accident. He lives with John Jones upstairs." This would convince the investigator that there really was a Marino and that he really lived there.

Now comes the accident. I picked up the flopper in my car, told him his name and address, and drove around for an hour to make sure I was not being tailed. Finally we got to the street corner I had picked. The truck arrived on schedule and the flopper went into his act. I paid him $10 for this. It was a good performance.

While my flopper was laying in the street groaning, a cop came up and wanted to know what is going on here. I stayed off in the crowd and watched the stage play. The cop called an ambulance, which soon arrived, and after the flopper was taken away the cop made out his report describing the accident. Now the accident was on the police record, which was important.

At the hospital the flopper made out that his elbow was badly injured. The act had to be very good in order for the intern to suggest X-rays. However, the flopper then refused to have X-rays taken there, saying he wanted his own doctor to take them. The intern then entered the case in the hospital records as a possible fracture. It was important for the intern to diagnose the injury as a possible fracture, since it opened the way for me to use one of my phony X-rays later. If the intern diagnosed the injury as contusions or abrasions I would have to drop the case, as contusions and abrasions are not worth the trouble.

One week after this phony accident I turned the case over to an attorney. This attorney was what you call book-smart, but he could not move around very fast and he did not know I was outsmarting him with a fake. All he was interested in was his check. The attorney sent a claim letter to the owner of the truck, which was forwarded to the insurance carrier. By the time the insurance company got the letter, there was already a lawyer in the case and they could not push us around.

In about ten days the adjuster from the insurance company called up the attorney and asked what the injury was. The attorney said it was a bad injury but that he could not tell him any more as he did not have a complete medical report. He then told the adjuster to arrange a physical examination with the insurance company doctor, but said it could not take place for several weeks since the injured party was not available just then.

It was important now to get a private doctor to put this fake case into his own files. I went to see a doctor who thought I was a legitimate insurance adjuster and told him things looked very bright for him in the future as I was interested in him and would like to see him picking up some extra change as an insurance-company doctor.

I then told him about the case and asked him to make out an index card for his files showing that he had treated the "injured." I told him he had nothing to fear so long as he did not give me anything in writing. All I wanted was for him to say he had seen the patient if the insurance company called and to tell them to call the attorney if they wanted more information. I paid him $50 for this, but before I left his office I lifted some of his letterheads and put them in my pocket.

The next step in this pattern was to make out a medical report on the doctor's stationery. I forged the doctor's signature on this report, which I wrote myself. The report stated: "This patient is under my care for the following injuries sustained on such and such a date: contusions and abrasions of right elbow; fracture of internal condyle of right humerus. X-ray examination reveals fracture of internal condyle. This patient will require further treatment."

I did not use the original flopper to take the insurance-company examination as I did not want to make him feel too important in the setup. I hired a thief instead from the Bronx who had the same type of build as the original flopper, and I gave this bum $15 to take the examination.

Eight weeks after the "accident" the doctor from the insurance company examined the patient. The reason it was eight weeks was that it takes about eight weeks for adhesive-tape markings to go away, and I could not appear in, say three weeks, with this bum who showed no evidence of ever being bandaged.

First, though, I took the bum to the scene where the "accident" happened so he could answer questions. I gave him his age and fixed his date of birth. I told him the name of the doctor who was supposed to have X-rayed him and treated him. I further explained to him when the X-ray was taken, when the adhesive strapping was applied, how often he saw the doctor, when the strapping was removed, the amount of bakings and massagings that followed, and the medical fees up to date.

At the examination the insurance doctor just looked at the phony X-ray and asked the patient to squeeze his hand to see if there was a loss of restriction. After this quick examination the insurance company settled for $1,750. That was as far as it went. In later cases I found that insurance-company doctors are usually too busy to be thorough, as they are looking to examine a lot of patients for purposes of money. I also found that big doctors are pushovers as they have big egos.

In the 15 years I worked this racket I came up against only a few thorough doctors. They were real heavyweights, but I had a system for them, too. When one of my injured was to be examined by a heavyweight I knew was thorough, I would use an old pickpocket's trick to discourage him. I just gave the "injured" a couple of shots of whisky and all the garlic he could eat and I have yet to see a doctor who could stand the smell when the patient blew in his face. The doctor would get desperate from this man's breath and would give him a fast onceover and tell him to put on his coat and wait in the outer office while he filled out his report. It was easy.

In all, I cashed over a million dollars' worth of insurance-settlement checks but I never kept any records. I never put a cent in the bank, even under an assumed name, as it would have been lost if I died. Sometimes I had as much as $20,000 in my apartment in the Bronx which I paid $60 a month for. I kept the money mostly in $500 bills and concealed them in a book called Ivanhoe, which was in a stack of other books in a closet.

My files were in my head. I had to be thinking all the time as it would have been fatal to backtrack on myself. I had to be careful that a flopper did not take two flops in front of the same cop or be picked up by an ambulance and taken to a particular hospital where he could be recognized as a repeater.

I also learned not to let a flopper or a diver take a car with a low license number, as this would indicate that the car belongs to an important individual and I did not wish to become involved in a lot of publicity. Once a flopper picked such a car in front of the Waldorf-Astoria, and when the cop came over to question the driver I heard him say, "Hello, Judge." I became somewhat nervous on hearing that this fellow was a judge so I eased over to the flopper and told him to get going. The flopper then picked himself up and said, "Sorry, I did not watch where I was walking," and we let the case go.

Another time one of my floppers was recognized by a cab driver who was a friend of his and saw him laying in the street after an accident. The cab driver yelled, "What's the matter, Johnny?" and it became necessary for me to go over to this cab driver and explain to him that this was no Johnny and for him to keep moving.

I also had to be careful not to let an insurance company maneuver me into a position where I would have to permit a re-X-ray since my client naturally had not been injured in the first place. If a company got suspicious and requested a re-X-ray, however, I would still not be licked. Luckily, an insurance company cannot get a re-X-ray without a court order, which they can obtain only by claiming fraud.

However, if the company got stubborn and tried to make me agree to a re-X-ray, I would immediately go up and see the company adjuster and would represent myself to him as a lawyer. I would give him a little bottle of Chanel No. 5 for his wife and then we would talk about the case. I would tell him I was short of money and was trying to settle the case in a hurry as I was selling my client out by not fighting for a bigger settlement for him and this naturally was to the company's advantage. This worked about 90 percent of the time. When it did not work and the company still wanted a re-X-ray I would drop the case as it would be too risky to argue any more.

I could do more tricks with my X-rays than a monkey with a peanut. By this I mean I could easily switch a right shoulder to a left shoulder or a right elbow to a left elbow. As I built up my file of X-rays I specialized in shoulders and elbows. When these X-rays got old and started to darken I would send them to a town in Pennsylvania or Indiana, and have fresh X-rays made from them by some process.

When I had X-rays taken of these Bowery bums, I made sure they were taken from an angle where the heart did not show. If it did show, I could not switch rights and lefts. Sometimes I would get a lady bum on the Bowery with a broken shoulder and would have her X-rayed. In cases like this I would make sure that the X-ray angle did not show her breast shadow as I could not pass it off as a man's picture if such a shadow showed.

In one of my early jobs I used an X-ray of a broken shoulder which I had stolen off a doctor's desk. Twenty-four hours after the insurance-company doctor saw this X-ray the company offered to settle with me for $4,500 if I would sign a release then and there. I was speechless for a moment, as this particular fracture was not worth more than $2,000, but I signed the release and left the insurance company very much disturbed.

I called the attorney on this case and arranged a meet on Thirty-fourth Street and Second Avenue. The attorney met me and I told him what happened. He thought we were in a trap. He wanted me to take the case out of his hands for the sole purpose that this amount was too excessive. Attorneys are the first guys to crack under these circumstances. I told him not to worry.

Later I went to see another doctor with this particular X-ray. I asked him what was on this picture. He said, "There is a fractured shoulder and *two fractures of the spine.*" I then realized the insurance company had gypped me. This fracture was worth at least $10,000.

There was another thing about this particular case. When the insurance-company doctor examined the X-ray he asked the "injured," who was with me, if his back hurt. Not knowing what to say as this part was not rehearsed, the injured said, "A little." The doctor never stopped to think that the injured would be in a hospital and not in a doctor's office if he had just had a broken back. To top it off, the doctor got so excited when he noticed the spinal fracture he never realized he was looking at the X-ray of a woman instead of the fellow beside me. When I looked at the picture later I could see the outline of a woman's breast.

If the cops or the insurance-fraud investigators could have trapped me with this phony X-ray in the doctor's office they could have saved over a million dollars, as this is the amount I took them for later. But I did not make this mistake again and it was fifteen years before I made another mistake.

confessions of a con man

"YELLOW KID" WEIL

One of the con games that helped Weil fleece his victims of an estimated eight million dollars was the faro bank pay-off. When investigated by a Senate Subcommittee on Juvenile Delinquency (1956), Weil admitted that some of his schemes sounded fantastic. He explained, however, that his confidence games had their great appeal because of the lure of a chance for easy money—without the avarice of his victims, he would never have succeeded at his trade.[1]

The confidence game known as the pay-off has been worked by many con men throughout the world. Undoubtedly the reason the pay-off has been operated so successfully in so many instances is that it is a game of chance where the victim stands to win a lot of money. There is perhaps no other lure known to man that has so much appeal—the chance to risk a little and win a lot.

Aside from the natural animal instincts that are inherent in every normal person, I believe nothing else is so powerful as the urge to gamble. That is the reason there have been so many attempts to legislate gambling out of existence. My own opinion is that you can do this about as easily as you can change human nature.

I venture to guess that there have been more laws against gambling than any other crime, with the possible exception of homicide.

These laws may have changed our habits, but they haven't done much to stop gambling. The net result is that we do our wagering furtively, just as we drank under cover during Prohibition. If gambling houses and bookmakers were licensed and allowed to operate openly and legally, some measure of protection for the public would be possible.

As it is now, the only "protection" is for the gamblers—against being

Reprinted with permission of Pyramid Publications, Inc. from "Yellow Kid" Weil—Con Man *by Joseph R. Weil as told to W.T. Brannon, (New York, 1957), pp. 122–33.*

[1]Additional autobiographies by confidence men include Hambly (1932), Irwin (1909), Smith (1923), and Slim (1969). For scholarly works on the topic, the reader is referred to Maurer (1940), and Roebuck and Johnson (1964, pp. 235–48).

raided. If a man is the victim of a dishonest gaming house, he can't protest to the law, because he was engaging in an illegal activity in the first place.

There are a number of reasons why gambling hasn't been legalized. One is that certain groups—generally, the same that forced Prohibition upon us—are against it. Another is that the racing interests, composed of influential people, do not want the handbooks legalized for fear that they could cut into their own fat revenues. These people oppose the legal book from purely selfish motives and not for any moral considerations.

Another group opposing legalized betting consists of politicians. They are the people who receive the protection money, which would stop coming in if the bookies became legal.

Now suppose we faced this realistically and recognized that you cannot stop gambling. Suppose we allowed each community to decide for itself whether or not it would have gambling. Those deciding in favor of it could license each establishment, as taverns are licensed.

There would be some abuses, of course. But one important element would be removed—the muscle man. Gambling is about all there is left to the powerful syndicates which flourished during Prohibition. Repeal reduced these gangs, and the number of murders they committed, and even caused the complete collapse of the smaller gangs. The licensing of gamblers would remove their last fertile field.

Moreover, the fees that would be collected by each city could be used for many good purposes. It has been estimated that Chicago alone could collect about $3,000,000 a year from gambling licenses.

The situation boils down to this. People want to gamble and they will, even though it is unlawful. Police have confessed that they are powerless to stop it. Then why not do the most sensible thing—make the gamblers pay for the privilege?

One of the oldest gambling games is faro bank. I don't know just when it first became popular. But I do know that it dates back to the Pharaohs of ancient Egypt, from whom the name was derived. It has long been popular in France.

In the early days faro was dealt from an open deck, without the box. Louis XIV was one of the first to try to legislate it out of existence. The French nobles gambled so recklessly and lost so consistently at faro bank that many became penniless. Louis issued a decree banning the game, but still it flourished. For centuries, it has been a favorite of Parisian and other French gaming resorts. It became a major attraction at Monte Carlo. In the early days of the United States, faro bank was popular in the frontier towns.

My own experience with the game began soon after my return from Baltimore. I was in Tommy Defoe's tailor shop in the Railway Exchange building. Tommy's place was a regular hangout for con men. If we wanted to pass the word along to a fellow worker, Tommy always obliged.

John Strosnider, who could be as smooth as silk, was sitting at a table shuffling cards. He was a wizard at cards. He could deal from the bottom and the average person would never know it. He also had a gadget for pulling a card up his sleeve which consisted of a wire extending from the foot, up through the trousers, under the shirt, through the sleeve at the shoulder, and out the coat sleeve. On the end of the wire at the sleeve was a clip-like finger. With this, John could palm the card he wanted and make any other card disappear faster than you could see it.

Now he was shuffling the cards, doing tricks and playing with his faro box. He had two new gadgets he was demonstrating. Both were bits of wire he manipulated with his left hand. He called one "the thief" and the other "the knife." With "the thief" he could remove any card he wanted from the deck, with "the knife" he could cut the deck and put the bottom card on top. He was practicing various other manipulations.

After a while I tired of watching him and picked up a newspaper. I turned to the classified column. I soon came across a want ad that interested me.

A Mrs. Kingston was going to California for six months and wanted to lease her nine-room apartment on the Gold Coast. I lost no time in calling on Mrs. Kingston. She showed me the apartment.

It was furnished luxuriously, and in excellent taste. The floors were covered with fine Oriental rugs. The large drawing-room was hung with priceless oil paintings. The other rooms were elegantly appointed, and there were two bathrooms.

The kitchen was completely equipped. Next to the pantry, there was a wine room.

It was an ideal setup. I succeeded in convincing Mrs. Kingston that I would take good care of her furnishings—and this was a prime consideration. I agreed to the $200 a month she asked, and paid her six months rent in advance.

Returning to Tommy Defoe's tailor shop I found Strosnider still practicing with his cards. I told him of the apartment and of my plans for it.

"We need a couple more good men to complete our organization," I added.

"How about the Deacon and Jimmy Head?" he proposed.

I had known Fred "The Deacon" Buckminster, one of Chicago's top confidence men, casually for a number of years but had never worked with him. Buck had been doing errands for Barney Bertsch, Chicago's big fixer. But things were hot for Barney, and Fred was ready to pull out.

He was a big, portly fellow, with the most innocent face you ever saw. Looking at him you would have sworn that he could not be anything but honest. His eyes were as innocent as a baby's and his features were positively cherubic. His demeanor was so decorous he actually radiated an air of piety. This had earned him the sobriquet "The Deacon" by which he is still known, although he is now an old man.

"He is a good detail man," Strosnider told me.

Fred seldom slipped up on the small things which are very important in any good con game.

Jimmy Head was from Texas. I have heard that he was from a good family and that his real name was not Head. He was a medium-sized man, nearing middle age, with a mild and pleasing manner and a slight Southern accent. In any crowd he would be inconspicuous, for he was a good example of the average citizen.

Head was also smooth. He was polite and his soft-spoken pleasantries made a favorable impression on the victims. He was the sort of fellow you would have expected to find in a teller's cage at your bank. We engaged a private room and I told Strosnider, Head and Buck of my plan. We would set up an establishment more lavish than any gambling club in Chicago. The story to our victims would be that it was a club maintained by the Jettison estate—one of a chain of such clubs scattered throughout the country.

They were enthusiastic about my scheme and agreed to play the roles I assigned to them.

As soon as Mrs. Kingston had vacated the apartment, we moved in. Of course there had to be some rearrangement. Buckminster arranged for a roulette wheel and I had a number of tables brought in. In addition to the roulette table, we set up tables for poker and dice and, of course, a table for faro bank.

In a corner near the entrance we set up a cashier's cage and installed Jimmy Head as cashier. He also kept the register and the membership book. This roster contained most of the biggest names in Chicago. Jimmy was supplied with large stacks of boodle, which were always in plain view. A victim always believes he has a chance of winning if there is a lot of cash in sight.

Strosnider was to be the manager of the club and also was to deal the faro bank game. Buckminster was the "overseer," an official whose headquarters were supposedly in New York. The story was that he went from club to club, checking to see that each was being operated properly.

The apartment was ideal. Only a very wealthy person, such as the millionaire Jettison, could have assembled such rich furnishings. It was not difficult for an outsider to believe that the club was frequented only by the socially elite. Indeed it would have been hard to convince the average person that anybody other than a millionaire was behind the club.

Strosnider became "John Steele," manager of the club. Buckminster became "Mr. McFetridge," the director from New York. My own place in the scheme was to pose as an outsider with inside connections.

As first victim I selected a man named Orville Hotchkiss. I had met him a year before when for a short time I operated a paint factory. Hotchkiss owned a retail paint store and had bought products of the factory. I knew he had no money to speak of, but I also knew that he was a fast friend of a man named McHenry, a sports promoter in Aurora. Though I brought in Hotchkiss, my ultimate victim was to be McHenry.

"Orville," I told him when I called, "I want you to help me out."

"Sure, Jim. What can I do?" Hotchkiss knew me as James R. Warrington.

"I have an uncle," I said, "who is the manager of one of the gambling clubs operated by the Jettison estate. You've heard of these clubs, haven't you?"

"Of course."

I knew he hadn't, but I also knew he had heard of the Jettison estate and the fabulous man who had founded it.

"My uncle has been with Jettison for twenty years," I continued. "He's served faithfully. He expected to get a raise last week, but what happened? They gave him a cut. He's plenty mad about it and wants to quit. But before he does he wants to make a killing."

"He knows that the New York overseer, a man named McFetridge, is back of it. McFetridge doesn't like my uncle and that's the reason for the cut. At the first opportunity he'll fire my uncle. But my uncle isn't going to give him a chance. He's going to clean up and retire."

"I don't blame him," said Hotchkiss. "What do you want me to do?"

"I want you to go in and make a big wager at the faro bank table. My uncle will be dealing. He'll let you make a killing—providing you split with him."

"Why don't you do it, Jim?"

"I would," I replied, "but they know me at the club. They know that Mr. Steele is my uncle. I couldn't get away with it."

"It's all right with me," returned Hotchkiss, amiably, "but what am I going to use for money?"

"Don't worry about that. My uncle will tell you how to do it."

I arranged a meeting with "Mr. Steele." He brought the faro box along.

"It's a case of rank ingratitude, Mr. Hotchkiss!" Strosnider said heatedly. "I've given Jettison the best years of my life. I certainly was entitled to a raise, if anything. But no, I get a cut." Strosnider was a good actor and there was bitterness in his voice.

"That's too bad," Hotchkiss commiserated with him.

"It's a rotten shame," Strosnider said with feeling. "But I don't intend to let them rub my nose in the dirt. I'm going to get even. Do you blame me?"

"Of course not," Hotchkiss replied.

"Ordinarily I wouldn't consider doing anything dishonest," John went on, "but this is different. I feel it's what I've got coming to me." He shuffled the cards. "Do you know anything about faro bank, Mr. Hotchkiss?"

"No, I don't."

"Well, you will when I get through."

For two hours Strosnider rehearsed Hotchkiss in how to play. He showed him how, by shielding the cards with his big hands, he could always see what was coming out before it was dealt. He arranged a series of signals so Hotchkiss would know how to bet. They went over it time after time, until Hotchkiss was letter perfect in receiving the signals.

"Now, I'll let you win all through the deck," Strosnider said, "but wait until the last turn to bet all your chips. I'll give you the signal just before the deal. Now is that clear?"

"Yes," Hotchkiss replied, "but there's one thing that isn't. What am I going to use for money?"

"You can write a check, can't you?"

"Sure, but it wouldn't be any good."

"Don't let that worry you," said John. "You can cover it the next day. It'll be plenty good with all the money you'll win."

"Suppose they won't take a check?"

"Oh, they'll take it. All the big men who come to the club write checks. You just hand me a check for $50,000 and I'll give you the chips."

Strosnider produced two elaborately engraved guest cards. He wrote "James R. Warrington" on one and "Orville Hotchkiss" on the other and handed them to us.

"Come in about ten," he said, shook hands and left.

Promptly at ten that evening we were at the Gold Coast building that housed the Kingston apartment. Hotchkiss knew he was in an aristocratic section. He knew also that only wealthy people inhabited this building.

We were admitted by a man in an impressive butler's outfit. He took our hats and escorted us to where the manager sat. Strosnider got up, shook hands, and greeted us profusely.

"We're happy to have you gentlemen as our guests," he declared.

He led us across the room towards the kitchen. The activities of the club were in full swing. My friend's eyes popped when he saw the lavish appointments. About two dozen men in evening dress were at the various gaming tables and with them a number of women in formal gowns.

Hotchkiss thought he had indeed landed in the very midst of Gold Coast society. He had no way of knowing that the men were all stooges, minor con men hired for the occasion. Each was paid $25. Each man furnished his own clothes and his own woman companion. I've no doubt that many of the girls thought the place a swank gambling club, just as Hotchkiss did.

Each man was plentifully supplied with chips. They strolled about the room, trying their luck at all the games. It didn't matter whether they won or lost. The chips weren't worth anything. But Hotchkiss didn't know that. He gaped at the piles of crisp greenbacks in Jimmy Head's cage.

We made our way across the room in leisurely fashion so that our guest could absorb all the atmosphere. Then, we went through the kitchen and into the wine room where we found a bottle of champagne in a bucket of ice. The chef—a genuine chef, incidentally—was preparing sandwiches to serve the "club members."

Strosnider poured the champagne. "Here's to the Jettison Club!" he cried. We drank the toast.

"You gentlemen make yourselves at home," said Strosnider. "I have to see if there is anything I can do for the guests. When you feel like it come over to the faro bank table and we'll have a little game."

For perhaps a half hour we wandered about the big room, watching the various games. The butler came in with a big tray of sandwiches and passed them among the "club members." Later he returned with the beverages. Hotchkiss was thoroughly sold on the idea that it was a high-class club.

"I see my uncle is not occupied now," I told him. "Suppose we go over and play."

Hotchkiss agreed, and we walked over to the faro bank table.

"I'd like to buy some chips," he said. "I don't have much cash with me. Will a check do?"

"Of course," said Mr. Steele (Strosnider). "How much did you wish to play?"

"Fifty thousand dollars."

"Just make the check payable to cash." He began to count out chips with an expression that implied this club thought nothing of a mere fifty-thousand-dollar bet.

Hotchkiss wrote the check and Strosnider handed him the chips.

"Step up, gentlemen, and place your bets," he said briskly.

Two or three stooges at the table put chips down on the board. Hotchkiss won small bets consistently, aided by Strosnider's signals, and had $75,000 in chips when the last turn came.

"The last turn, gentlemen," Strosnider called. "There are three cards left. You must call the first two to win. The winner gets four to one."

But the other players apparently had had enough. They left the last turn entirely to Hotchkiss. Strosnider signaled, and he put his chips down on low-high. The last turn was dealt and the first two cards to appear were Four-Queen.

"I congratulate you, sir," said Strosnider, pushing $300,000 in chips to Hotchkiss. "You have been—"

He didn't finish the sentence. He looked up and there, standing behind Hotchkiss, was a big, imposing figure. He was immaculately groomed and he watched with great interest as Hotchkiss picked up the chips and walked to the cashier's cage.

"Hello, Mr. McFetridge," Strosnider greeted him with a sickly grin. "This is an—ah—unexpected pleasure."

"Mr. McFetridge" nodded curtly and followed Hotchkiss to the cashier's window.

Hotchkiss unloaded his chips and Jimmy Head counted them. "Three hundred thousand," he said. "Is that correct, sir?"

"Yes," Hotchkiss replied, obviously with a lump in his throat. You could tell that the mere thought of $300,000 all in one bundle frightened him.

Jimmy Head reached for the pile of boodle and started counting out crisp hundred-dollar bills.

"Just a moment!" It was the commanding voice of Mr. McFetridge.

"Mr. McFetridge!" Head exclaimed. "When did you get in?"

"I just came in as this gentleman called the last turn," the big fellow replied. "Are you a new member, sir?" he asked Hotchkiss. "I don't seem to recall you."

"Why, no," Hotchkiss replied. "I'm a guest."

"I see," said McFetridge. "I was over at the faro bank table and I noticed that you bought your chips with a check."

"Yes. Isn't that all right?"

"Of course," Mr. McFetridge replied. "Our members do it regularly. But we know them and we know their checks are good. But the rules of the house require that a guest pay cash for his chips."

"I can do that," Hotchkiss retorted crimsoning. "If you'll just wait until I collect my winnings, I'll be glad to redeem the check in cash."

"I'm sorry," said Mr. McFetridge, gently but firmly. "That's against the rules of the house too. I am sure that you can see our position. Suppose you had lost. Would the check have been good?"

"Certainly it would!" I cut in.

"I have no doubt that it is good. But we must be sure before we can pay your winnings."

"What do you want me to do?" asked Hotchkiss.

"Just let us put your check through the bank," the overseer said amicably. "It will take only a couple of days. Then we'll be very glad to pay you your $300,000."

"In other words," I said, "if Mr. Hotchkiss can prove he had $50,000 in cash, you will pay him?"

"Certainly," said the overseer. "The money is his. He won it. All we ask is that he demonstrate his ability to pay if he had lost."

"Then why not give him back his check? He can cash it and return tomorrow with the money."

"That is agreeable to me," said Mr. McFetridge. "If he brings in $50,000 in cash tomorrow, we'll gladly pay him what he won." He turned toward the faro bank table. "Oh, Steele!"

Strosnider came over, a hang-dog look in his eyes.

"You know the rules of the house," McFetridge said sternly. "You know that only members are allowed to use checks to buy chips."

"Yes, sir," the other murmured abjectly. "But Mr. Hotchkiss has a guest card—"

"I have no doubt that Mr. Hotchkiss is as good as gold," McFetridge cut him off. "But the rules of the house must be obeyed. I'm afraid I'll have to report this infraction of the rules to the New York office."

"I'm sorry," the faro bank dealer apologized.

"Now give Mr. Hotchkiss his check back," the overseer ordered.

Strosnider handed the check to Hotchkiss.

"We'll be in tomorrow with the cash," I said. "Please have the money ready."

"It will be ready," returned the big fellow, with a sweep of his hand toward the pile of boodle in the cashier's cage.

Once we were outside I muttered, "It would be just our luck to run into that overseer."

"What are we going to do now?" Hotchkiss asked.

"What can we do?" I shrugged. "I haven't got $50,000 and I don't know anybody who has."

"Well, I do," he said. "And I don't intend to pass up my share of that $300,000."

"You do know somebody with that much money?"

"Yes. You remember McHenry?"

"McHenry?" I hesitated. "McHenry. Oh, you mean the man who helped you in the paint deal?"

"Yes. He's got $50,000. If I give him half of my share, he'll come in with me. Or I think he will."

"So what are you going to do?"

"I'm going to Aurora first thing in the morning."

"Good! We'll put one over on that McFetridge yet."

I parted from Hotchkiss after arranging to meet the one o'clock train from Aurora on which he expected to return. As I have said, we had slated McHenry as the real victim and Hotchkiss was doing exactly what I expected him to do.

When the train came in I was there. Hotchkiss got off and so did McHenry. We shook hands and went into the station restaurant for lunch.

We discussed the deal and McHenry took the bait. "Suppose we go up there now," he proposed. "Will anybody be in?"

"Yes," I replied. "My uncle is always there in the afternoon."

"All right," said McHenry. "Let's go."

We took a cab to the Gold Coast apartment. Strosnider admitted us.

I introduced him to McHenry and said: "We've come to collect. Mr. McHenry has the $50,000."

"McFetridge isn't here, the dirty rat!" Strosnider said bitterly. "He's got all the funds locked in the vault. You'll just have to wait until he comes. He's threatened to fire me."

"Well," I declared softly, "after this deal you won't have to work for him, Uncle John."

"I have a better idea," offered Strosnider. "You gentlemen come with me."

He led the way to a sun room which was comfortably furnished with tables and chairs. "Have a seat and I'll be right back."

When he returned he had his faro box.

"Do you know anything about faro bank?" he asked, addressing McHenry.

"Not much," McHenry admitted.

"Well, we've got plenty of time. I'm going to teach you."

"What for?"

"I'm going to give that McFetridge a real double-crossing," Strosnider replied. "You've got $50,000 in cash. You can buy chips with that and I'll let you win. You can win $300,000 and give Mr. Hotchkiss $50,000 and let him collect his bet, too."

All afternoon Strosnider rehearsed McHenry in how to play faro bank, how to bet, and the signals. Finally McHenry said he had practiced enough.

"Are you sure you understand it?" John asked.

"Positive," McHenry insisted.

"All right but I don't want any slips. Are you sure you don't want to go over it again?"

"No. There won't be any slips. I understand it perfectly."

He didn't, of course, but we didn't want him to. Strosnider wrote out a guest card for McHenry and we departed. I took them to dinner and at nine that night we went back. Our purpose in going early was to allow McHenry to make his play before McFetridge showed up.

The same group was on hand, going through the same motions. McHenry, like Hotchkiss, was very much impressed. But there was a difference between the two men. Hotchkiss frankly admitted he didn't know his way around gaming circles. But McHenry was the type that would today be called a "wise guy." He looked upon everything with a knowing eye.

When he approached the faro bank table he was set for the kill. He put down $50,000 in cash and received the equivalent in chips.

The game started, with a few stooges playing alongside McHenry. They all dropped out before the last turn. He won regularly with the help of Strosnider's signals. He had more than $75,000 in chips when the last turn came.

"Step up, gentlemen," Strosnider called. "It's the last turn. You can bet any of six ways. There are three cards remaining in the deck—a King, Ten, and Ace. You can call it high or you can call it low. If you call the cards, you get four to one."

This was the signal for McHenry to bet. The cards were in the box exactly as Strosnider had called them. But McHenry got his signals mixed when John said, "You can call it high or you can call it low." That was in reality the signal that high card would be first.

McHenry put all the chips he had on Ace-King to show in that order. Strosnider started to deal, then looked up. Behind McHenry was the formidable bulk of Buckminster (Mr. McFetridge). Strosnider signalled frantically to McHenry to withdraw. This was to make it seem realistic to McHenry.

Buckminster spoke up. "The bet stands," he said icily.

Strosnider hesitated, looking from McHenry to McFetridge, with a harried expression.

"Deal the last turn!" McFetridge commanded.

"Sure, go ahead and deal," McHenry said confidently.

Strosnider dealt the cards. The first was a King, the second a Ten, the last an Ace.

Sorrowfully, Strosnider raked in the chips. McHenry turned pale, as if he could not believe his eyes.

"I've been cheated!" McHenry muttered.

"Come on," I said, grabbing his arm. "Let's get out of here."

"You can go with them," said McFetridge. "Steele, you're fired!"

The three of us went out and stopped in the nearest buffet.

"Whatever possessed you to bet on Ace-King?" Strosnider demanded as soon as we had been seated.

"You signalled to bet on the high card," McHenry defended himself.

"Certainly I did," Strosnider replied. "Why didn't you?"

"But I did. I bet on the Ace—"

"The Ace? Why, you stupid idiot, everybody knows that the Ace is low card in faro bank."

"I didn't."

"Well, why didn't you ask?" Strosnider demanded bitterly. "I thought you said you knew everything about this game."

"I'm sorry that I muffed it."

"A lot of good that does now. Not only did you muff our chance to make a killing but you caused me to lose my job. I hope that I never run into anybody like you again!"

On this note we parted company. I later saw Hotchkiss many times. He laughed about the whole thing when he learned my real identity.

i stole $16,000,000

HERBERT EMERSON WILSON

In this selection Herbert Wilson, safe-cracker, discloses some secrets of his trade. Wilson describes two separate incidents: one of his successful jobs (cracking the difficult cannonball safe) and one of his more spectacular failures, in which he almost cracked a safe containing $14,000,000. During his career as a thief Wilson attained a multi-million dollar bankroll.[1]

The doors of some safes are so tremendous that the small portion of soup which it is possible to inject into the cracks surrounding those barriers could not possibly do more than jar them. Cutting, by means of my oxygen-acetylene torch, was, therefore, of immense help.

Of course I could have purchased large and cumbersome contraptions, but one can scarcely cart around such bulky armament at night without arousing the curiosity of passing pedestrians, and who knows, even the police. I conceived the idea of designing a torch that could answer all my purposes and yet be tucked in my small traveling bag.

After exhaustive study, I drafted a plan for a torch that would meet my requirements. I took the sketch to the Oxweld Acetylene Manufacturing Company, in Chicago, one of the largest manufacturers of steel-cutting implements in the world. Going directly to the head of the firm, I enlisted his aid with a carefully trumped-up story. I claimed to be the manager of a kelp-gathering company, engaged in salvaging that seaweed from the tidal waters on the Pacific Coast. I explained that we extracted potash from the kelp, which was used in the production of high explosives for the Government, with whom we had a contract.

When you lie, tell a good one, was my belief.

I went on, pointing out to the head of the firm that our raw material was stored in huge septic tanks for certain treatment, and as those tanks were on tidal waters we found it necessary to seal them up to guard against the intrusion of high water. I told him that I wanted the torch I had

Reprinted from Herbert Emerson Wilson, I Stole $16,000,000 *(New York: The New American Library, 1956), pp. 64–66, 73–81.*

[1]Additional autobiographical information can be found in Martin (1952).

sketched to render convenient the reopening of those tanks, as the work had to be done by men laboring on stagings.

He swallowed all of it, hook, line and sinker. Then he called in the head engineer who went over my blueprint with me, and ten days later I had one of the most compact torches ever devised. Next to my Thermol Solution, that little darling of destruction was the greatest factor in the success of my criminal career. I ordered a specially constructed traveling bag which was divided into compartments. They accommodated the necessary tanks, fifty feet of fireproof hose and my torch. I took it with me on every job where a traveling bag might be carried.

It was with the aid of that torch that I became known as the only crook in history who beat a "cannonball" safe.

The money compartment is a large egg-shaped safe attached to a lower stand of solid steel, about four feet in thickness. Such a stand should prove formidable to any safe-cracker, and butterflies did a spring dance in my stomach when I first saw one. The weight of the upper part of a "cannonball" safe is tremendous. The door of the money compartment is made of twelve steel plates, each having a thickness of two inches and being securely bolted to another. The door does not open as would an ordinary safe or vault door. Instead, it "screws" open when the wheel attachment is turned in connection with the combination. Because of the manufacture of this door, it is impossible for the safe-cracker to penetrate the first plate and put in his soup.

When I was first told of this particular type of safe, I was anxious to see one, and with Doc De La Pena I journeyed to a city to see a newly erected bank building which had one. I went into the bank, asked for change for a hundred-dollar bill, cased the "cannonball," then returned to De La Pena who sat in my Packard.

"What do you think?" were his first words.

"I don't know, Doc. I'll sleep on it and let you know tomorrow."

But that night I couldn't sleep, my mind turned continually to the "cannonball." I hated to admit that I had come up against something that could beat me. Then on the following morning, while shaving, I got that flash of light which showed how I could turn the trick. I was in the act of lathering my face when I remembered how back in my Boer War days we soldiers used to break open the large ostrich eggs we found on the South African veldt. With a small hatchet we'd crack the shell on the large end, going completely around the egg. Then one last blow with the hatchet, a little pressure with one hand while the other seized the opposite end of the egg, and the two pieces came apart as the contents went into the frying pan.

"That's it!" I exclaimed to the man in the mirror. Myself.

I got busy; I visualized the first successful "cannonball" robbery in America and perhaps in the world. Then I sent for my men and had a crossroads blacksmith hammer me out a hatchet, somewhat like the ordinary kind but not with so sharp an edge. George Redding cased the bank for several nights, got the low-down on the movements of the night watchman, and learned that he tried all the doors every hour up till midnight, and every two hours thereafter till daylight.

After numerous though usual preparations, we were ready to strike.

A few minutes after 4 A.M., on a Monday morning, my brother Lou, Tony Masino and I drew up near the bank. Cox had "bridged" all the electric burglar alarm wires, and three more members of my mob were in strategic positions near the bank, ready to handle any busybody. While Lou and Masino were making our "in" through the front door, by boring a hole near the lock, and opening it by putting a hand through the hole, I was moving my equipment from the car. Safely within the bank I went directly behind the lighted safe, took out my torch and got ready.

This is how I beat a "cannonball" safe:

First I applied the tongued flame of my torch to the chalkmark I had made directly around the safe—the big end of my "egg," as I was mentally calling it. Great care had to be taken, however, for if I were to let the flame get out of hand, the paper money and securities within the safe could be destroyed. Burned to a crisp. So I cut only a one-inch groove all the way around the safe. When I had finished, Tony Masino poured cold water on the heated metal. This casehardened my egg and I was ready for my next movement.

Into the burned groove went the edge of the new tool, the hatchet the blacksmith had made for me. Then as Lou swung an eight-pound copper hammer against the hatchet, I methodically followed the groove till we had circled the safe. There was not much sound, since copper against steel makes little noise. With that work completed, and while Lou and Masino looked on, somewhat dubious of the success of the job, I took aim with the blacksmith tool, prayed that my hunch was right, hit the groove at the top of the safe only one sharp blow, just one and. . . .

Lo and behold! Just like the South African ostrich eggs on the veldt, when properly attacked, the big end of the "cannonball" safe gave way and fell upon the floor at our feet.

The haul came to a hundred and seventy thousand dollars!

• • •

"Well that's the story," George Redding concluded, "and it's just like I told you. Outside of the Treasury, there isn't a crib in the world like the one at the Maccabees! It's dangerous as hell and it's almost impregnable, but if any man in the world can crack it, Herb, you can, and if you get in there you'll be able to lay your mitts on the biggest haul in the history of crime—$14,000,000!"

If I hadn't known him to be the best caser in the racket, I would have thought that he had suddenly gone crazy. But as usual George Redding was right. There had been $14,000,000 in cash and bonds in the safe of the Maccabees the night I raided it. Yes, $14,000,000—the organization itself admitted that to the press on the following day. And why didn't I get it?

Well, this was one time, for all my planning, that we came out second best, even though we had been working on our master stroke for nearly four months.

In imagination Tony Masino had already spent his share of that $14,000,000, and for weeks before the raid the handsome Italian was saying: "I'll build a castle on the Nile, bring in a harem of redheads, swim in a pool of champagne and eat mockingbirds' tongues on golden plates—while J. Pierpont Morgan waits on the table!"

At best it was bad enough to miss out on that veritable king's fortune, but what made it all so downright maddening to me was the fact that I was less than an inch and a half away from it when catastrophe fell. Just another inch and a half and twenty minutes more, and that $14,000,000 would have been ours!

I had been in New York when George Redding first told me of the Maccabees and their safe in Detroit. The Maccabees, a well-known society that specialized in fraternal insurance, maintained its national headquarters in Detroit. The order was, and still is, immensely wealthy. In fact a recent report I had disclosed the staggering sum of insurance in force to be close to three-hundred-million dollars, with cash on hand of more than seventeen million.

At the time of my raid the thriving and ambitious Maccabees' Association apparently believed it was good advertising to broadcast the happy knowledge that, stored away in its impregnable vault, was the ready cash used to pay off its policy holders. I felt it was a prize well worth going after. I called in my entire ring from all points of the compass, and in Detroit's Cadillac Hotel we sat in solemn conclave and set the wheels in motion for the raid.

On three occasions Helen Gillespie and I had driven out on Woodward Avenue and looked over our contemplated target. You couldn't miss the place—at least at that time you couldn't—because it had a wide lawn on which were cut four large letters, K.O.T.M.—Knights of the Maccabees. The building itself looked like an ancient fortress, a mighty castle with gray granite walls and turrets on the roof. All they needed was a few knights in armor walking around and you would have thought you were back in the days of King Arthur. Behind the building was a whitewashed stone wall about twelve feet high.

To detail the thousand and one kinds of ruses employed by my ring during the following four months, in their efforts to gain a thorough knowledge of the lay of the land, would prove that we all had wills of iron. Seemingly we overlooked nothing; certainly we spared neither time nor expense. And the necessary information did not come easily as our subtle maneuvers, again and again, proved futile. But we were after the greatest crime haul in history, and we were not going to give up until we had exhausted the last ounce of cunning, had employed every wile at our command.

One of the first unwelcome discoveries had been when we learned that it was almost impossible to place an inside "plant" in the establishment. That had always been a big help to us and we were usually able to arrange it, but in this case it was impossible. Their complement of help was filled, and though we had both men and women operators on the waiting list of the executive who did the hiring, they were never successful in obtaining positions.

"We've just got to get someone in there," I told Helen. "Someone who can gain a thorough knowledge of the ins and outs of the place."

"If we can't, at least let's do the next best thing," was her opinion. "We'll get to know some of those who are in there. They can drop a lot of tips, unknowingly, if you go about it in the right way."

So Helen, who was just the girl to "go about it the right way," managed to strike up an acquaintance with two young women employed in that castlelike structure, and under one pretense or another she would call on them from time to time. Helen posed as a rich divorcee who enjoyed playing around and was not averse to male company. Neither were her acquaintances, and as she paid all the bills to theater parties and some dubious clubs, she naturally became quite popular with the pair. But they knew just so much and no more.

It seemed that the one with all the answers was a certain spinster who had been a trusted employee in the establishment for many years. She also possessed keys for unlocking certain doors, including an entrance into the place. But here was the catch. In her mid-forties, stern featured and tight-lipped, she was suspicious by nature, frowned on all frivolity and, after concluding her work, she would return to the small house she shared with her sister, where the two would wind up the clock, put out the cat and cover up the canary before retiring. Helen couldn't get to first base with her.

So I called in lover boy, Tony Masino.

Helen had pointed the woman out to me and I knew the small restaurant, as well the booth she always sat in, when she went to the place every noon for her soup and coffee. She brought her own sandwiches. One day I took Tony to the restaurant at noontime, we sat at the counter and I said:

"You have been telling what you are going to do when you get your share of the Maccabee split—your castle on the Nile, harem of redheads and all that."

"Right."

"You'd really like to have that kind of money?"

"Right."

With a nod of my head I gestured towards the lone occupant at the far end of the restaurant. "See the girl in that end booth?"

His eyes followed my gesture, then returned to me. "I see the old bag in that end booth."

"Well from now on she's your flaming flapper," I told him. "I want her to fall so hard for you, she'll bounce!"

"What have I done to deserve this?"

"She knows every damn move that is made in the Maccabees, has worked there for years and carries some important keys. She's the ticket to your castle on the Nile. Catch on?"

He was already on his feet as he swung into action with a gusto, walked towards her and the next moment I heard, "I beg your pardon, but haven't we met somewhere?" He had removed his hat, and it revealed the wavy jet-black hair girls fought to run their fingers through.

We continued to learn more about the castle of the Maccabees. We discovered that the big burglar alarm that helped to guard the place was hidden behind a festooned high wall beside the main office, and was kept charged from a storage battery in an adjoining private garage. The night watchman went on duty promptly at 6 P.M., just as the day force left.

On the night of the fourth day after I had given Tony his instructions regarding the frigid spinster, he made a phone call to let us know that he had taken her to a theater and between acts had secured the key impression for the entrance into the Maccabees—cleverly stealing it from her purse and making the impression on soap. We quickly filed out a key and before midnight had solved one problem—the matter of obtaining entry. We drove out to the place and tried the improvised key in the door lock, while the night watchman was on one of the upper floors making his rounds.

It worked!

Previously I had had a look at the colossal vault of the Maccabees. This opportunity came one morning when I had called on Daniel Markey, the head of the organization.

Yes, I was considering the possibilities of taking out a substantial policy. I might even be interested in opening up new territory for them out in the West and investing some of my own money in the project if the right inducements were offered. A profitable conference followed. In a comprehensive manner he outlined the advantages of insurance, particularly the fraternal variety in which his society specialized. He convinced me that the comparative rates—and they were low—of mutual insurance were justified, and that the financial statement he proudly exhibited indicated a healthy business condition. He told me:

"Our company's strongest argument has always been, and always will be, the swiftness with which we discharge all obligations. We are not only glad to extend immediate service—we always have the cash on hand to meet all demands at a moment's notice!"

I tried to put a tone of surprise in my, "But is it safe to keep so much money on the premises?"

"Absolutely, my dear Sir, absolutely! We have no apprehension on that point, believe me." A thought seemed to strike him. "If you feel the slightest alarm, please follow me and I will show you our gigantic, burglarproof vault. The mere sight of it will comfort you."

"It might at that," I agreed and accepted his invitation. He showed me the vault.

It really was something, the most gigantic and magnificent specimen of steel and masonry I ever laid my eyes on. With its steel door, twenty-two inches thick, it resembled a blockhouse rather than a vault, and it was loaded with alarms. But I knew what would be inside of it. There could have been a dozen lions serving as watchdogs, and I still would have raided it. As I talked to Markey, I made mental notes on the general layout and approximate dimensions of one kind or another. I left the cordial executive with an assurance that when I could wind up my business affairs in the West he would probably hear from me.

I told myself that I was getting somewhere at last, though the brief inspection I had had of that daddy of all vaults convinced me that my torch, and not my soup, would have to be the weapon employed. With such a prize in sight and wishing to brush up on my technique, I enrolled at Detroit's Y.M.C.A., where I took a course of practical training in the oxygen and acetylene department of their mechanical arts school. The course lasted four weeks, I was voted honor man and beamed on the bald-headed man with three chins who handed me my certificate.

With everything in readiness, we decided to raid the great structure on a Saturday afternoon after the office closed for the day at 4 P.M. Detroit was suffering a minor heat wave, furnaces were no longer running and we learned that the night watchman had suddenly changed his schedule. He was not arriving for his duties till 8 P.M. during the hot spell. I called in the boys for one last conference, everything was planned to split-second timing and we were all set.

With me on the night of the big raid were my brother Lou, Herb Cox, Tony Masino, Doc De La Pena, George Redding, Joe Bertsch and big Harry Woods—the cream of my mob!

At 5:30 sharp on a momentous Saturday afternoon—after the departure of the employees and before the arrival of the watchman—a large truck pulled up in front of the Maccabees and came to a sudden stop at the curb. A husky driver and his two helpers got down from the truck and set about the task of delivering four rough-looking boxes to the establishment.

The two helpers, seemingly colored men, were actually George Redding and Joe Bertsch in blackface. Harry Woods was the driver.

The boxes, six feet long, two in height and three in width, were the approximate dimensions of coffins. From the manner in which the men were straining and struggling with their burdens, it was evident that those large containers were heavy, but the movements of the trio aroused neither concern nor comment from the dense throng of pedestrians who were passing along nor from the traffic cop, a half block away. He had his hands full directing the Saturday afternoon rush of vehicles. True, a couple of sidewalk superintendents gave brief bits of advice in passing, but on the whole the three men were ignored.

We entered, using the key we had secured, and the trio carried the boxes into the basement. They immediately left the premises, to all appearances three cartage men who had been obliged to work overtime. The long boxes lay on the floor where the three had set them down. In a nearby room, the entrance of which was blocked by a huge door, was the massive vault of the Maccabees. The minutes ticked slowly along, and then there was a sound, a faint sound followed by a movement from within one of the boxes. The next instant came a click and the lid on the box nearest to the doorway began to rise. Gradually it rose higher, then a hand came up with it—and I followed that hand!

Quietly I stepped from the box and on tiptoe walked over to the one nearest to me then rapped softly on the lid. The next moment it was also rising and Tony Masino stepped from it with the whispered comment:

"Now I know what it feels like to be dead!"

Drawing a few breaths of fresh air, for it had been very close within the boxes in which we had been confined for more than an hour, we stretched our cramped arms and legs and proceeded to get down to business. It consisted in the unpacking of the other two boxes that contained my torch, hose and necessary equipment, as well as two large tanks of oxygen and acetylene. This being done, and the watchman not due to arrive for nearly two hours, we employed our time to some use in a thorough search of the premises for concealed burglar alarms.

Five minutes before 8 P.M. the watchman put in his appearance. Tony Masino stepped out from behind a door and rammed a gun into the man's stomach with the comment: "You look tired, pal. You better lay down and have a long rest!"

Apparently he didn't relish the opportunity for such leisure, but we were insistent. Bound and gagged, we left him lying on a piece of felt padding, and five minutes later, in response to a ring from the main entrance, I opened the door and there stood Herb Cox, dressed in the garb of an up-to-date watchman. "Right on the dot," I acknowledged, and he smiled. Then securing a ladder our electrical wizard placed it under the giant burglar alarm bell concealed beneath the foliage on the festooned wall adjoining the main office.

He ascended the steps and "spiked" that dangerous contrivance by the simple method of gumming the open space between the base of the bell and the gong. Then he filled it with fine bird sand. This done, he was again admitted into the building and reported that all outside connecting electric wires were dead. He had once more accomplished his "bridging" operations.

We waited till 10 P.M. Then Cox stepped out once more and ran the wires of our buzz system to a secluded spot where George Redding was waiting. Cox returned with Lou who had been hiding in the shadows, and the pair went to the basement where Tony Masino and I were waiting. Outside De La Pena, Redding, Bertsch and Harry Woods kept their eyes open for any inkling of trouble.

Within the building we hung black cloth over the basement windows to hide the flare of the torch. Then, with my little beauty in my hands, I stepped up to the safe and sank to one knee, looking like the Grand Wizard of the Ku Klux Klan, for I was dressed in a white apron of asbestos that covered most of me, and wore a hat and long gloves of the same material. I adjusted my welding mask and turned to the task before me—the big one!

"Fourteen million—here I come!"

The streamlined and fiery tongue of my torch went to work, but it was a long and tedious task. Somehow everything about that night seemed slow and tedious—dragged out, endless. I don't know why it appeared to be that way; maybe I was trying too hard, too impatient to get at the fabulous riches only scant inches from me. But I couldn't seem to get started. Every inch I burned with my torch and everything I did seemed to require double time to accomplish.

Behind me, Lou, Cox and Masino looked on in silence. Every hour on the hour Lou made the rounds and rang the nine A.D.T. bells for the watchman.

The night was oven-hot, and with the heat from the torch it wasn't long before the basement was like a Turkish bath. My welding mask kept getting fogged up. To my annoyance I had to wipe it almost constantly and swore softly to myself as I did so. There was also another interruption that could not possibly be avoided. Steel can absorb only so much heat before it gets too hot to work on, and at regular intervals I was obliged to halt while the others sprayed the vault with water, attempting to cool it. Then I would return to my work, while the torch flared steadily as it ate its way through metal.

That damnable heat! It was draining the life out of me by inches, while each passing second seemed a minute and every minute an hour! No one spoke.

There had always been something soothing to me about the lullaby of my torch, but that night its song was annoying and monotonous, and apparently without end. I could hear the three behind me shifting around as they awaited the outcome. They too were keyed up and restless. Eleven o'clock came and then twelve while I continued to battle with that mighty metal monster. Then twenty minutes after midnight we suddenly heard it, the last thing in the world that any of us wanted to hear—then or ever!

From the street George Redding buzzed us three times. The danger signal!

I killed the torch and sprang to my feet while the others whipped out their guns. None of us breathed. A minute passed, another followed. I thought that if it were possible for me to yell once, long and loud, I would feel much better. Finally, from the street came another signal—one that told us to go on with our work. We didn't know it at the time, but an approaching drunk had alarmed George Redding.

It was a pale and wide-eyed foursome who stood in the basement of the Maccabees, and it was a good ten minutes before I could return to my work, because my hands were still shaking. Cox swore that if he ever got out of this one alive he would return to his beach home in California and never leave it, while Lou said something about being sorry that he hadn't taken his mother's advice and become a clergyman. Frankly, the old pulpit wouldn't have looked too bad to me at that moment, but I believe it was Tony Masino who expressed the thoughts of all of us when he said:

"The way I feel now, another danger signal from the street and I won't have to run. I'll just cut my suspenders and go straight up!"

We all gave nervous titters.

It was close to 3 A.M. when I discovered that the first tank of oxygen was almost empty. I had Lou switch the hose to the reserve tank and told them that I was almost there. "Another twenty minutes will do the trick," I said. "I'm down to the last of the twelve steel plates now! I've even cut into it a bit!"

Lou turned on the tank cock and I started again, but something was wrong. I wasn't getting any oxygen! "Turn it on!" I ordered. "I'm not getting any flame!"

"I did," came from Lou.

"Then turn the damn thing on harder. We haven't got all night. Turn it on all the way!"

He fooled with the tank for a minute—but nothing happened. No flame would come from the torch!

Webster defines oxygen as a "colorless, tasteless, odorless, chemically active gaseous element, which produces a very hot flame." It certainly does—when it is fresh and still retains its virile qualities. When properly mixed with acetylene and shot from the right kind of torch, there is no safe or vault metal that was ever made that can withstand its cutting flame. But I was quick to realize what had happened. The contents of this particular tank had deteriorated from age or had suffered pollution. It was useless.

We had stolen it from a city warehouse, and even now I get angry when I think that maybe some grafting contractor was cheating the city with a lot of dead oxygen tanks. The nerve of the man!

Frenziedly I tried to do everything I could to break through that last inch and a half of remaining steel—the inch and a half that stood between us and $14,000,000!

It was nearly 4 A.M. before I would admit that I was defeated, and it was foolhardy to remain there any longer. We were way past our deadline. The bubble had burst. It was all over!

We went about the necessary task of wiping off all finger marks from the articles our hands had come in contact with. How despondent we felt in the approaching dawn of that warm Sunday morning! It was with heavy hearts that we slunk out of the back door of the temple of the Maccabees in a typical "tail between our legs" manner, while the great wealth, still untouched, lay within the security of the vault. It had cost me dearly to learn that all materials should first be tested and proved worthy before being used.

The price of that lesson was $14,000,000!

PART TWO

Prison

Most people who break laws never go to prison. Reasons for this include: (1) society's failure to recognize the existence of a committed crime, (2) failure to take action on a complaint, or failure to secure an arrest in cases where official action *is* taken, and (3) further attrition in the legal process as an offender is charged, brought to trial, sentenced, and convicted.[1]

Because criminals not apprehended and incarcerated may open themselves to prosecution or censure by writing about illegal activities, we have comparatively few autobiographical statements from the truly "successful" criminal. On the other hand, the imprisoned criminal often has both the leisure and motivation to write. Thus, most available writings by self-acknowledged criminals are by those that have been "caught." In addition, the incarcerated writer often writes to tell the "outside world" of the conditions of his prison life in the hope of stimulating prison reforms. He often makes a special appeal for his own case as well, claiming that he was "framed" or "railroaded" on false charges.[2]

This is prison life as seen by prisoners themselves. (For an overview by administrators and social scientists, see Cressey, 1961; Clemmer, 1958; and Sykes, 1958.) The primary aim is a description of prison conditions. For historical

[1]For more complete discussion and statistical data on the legal process and offense clearance, the reader is referred to Bloch and Geis (1962, pp. 143–49), Korn and McCorkle (1961, pp. 56–61), Ennis (1967, pp. 36–44), and *Uniform Crime Reports* (1968, pp. 100–106).

[2]We include only statements by criminals who have *admitted* to criminal activities. This excludes some sources of autobiographical statement which might otherwise be included in this volume. In order to be included in this collection, the prisoner did not necessarily have to admit to the justice of his imprisonment nor to the correctness of the charge which brought him there, so long as he acknowledged *some* criminal activity.

perspective, two of the pieces describe prison conditions near the turn of the century. The first selection, written from inside a British prison, shows how broad the variation in prisoner treatment could be. It is in marked contrast to the second piece by John Reynolds which probably represents more accurately the lot of most prisoners during that period.

Prison conditions have vastly improved since Reynolds' time. But prisoners today still react to the place where they must "do their time." The next three pieces give a general picture of prison today. The first, by an anonymous author, comes out of a Federal prison; the second, by Barbara Deming, recounts her experiences in a city jail; and the third, by Dorothy West, tells a personal horror story of rape and torture in a county jail. The pieces by William Doyle and Nathan Leopold describe the deprivations of prison life, the first concentrating on the sheer physical discomforts—hunger, unbearable heat or insufferable cold, noise, total lack of privacy—the second on the psychological discomforts. Two selections describe a significant aspect of prison life: the sexual problems encountered by the prisoner. Patterson writes of sex in a male prison, and an anonymous female prisoner delineates the problem in a women's prison. In the final selection, Labat speaks of the special difficulties of the man on death row.

prisoner privileges in the 1800's

JAMES HARDY VAUX

In his autobiography James Vaux, professional pickpocket and shoplifter, discusses some of his experiences as a convict. Confined in six different prisons and work-houses in London, Vaux was treated as a gentleman convict during his incarceration. He describes the discrimination according to status or wealth which existed in the prisons of his day—pointing out that prisoners who could afford the privilege were allowed to have their wives live with them or stay for a night, a practice much discussed recently in penology.[1]

On entering the gates of the gloomy receptacle to which I was now consigned, and which on many accounts has not been unaptly named the Bastille, the sensations I felt may be more easily conceived than described. Besides that this was the first prison I had ever entered, every thing around me had an air of unspeakable horror. After being viewed and reviewed by the surly Cerberuses of this earthly hell, I was conducted up some stairs to a long gallery, or passage, six feet wide, having on either side a number of dismal cells, each about six feet by nine, formed entirely of stone, but having a small grated window near the roof, at the further end, which admitted a gloomy light, and overlooked a yard, in which other prisoners were confined; there was also a similar grate over the door; but, owing to their height, both these apertures were very difficult of access. The cells on the other side the passage, were exactly similar, but overlooking another yard, and the doors were immediately opposite each other. The only furniture of these dreary apartments was an iron bedstead, on which were a bed, blanket, and rug, but all of the coarsest kind. I afterwards found, that by paying an extravagant price, I might have had better accommodation; but as I had then

Reprinted with permission of William Heinemann Ltd. from The Memoirs of James Hardy Vaux *by James Hardy Vaux, edited by Noel McLachlan (London, 1964), pp. 74–75, 187. (Footnotes omitted.)*

[1]For a discussion of conjugal visits for prisoners see Zemans and Cavan (1958, pp. 50–57), and Cavan and Zemans (1958, pp. 133–39). See also Hopper (1969) for a discussion of conjugal visiting in Mississippi.

only a few days to stop, and I found no want of cleanliness in my present lodging, I declined the favour.

My conductor having given me a pitcher of water, without vouchsafing a word, locked the door, and left me in utter darkness. I retired to my homely couch, and having well refreshed myself before I left the Brown Bear,* I soon forgot my misfortunes in the arms of Morpheus, and did not awake till I was roused by the turnkey, at a late hour in the morning. This personage now behaved with some little civility, and let me know that if I had any money I might be supplied with a good breakfast; at the same time tossing upon my bed a small loaf (about fourteen ounces), of bread, which he told me was the daily allowance of the prison. I gladly accepted his offer, and desired to have some tea, which was presently sent up to me; and I continued to have three tolerable good meals, (at least in quantity), every day during my stay here; but I paid for each on delivery, and through the nose.

• • •

I was then finally committed to Newgate, as the Session was to commence on that day week (the 15th). My unhappy wife was waiting the issue of my examination, in the neighbourhood of the public office, and on learning the result, took coach, and was at the door of Newgate as soon as myself. The officers who escorted me having retired, both my wife and I were very kindly received by the principal turnkey, who instantly recognised us as Mr. and Mrs. Hardy, and expressed his concern at my so soon becoming again an inmate of Newgate. He then ordered me to have a light iron put on; and requesting to know what ward I wished to go into, I chose the same I had before been a member of, and to this room my wife accompanied me. After receiving the compliments of such of the prisoners as were before my fellow-lodgers (among whom were the two brothers), all of whom vied with each other in contributing to our accommodation, we partook of some tea; and having been a fortnight separated from my beloved wife, I would not suffer her to quit me until the next morning.

I had now but a few days to prepare for my approaching trial; and though I entertained no hopes of escaping conviction, I determined to employ a counsel; and who so proper (thought I), as my good friend Mr. Knapp, who had so adroitly brought me off on a late occasion. I, therefore, drew a brief, in which I dwelt strongly on some particular points both of law and fact, and enclosed it, with the customary fee, in a letter to that gentleman, reminding him of my being his client in November session, and trusting he would do all in his power to extricate me from my present embarrassment.

*A public-house near the police-office, where prisoners are confined until their removal to prison by the officers, who seldom hurry a *gentleman, if he behaves like one*, as their phrase is.

Mr. Knapp assured my wife that I might depend on his best exertions, and I now waited with patience for the event. My affectionate partner was unremitting in her attention to me, being never absent but when she had occasion to look into our affairs at home, and her sister having undertaken the care of our house till my fate was determined, she slept with me every night, as I had reason to fear I should soon be removed to a place where I could not have this indulgence.

the punishments of prison

JOHN N. REYNOLDS

An account of life in prison very different from that of James Vaux is presented by John Reynolds, a prisoner in both Kansas and Missouri in the late 1800's. Reynolds discusses the discipline and brutality he found in the prisons of his day.

The discipline of this institution is of the very highest character, and is unequaled in any similar institution of the United States. The officers are very watchful and strict. The inmates who work on the surface are not permitted to converse with each other only within the hearing of an officer, and then only with regard to matters that pertain to work. The convict attends to his duties, observing the strictest silence. When visitors pass about the prison the inmate is not permitted to lift up his head to gaze at them. Not even is he permitted to take a drink of water or to leave his place of work for anything without the permission of the officer in charge. As soon as a criminal enters the prison and is clothed in stripes, a copy of the rules and regulations is placed in his hands for perusal. If he cannot read, an officer reads them to him. On the first day of his admission the prisoner receives certain tickets, which are permits for privileges granted to him. One of these tickets allows him to have tobacco if he used the same before coming to the penitentiary; one allows him to receive visits from his friends; another to write a letter, monthly, to his relatives; and still another gives

Reprinted from The Twin Hells *by John N. Reynolds (Chicago, Illinois: The Bee Publishing Company, 1890), pp. 90–95.*

him the privilege to draw a book from the library, weekly. These privileges are highly appreciated by the prisoners. For the first offense in violation of any of the rules and regulations the refractory prisoner is deprived of his ticket; and in extreme cases these tickets have been kept from the prisoner for six months. To deprive the convict of his tobacco for a month or two, if he uses it, and many do, is a severe punishment. This kind of punishment is usually effectual in securing good discipline. There are extreme cases, however, that require severer punishment. To meet this contingency, dungeons are provided. As their name implies, they are dark. They resemble an ordinary cell with the exception of the door, which, in the common cell, contains open spaces for the admission of light; but the dark cell admits neither light nor a sufficient quantity of air. There is no furniture in this dark cell. While undergoing punishment, if a prisoner desires to rest, he can do so by reclining on the stone floor. No refractory prisoner ever grows corpulent while confined in these dark cells, as he only receives one meal of bread and water in twenty-four hours! The prisoner is often kept in these cells from eight to ten days. Sleep is almost impossible. When a prisoner enters the dungeon he is required to leave behind him his coat, cap and shoes. During the winter months it is often very cold in these cells, requiring the prisoner to walk up and down the dungeon in his stocking feet to prevent his freezing, and this for a period of ten days, in nearly every instance compels submission. After the dark cells thaw out, during the summer months, they are excessively hot. Sometimes in winter the temperature is below zero, and in summer it often rises to one hundred degrees. They are then veritable furnaces. Generally, after the prisoner undergoes the freezing or baking process for eight or ten days, he is willing to behave himself in the future. They are sometimes so reduced and weak when brought out of the dark cell that they can scarcely walk without aid. I have seen them reel to and fro like drunken men. They are often as pale as death. That in many cases the prisoner contracts cold which later on terminates fatally, is one of the principal objections to this mode of punishment. There is no doubt that the dark cells of the Kansas Hell have hastened the death of many a poor, friendless convict. If a person in the mines does not get out his regular weekly task of coal, on Saturday night he is reported to the deputy warden by the officer in charge, and is sent to the blind cell before supper, and is kept there until the following Monday morning, when he is taken out and sent to his work in the mines. While in there he gets only bread and water once in twenty-four hours. This is a great inducement to work; it certainly prevents criminals from shirking their labor, and soon converts a lazy tramp into a rustling coal miner. There is one thing, however, that is connected with this system of punishment that I will criticise. The officer under whose immediate control the prisoner is placed fixes the period of his confinement in the dungeon. It gives the officer a good opportunity to abuse a prisoner he may dislike. These subordinate officers are not all angels. Some of them are lacking in sympathy. They have become hardened, and frequently treat their men like beasts. These persons should not possess such a dangerous power. The warden or deputy warden should decide the character as well as the period of punishment.

If in this dark cell ten days and nights is insufficient to subdue the rebellious spirit of the convict, he is taken out and placed in the solitary cell. This is similar to the ordinary cell, with the exception that it contains no furniture. Here the convict remains on bread and water until he is starved almost to death, or until he is willing to submit and do his work as ordered.

Another mode of punishment resorted to in a few cases, is even more brutal than the dark cell. The obdurate prisoner is stripped naked and tied to a post. The hose which is connected with the water-works is turned upon his naked body. The water pressure is sixty pounds to the square inch. As the water strikes the nude body the suffering is intense. This mode of punishment is but rarely resorted to. It is exceedingly wicked and barbarous. It is a shame to treat a human being in such a manner. There are many hardened criminals and desperate characters in the penitentiary, and it may sometimes be necessary to resort to extreme measures, but there have been many instances when, as it seemed to me, these excessive punishments might have been avoided and still the good discipline of the prison maintained. "Blessed are the merciful, for they shall obtain mercy." But the author would have you recollect that the punishments of the Kansas penitentiary are not as severe as the discipline in her sister institutions. Many of the inmates of this prison who have formerly served terms in others of like character, have shown him the scars and marks of brutal punishment. One of these poor unfortunates showed me his back, which is covered with great furrows in the flesh caused by the cat-o'-nine-tails in the hands of a merciless official of the Missouri penitentiary. Another prisoner carries thumbs out of joint and stiffened by the inhuman practice of hanging up by the thumbs in vogue in a former place of imprisonment, and still another carries about with him ugly wounds inflicted by bloodhounds which overtook him when trying to escape from a Southern prison.

how it feels to be a convict

ANONYMOUS

This document was addressed to the prison doctor of the institution in which its author, a federal prisoner, was incarcerated. A rather atypical inmate in terms of his education and cultural background, he gives his reactions to being confined in prison.[1]

Dear Doc:

You have asked me to do an impossible job. If the prisoner's look at prison life is to be valid for others as well as himself, I am probably the last man who could give you the right answers. By the grace of Providence I am, for better or for worse, far different from the general run of convicts. So, if what I say here seems to you neither objective nor even fair, you have brought it on yourself.

It is not true that "stone walls do not a prison make." It is precisely they which do make a prison. I, at least, remember the cold apprehension with which I looked at the gray walls surrounding the penitentiary when I first arrived here in the company of a slightly drunk and hence highly sympathetic marshal. If prison authorities had any creative imagination, they might think of hiring someone like Diego Rivera or even John Steuart Curry to cover the frosty, unpleasant, no-color surface of these walls with fresco paintings. Dante and I could give them some excellent suggestions on composition.

And that isn't just a first impression. All through your life here the consciousness of the wall runs through the stolid symphony of your days and nights like an ever-present discord. In summer, when some parts of it are covered with creeper, you can fool yourself for a brief while. From the main corridor, the large windows on the south side give on fair-sized plots of meticulously groomed lawn, framed on both sides by the dull red brick of the buildings and by vividly colored flower beds. What you look at might well be an English garden. But if, like John Donne, you see "the bone beneath the skin," the illusion doesn't last long.

Reprinted with permission of The American Mercury *from The American Mercury* 58 *(April, 1944), pp. 472–79.*

[1]For similar autobiographical accounts see Cantine and Rainer (1950), Wilde (1909), and Witherspoon (1968).

The admission formalities are simple and thorough enough. You are examined physically as completely as you have ever been in your life. They look under the bridgework in your mouth and even through your hair to see if you have any "dope" on you. Then, after a shower, you are clad in the dun uniform of quarantine and relegated to a whitewashed cell containing a cot, a chair, a locker, toilet facilities and a washstand. All your belongings—I mean quite literally all—are taken from you and sent to your people, and a provident Government furnishes you with a comb, tooth brush and powder, a safety razor and blades and a shaving brush. (Shaving twice a week at least is obligatory.) During all that time, you are conscious only of a dull and hopeless indifference.

And then, curiously, comes relief. You are alone, undisturbed, in your cell. It is clean, aseptically, painfully clean, and unmarked like a room in a hospital, an army barracks or a monastery. They show you how to make your bed in accordance with regulations; it becomes a deft automatic chore in the weeks that follow. You lie down on it, and for the first time in months you feel something like peace stealing over you. The confused solemnity of the courtroom, the hot humiliation of the fingerprinting and "mugging," the clanking of your handcuffs, the unspeakable filth and misery of the county jail, the noisy rush of your railroad trip—all these are far behind you, and you know that you have entered upon a new phase of your life.

The first week in quarantine is not hard to bear. Every day you are called for some investigation or examination. They take your blood pressure, your pulse beat, your IQ, your parole application; they pump blood out of you and typhoid bacilli into you. In the intervals, the prison library sends you some books—a curious enough selection of blood-and-thunder Westerns, sober classics and lurid detective stories. And you read them all; it is the only escape left open to you. You read again with the insatiable curiosity of your youth, and you never seem to get enough.

There are no newspapers or periodicals in quarantine—not because they are forbidden, but because it takes a month to make your subscription effective. The result is that you live as on an island, completely divorced from all that goes on in the world, thrown upon your own intellectual and emotional resources, much as a monk or a lay brother might be in some ecclesiastic retreat of medieval times, and the illusion is heightened by the austere simplicity of your cell and your clothing.

Sometime, during your first day, the quarantine officer's shrill whistle reminds you of eating, and you line up with your fellows to march, in a silent shuffling procession of twos, to the dining room. Through interminable, tortuously winding corridors, down an incline, up some steps, you march into an immense vault of a hall, large enough to seat and feed fifteen hundred men at one time, constructed in severe prison Gothic—probably the most loathsome and depressing architectural style in all history.

Of course, it is meticulously clean, as all things are clean in this place, but not with the fresh and wind-swept cleanliness of a house inhabited by self-respecting people. There is about it the self-conscious sterility of an operating room. The fragrance of cabbage and hot grease is fighting a brave but losing battle with the acrid smell of strong laundry soap, which reigns uncontested everywhere.

The food is served, cafeteria-style, on flat, chromium-plated trays. It is surprisingly good and there is plenty of it, but it is, as the Spanish say, somewhat *desabrido*—flat in taste, without pleasant surprises, and of a deadening monotony. If you don't want to consult a calendar, you can always tell by the food at dinner just what day of the week it is.

At meals, and during the brief rest periods after meals, you first learn to know your fellow inmates. You can spot the first offenders among them right off; the stigma of their sudden and drastic removal from decent society is plainly on them. There are doctors among them, and ministers, lawyers, bankers, a university teacher or two.

In quarantine they keep to themselves and form little cliques, to which a young psychopath occasionally attaches himself, thinking he can learn something from them, or he can get a job through them. Later on, when they have passed through the purgatory of quarantine, the differences in manner, in speech and in apartness tend to disappear. Prison is a very democratizing institution: soon the psychopaths talk like the lawyers, and the lawyers like the psychopaths.

• • •

This place, I believe, was originally intended to accommodate chiefly first offenders. But all of the laws of your New Deal notwithstanding, there just aren't enough of them so there has been and continues to be a steady infiltration of habituals until by now they form a large majority. They are the ones who give the prison its tone and its color. Even in quarantine, they know their way around. They get messages through to old "rap partners" or friends who are in blue, and the friends respond by sending them cigarettes or candy.

You can buy these at the commissary, but the first week or so in quarantine you have no commissary book, and so you are denied the wonted comfort of smoking. Somewhat gingerly, you begin rolling your own with the issue tobacco of which the Government supplies you (one small sack a week, known in prison parlance as "rip"), and you find you like its rank and biting taste better than you thought you would.

If you have the misfortune of being able to listen to the troubles of mankind in four languages, as I can, you are soon sought after. You observe the quarantine officer trying to explain some of the intricacies of daily routine to a Brazilian seaman, who doesn't yet know why these crazy Yanquis put him into a lovely place like this, where you get three enormous meals daily, and don't have to either pay or really work for them. He looks at the officer uncomprehendingly out of ox-like round eyes. The officer gets desperate; he raises his voice and gesticulates wildly, until finally you can't resist stepping in and helping out a little. His gratitude is out of proportion, and highly articulate. He begins sending you customers, and presently you find yourself translating and writing letters for Italians, French-Canadians, Puerto Ricans to waiting Micaelas, Helenes and Mercedeses.

One Italian, in particular, is extraordinarily persistent; he harbors the most passionate and uninhibited feelings for his soul-mate and insists on having you put them on paper in plain English. You explain to him with some difficulty that the Americani are quite priggish people, and that you cannot get a letter past the censor if it refers with approval to certain qualities in a woman, which, though highly appreciated are not much talked of in Anglo-Saxon countries. Fortunately, the total number of letters a man may write is two a week (though he may receive seven), or you would have to neglect your own correspondence. At first, your own letters are restrained, brief, somewhat embarrassed; it takes time for you to lose the self-consciousness which comes from knowing that it will be read first by a censor.

Finally, all too slowly, dawns the day when you are released into the "population." You turn in your khaki and receive a set of "blues"—a blue shirt and trousers of a lighter blue—the uniform and comfortable garb of all inmates save those working in the hospital, who dress in pristine whites. For thirty days or so, you haven't been able to go to church, to see a movie, or to do any regular work; all of these are privileges reserved for the "blues." Now your life in prison begins in earnest.

At first everything is a little confused. You pack all your belongings into one of your gray bed blankets and lug them over into a dormitory—a large, oblong, crowded room, bed on bed in military precision, filled with smoke and men's talk and laughter. While you are arranging your things in the locker assigned to you, and making up your bed, you begin to get acquainted. One or two of your immediate neighbors (you don't know them in the least, but they are as friendly as puppy dogs) offer to help you. Afterwards they show you around and volunteer some sage counsel as to your future conduct in the institution.

From the officer in charge you learn with dismay that your background, talents and education have obtained employment for you in the kitchen. The next morning at five, someone rudely pulls your foot, and while the rest of the dormitory keeps on sleeping until the whistle, you slip into your clothes, get over to the kitchen and, after a hasty breakfast, start the day's work by getting the dining room ready for the first meal of the day.

And pretty soon the bugle sounds the call to mess. From cell blocks and dormitories, from honor rooms, from everywhere, through the wide open doors of the dining hall a stream of blue-clad humanity pours itself. They advance with measured steps; there is nothing precipitate about it; they simply come to be fed another meal. But they march in the indescribably sad rhythm of the jailhouse. Day after day, three times a day, they make this trip: advance to the steam tables, get their victuals, walk back to their tables, sit down and begin to eat. Ordinarily, prisoners have faces, even as you and I have faces—they look vivacious, melancholy, intelligent, stupid, lively or slow-witted. But when they march in this aggregation, they are reminiscent of nothing so much as the characters in O'Neill's *Great God Brown*; they wear the vacuous and sullen masks of prison, and they all look alike. It is a depressing spectacle to which only a William Blake could do full justice. You shudder when you think of the sum of human misery—the thousands of years of wasted living; the urgent and repressed desires for freedom, for light, for air, for love; the amount of human energy laid barren, represented by this mass of men, shuffling in dispirited regimentation to get their sustenance. Your own troubles seem insignificant enough by comparison.

Otherwise, the kitchen is not too bad. True, the working hours are badly arranged, but the work is spaced and there are long intervals when you have nothing to do. That isn't any longer the liability it used to be in quarantine, for now you can go out on stockade for two hours at a time; and you can also go to the library at stated periods and select your own books.

In your new job you have to know how to get along with people. Most of your fellow-workers are confirmed psychopathic cases, since transfer to the kitchen is supposed to be a form of punishment for men who don't do well in other jobs. Often enough the atmosphere is tense with resentment likely to flare up into a fight; sometimes with fists, rarely with a knife, which in the kitchen is more easily available than elsewhere. But if you mind your own business and display a reasonable amount of unruffled courtesy to everyone you won't run into any trouble.

Soon you are moved again; this time to one of the kitchen dormitories. Here your neighbors are more lively. Many of them are Southern boys, and in the evenings the twanging of their guitars, mandolins and jews'-harps is counterpointed by the soft drawl of their hushed singing voices. I like them when they sing the songs, at once ribald and melancholy, of prison. But when they whine about their lost loves, in one of Mr. Berlin's or Mr. Kern's potboilers, they are pretty awful. In a dormitory you may play checkers, occasionally a good game of chess, and you can almost always get into a surprisingly competent bridge game.

After you have worked in the kitchen for about a week, one day early in the morning your officer (in prison speech always referred to as "the hack") hands you matter-of-factly a pass: at eleven you are to appear before the Classification Committee which will assign you to a permanent job. This is a matter of great moment. For days it has been the subject of concerned and tortuous discussions among the newly arrived. "Where are them guys goin' to put me? I can't make my time in some screwy place like the laundry issue. I'm liable to blow my top!"

As for yourself, you keep hoping. You want to get into the hospital, and through the grapevine you have learned that you stand a good chance. The hospital is going to lose a man and they have to break in a successor. Since psychology has been the hobbyhorse you have been riding (with more enthusiasm than skill) since your college days, you feel qualified enough. Besides, there are the unforgotten achievements of your youth: shorthand and typing. So you join the long line of your melancholy fellows on a long bench in the center hall of the main corridor, which is known as the Captain's Court, waiting with that dull patience which is the first prison virtue.

Finally your call comes, and, with some trepidation, you step into a large room completely filled with brass-hats. They all stare at you. For a moment you feel as if you were a mannequin in Macy's window. Without much ado, someone tells you presently that you have been assigned to the one job you coveted, and that you are to begin working as soon as it is practicable to transfer you. You can hardly believe your good luck, you've heard so much about the stupidity with which other assignments have been made. Before they have a chance to change their minds, you slip out in a state of high enthusiasm.

The first chill on your delight materializes right away. It appears that the kitchen is too short-handed to spare you. The ensuing two weeks are the hardest in your whole prison career. Every day, every hour, you hope your transfer will come through; every day you are disappointed. Finally, with the help of a loudly protesting medical department, you make it. You get yourself a set of white clothes and present yourself to your doctor.

• • •

Your work begins to absorb your interest. Every week, the newly arrived men come up from quarantine for intelligence tests and behavior analysis. It will be your job to give the former, and fill in on the latter. It seems ludicrously easy, but you soon discover that it isn't; there is a knack to it you have to learn. Aside from the technical angle, your temper has to be equable and unruffled; and you have to have a reasonable amount of human sympathy and understanding. The miseries of a thousand people unfold before you, as you interview these men, week after week. You must know how to keep discipline in a room full of mischievous boys, to whom the group IQ test seems like a lot of esoteric nonsense (they have a much stronger, monosyllabic word for it), and how to give a consoling word to the troubled in heart, who come in pride, and leave in tears.

While you are in the hospital, you are thrown into contact with the rest of the staff. Most of them are very decent people, particularly the doctors, who are uniformly softies (all doctors are) and who hide the tenderness of their hearts beneath weary profanity. If you are even reasonably competent, you soon assume the dignity of a fellow-worker; and the feeling of social degradation, with which you were infected when you first came here, disappears almost completely.

Even the officers assigned to maintain order and discipline in the hospital wing have a tendency to relax somewhat in its mellow atmosphere. As a matter of fact, most of the "hacks" are not at all what your imagination has pictured them to be. The large majority of them strike you as rather good-natured, slightly bewildered men, somewhat underprivileged as to intelligence, who are trying hard to do their best. When they first get into their uniforms, they are as scared as the men in quarantine; after a while some of them develop the arrogance typical of the military mind and begin to order you around. These are the ones who love beyond all other things to blow their whistles, the sole outward token of their authority. But most of them learn, sooner or later, by practical experience, that an overbearing attitude does not get them anywhere in particular.

Soon you are established in your routine, and the even tenor of your days goes on and on. You have weeks when the work is all-absorbingly interesting—as when you get some special cases (the psychiatrist ghoulishly speaks of a "beautiful" paranoia). There are other times, when your days and nights drip, as water drips from a leaky faucet, into the vast sink of time, and when you have to muster all the resources of your brain and spirit just to keep on living.

Not that there aren't any diversions. In the evening, you have your bridge game. Once a week, on Saturday or Sunday, you go to see a movie. Most importantly, there are constant excuses for laying off work, if it isn't too important, because one or another prisoner furtively comes into the office to ask you to write a letter, advise him on some problem, or intercede for him in one or the other direction. For by now you are known as a "right guy," and a valuable "connection." There is hardly a word in the language which is more extensively used than that word "connection."

The truth is that the institution is run by the inmates—the civilians and officers only give the orders. From the Warden's office on down, the whole penitentiary would be a shambles of confusion if for some reason or other the inmate clerks or attendants would not or could not function. Many of these men are outstandingly competent and capable, used to serious responsibilities in the outside world; not a few of them have commanded and will again command salaries of substantial size. No intelligent civilian or department head would refuse his key man a small favor. And there are so many stupid, pettifogging, illogical and meaningless little rules and regulations, that it would be utterly impossible to live in the place unless you could occasionally soften their impact. Sometimes these connections are on a very simple mercenary basis: a "pack" (that is, a pack of cigarettes) will fix you up. More often it is not a question of paying off: favor for favor.

Against the high IQ men, the first offenders, the men who have occupied a somewhat superior position in their outside life, there reigns a scarcely disguised dislike and distrust on the part of many of the civilian and custodial employees. It is, of course, merely the result of a persistent inferiority complex. Some of them will treat the most unruly, undisciplined and incorrigible pimp with more courtesy, decency and consideration than some of the men whose shoes they are not fit to shine, and whose intelligence, honesty and earning power they could not begin to match.

Even the Parole Board seems to hold that general attitude. Their coming (four times a year) is an occasion similar to that first Classification Board meeting. The hopes and fears of the men who go up to be examined with you are so intense that they are almost like a tangible pall that hangs over their heads. The great day dawns. You get your pass. Once again you interminably wait your turn. This time it isn't so hard. By now you are used to waiting.

When you go in, you cannot possibly judge your examiner's reaction; he doesn't give you enough time. To be fair to him, he hasn't enough time to give you. In the limited period at his disposal he must see fifty or more men a day. Each of these people represents a special and individual problem; it would take the memory of a Caesar, the mind of a Socrates and the judicial qualifications of a Solomon to do them justice. After a few minutes, you are curtly dismissed. Then you wait for the final decision.

Some make it, some don't; why and wherefore, no one appears ever to have discovered. You see men with three previous convictions go out on parole; you see others with a life-long record of decent living, recommended by the prosecuting attorney and the sentencing judge, refused without reasons being given. Being a pessimist, you don't really expect to make it. So, when the verdict comes down: Denied!—you only feel a momentary pang of hot bitterness. Then you settle down to pull your time.

By now you are an old-timer. When you first came in your principal emotion was a bitter resentment against your fate. But now your attitude has changed into a sort of resolute melancholy. You have done a year, so another seven months will not be too hard to do.

prisoners don't exist

BARBARA DEMING

In this very personal account Barbara Deming, a member of an integrated cross-country peace walk, relates her experiences after being jailed along with several others while attempting to walk through the business district of Albany, Georgia. Jailed twice, she remained incarcerated for almost two months—fasting most of this time—until the group succeeded in altering the city's stand on the route of the march. She relates how her jailers, through indignities, attempted to deny the existence of herself and the other prisoners.

January 27, 1964

Albany city jail, Georgia. The cop locks the door on us and walks off. Now we're out of mischief. The barred steel door has banged shut; the big key has made a lot of noise; they have "put us away." People still believe there is some magic in the turning of a key.

He walks past some other cages, running his night stick, clattering, along the bars; and then we hear him make a curious little clucking noise to the prisoners—as though human speech were not quite appropriate to cross the distance between us. Magically, now, we are no longer quite of the same species.

As he goes, he glances down at his boots, and he puts his hand—as if to be sure of something—upon his wide leather belt with its creaking tooled-leather holster.

"Sonofabitch cop!" a prisoner rages, and grasps the bars and rattles them. "Oh goddam motherfucking sonofabitch! Wait till I get out of here tomorrow!"

I am reminded of a fairy tale I once heard about a miser and his old slippers. One day they cause him embarrassment and he tries to throw them away. He isn't able to. He throws them out the window, he buries them in the garden, he tries to burn them, he travels to a distant country and drops them in a pond; but each time fate returns them to him, and

Reprinted with permission of Grossman Publishers, Inc. from Prison Notes *by Barbara Deming (New York, 1966), pp. 1–7.*

each time in a way that causes him mischief. They are too much a part of him. If the miser could not get rid of his old slippers. . . But people persist in believing that they can put other people from them.

Yes, they manage to sound very reasonable to themselves as they talk of deterring others from crime; but the act of putting a man in jail remains essentially the act of trying to wish that man out of existence. From the moment of arrest one begins to feel against one's flesh the operation of this crude attempt at sorcery.

I remember suddenly the first time I was ever arrested, in New York City, 1962. As I begin to write about time I have served in Albany's jail, my earliest impressions of the world of jail crowd upon me.

A bitter March morning. The United States has just announced resumption of nuclear testing, and in protest I have sat down with a group of pacifists in front of the A.E.C. building on Hudson Street. A small group of us sit, expecting arrest; a larger group circles there, immune from arrest, in a simple picket line. The arrests are swift. Before we have time to shiver on the cold sidewalk, we are picked up and dumped into a paddy wagon waiting at the curb. We are dumped into the back, but we crowd that section, and one of the cops tells three or four of us to crawl over into the space up front in the wide cab. Up there we can stare out the open door at our friends walking past, almost within our reach. And they could look in at us easily, exchange a few friendly glances. But not one of them does, though we sit there for quite a long while before we are driven away, and they circle past us, circle past us again. With our arrest, we have become invisible, even to them. My friends are being dignified, of course; but there is more to it than that. When people are arrested, a kind of primitive awe can take hold of everybody involved. They are caught up in spite of themselves in the ritual act of denying our existence.

I remember the woman guard sitting outside the detention cell in which some of us were held before being taken to the Women's House of Detention—remember her uneasiness every time she noted in us signs of life. She spies dangling from my lapel the lettered white ribbon we have all worn that morning: NO TESTS EAST OR WEST. She snatches for it. "No banners in here!" A little later she says that she can make one telephone call for each of us. One young woman in the group writes out a message to her sweetheart. She makes it, carefully, very brief, but her feeling for him is clear in it—it flies this banner. The guard gives a little start as she reads it, takes a pencil, swiftly edits. Nothing of the young woman's self now remains in the message.

Nobody has to print in a manual for guards that the prisoner must be wished out of existence for society's sake; this magic principle is grasped as if by instinct. Prison routine varies from place to place, but the one blind effort shapes it everywhere. Here is part of the routine of our "admission" that day:

A policewoman takes us into a small room in the building where we are arraigned. She searches our handbags for sharp objects; we take off most of our clothing for her, unfasten the rest as she peers at us. The guard outside the temporary detention cell examines our bags for a second time, removes a few more possessions. At the House of Detention, a third guard empties the bags, keeps every remaining article. We have packed a few things with which to keep ourselves decent: comb, toothbrush, deodorant, a change of underclothes. She takes them all—even, in my case, some pieces of Kleenex. And if I have to blow my nose? "Find something else to blow it on," she tells me cheerfully. She explains then: I might be smuggling in dope this way. I am led into a large shower room and told to strip. Another guard shakes out each piece of clothing. Hands on her hips, she watches me closely as I take my shower, and I struggle hard now for self-possession. Her stance reminds me a little of that of an animal trainer. Now she asks me to hold my arms wide for a moment, turn my back and squat. I ask the reason. She, too, is searching for dope—or for concealed weapons. One of my companions has been led in by another woman and has stripped and is sitting on the toilet there. Her face is anguished. She explains her predicament to the guard: she is menstruating, but her extra sanitary napkins have been taken from her. "Just don't think about it," the woman tells her. I don't know how to help her; catch her eye and look away. I am given a very short hospital gown and led now into a small medical-examination room. Another of my companions is just leaving the room and smiles at me wanly. I climb up on the table. I assume that the examination performed is to check for venereal disease. The woman in the white smock grins at me and then at her assistant, who grins back. No, this too is a search for concealed dope or dangerous weapons.

I hear myself laugh weakly. Can they frisk us any further now? As a matter of fact, if their search is really for dope, they have neglected to look in my ears, or up my nose, or between my toes. They wouldn't be able to admit it to themselves, but their search, of course, is for something else, and is efficient: their search is for our pride. And I think with a sinking heart: again and again, it must be, they find it and take it.

Sometimes, all of a sudden, one of them will give it back. People are everywhere, happily, unpredictable. I am told to dress again before going to my cell, but I'm not allowed to wear my tights (because I might hang myself with them?) or my fleece-lined English snowboots (these are labeled "masculine attire," forbidden). A young Negro guard tells me to find some shoes for myself in an open locker she points out. I stare at the heap of old shoes and tell her wearily, "It's hopeless. Most of these have heels and I can't wear heels. Also, my feet are very big."

She looks at me and smiles. She says, "If you thought anything was hopeless, you wouldn't have been sitting down on that sidewalk this morning!"

I smile at her, astonished, and feel my spirits return. I tell her, "Thank you. You're right. I'll find a pair."

Before I can, she kneels, herself, and fishes out some floppy slippers that will do.

But more often the guards are caught up altogether in the crude rite of exorcism. I remember the ride to jail in Macon, Georgia, this past November. We are peace and freedom walkers this time. A number of us who will go to jail again in Albany have been arrested for the crime of handing out leaflets.

The guard who drives the paddy wagon begins to chatter like an excited boy to the second guard as soon as we are locked in, seated in back on the lengthwise metal benches against the sides of the cab. He suddenly lurches the car forward, then, with a gnashing of gears, backward, then forward again, swerving the wheel. Knocked against the metal walls, we link arms quickly; brace our feet, not to be tumbled to the floor. Later we'll meet prisoners who are black and blue from such falls. "Something seems to be the matter with the gear shift!" he shouts, delighting in the pretense. There are railroad tracks to be crossed; he manages some good jolts here by zigzagging, then takes the car on two wheels round a curve. "Yes, something seems to be the matter with this car!" As the drive ends, and he jerks us again in the prison yard, forward, backward, forward, backward, forward, we put out our hands instinctively to touch one another: you are still there. But the exulting excitement in the driver's voice betrays his opposite conviction: we cannot be people any more. He has shaken that out of us.

Now it is Albany, Georgia. This is the city where the police chief, Laurie Pritchett, likes to boast that he has defeated Martin Luther King nonviolently. When we are arrested for walking peacefully down the sidewalk with our signs, and in protest we sit down, conspicuous respect is shown for our persons: we are carried to the paddy wagon on stretchers. But the familiar instinct persists, for all this show. Ralph has been dumped into the wagon gently enough, and I have, and Kit and Tony and Michele. They are bringing John-i-thin. One cop looks at another. Suddenly they tip the stretcher up, the wrong way round, standing John-i-thin on his head.

Magic: Shake it out of them—the fact that they are people. Or tip it out of them. Or frisk them of it. And put them away. Has the relation with them been a difficult one? Now they don't exist.

Our cage in Albany is seven by seven by seven. Three bolted steel walls, a steel ceiling, a cement floor. For bunks, four metal shelves slung by chains—two on one wall, double-decker, two on the wall opposite. Thin filthy mattresses. No sheets, no blankets, but, very recently, muslin mattress covers have been added. The chief expects publicity, perhaps. Against the third wall, a tiny washbasin. Cold water. Next to it, a toilet without a lid.

The mattress of the lower bunk rests against the toilet. The upper bunk is so close above the lower that one can only sit up on the lower bunk with a curved spine. The floor space allows one to pace one short step—if there are not too many inhabitants. We are six at the moment, but we'll be more. Other cells are more crowded. It is not by stretching out that the prisoner here will recover himself.

The fourth wall is made of bars and a thick barred door, centered in it. In the corridor outside, guards and plainclothesmen come and go, day or night. If one is sleeping, a sudden knock at the bars: "Hey!" Or a little tug at the hair of the sleeper's head: "What's this one?" No corner of privacy in which to gather oneself together again.

The dirty windows in the corridor look out upon an alley and a brick wall. (They are very dirty. A prisoner long ago has flung a plate of spaghetti against one of them. Shriveled tatters of it still hang there. On the window next to it a shrunken condom hangs.) A little weak sunlight filters through to us at certain hours, but there is no real day.

And no real night. Our only other lighting is a naked bulb hanging in the corridor out of reach, and this burns round the clock.

Not enough space. No real time.

i was afraid to shut my eyes

DOROTHY WEST

Dorothy West relates her frightening experience in a county jail in which she became so afraid of attack from the other inmates that she was unable to sleep. While in jail, she was beaten, set afire, and raped by her fellow prisoners.[1]

I was sitting on the bunk of my cell in Women's Tier A-4 at Chicago's Cook County Jail when Ruby Yarbro appeared in the doorway. She was six-feet-two, weighed 190 pounds and was the "barn boss" of our tier.

Reprinted with permission of The Saturday Evening Post Company from The Saturday Evening Post 241 *(July 13, 1968), p. 23.*

[1] A discussion of prison violence can be found in Kinzel (1968), and Conrad (1966, pp. 113–19).

Behind Ruby were seven other husky women. "The boys below are worrying about you," Ruby said. "We gonna make sure they don't have to worry about you no more." I made a dive for the open cell door, but Ruby grabbed me by the hair and pulled me back. I screamed for the matrons, but all four of them were off the floor. The other women filed into the cell and closed the door. The memory of that final nightmare still makes me wake up screaming.

I had been taken to the jail eight weeks before, in December, 1965. I had been charged with the armed robbery of a Chicago currency exchange, a store where checks are cashed. I was 39 years old. I come from a good West Virginia family, I'm considered to be an expert bookkeeper, and I never was in trouble until after my husband died of tuberculosis in 1957. In the early 1960's I had problems with bad checks, and then came the hold-up charge.

When I first arrived at the jail, I had to strip and stand naked and shivering in the windowless infirmary with six other naked and shivering women. We were all waiting for the physical examination we had to have before we could be admitted to our cells. Two of my fellow prisoners were obviously in the first stages of narcotics withdrawal, one had gaping sores over most of her body, and a fourth showed evidence of having been beaten around her head and shoulders.

The "physical examination" the doctor finally gave us consisted first of fingerprinting, and then vaginally examining us. He used the same instrument on all seven of us without sterilizing it. Then we got dressed, and a matron named Mrs. Fritz herded us into a back elevator and took us to the fourth floor. My cell on Women's Tier A-4 was approximately 14 feet by 9 feet. For eight weeks I had to share those filthy cramped quarters with five other inmates, plus an assortment of cockroaches, rats and water bugs.

Within minutes of my arrival, a notorious drug supplier named Opal opened my purse and took what little money I had, my toothbrush and a clean change of underwear. I also witnessed a vicious attack on one of my cellmates, a pretty heroin addict who was desperately ill and totally unable to defend herself. When I tried to help the young girl, two other women grabbed hold of me by the hair, hit me a few times, and then burned my hand with a lighted cigarette.

That night the food consisted of pigs' tails and half-raw lima beans and scalding-hot cocoa. Ruby Yarbro and Opal refused to eat and threw the pigs' tails and the boiling cocoa all over the dayroom. The food hit some of the other prisoners, and several were burned by the cocoa. Warden Jack Johnson was summoned by the matrons, and finally he managed to calm Opal and Ruby by sending down to the kitchen for potato salad, cold cuts and hard rolls.

On my second day in jail there was a shakedown in Women's Tier A-4.

We all were locked into certain cells. Then the matrons, accompanied by male guards ordinarily not permitted on the women's floor, confiscated razor blades, hypodermic needles, hair spray and male sexual devices. Because I had been seen talking to Warden Johnson the night before to ask if I could have some magazines, I was blamed for the unusual search. That night four women set fire to my mattress and to my hair. When I shrieked for help, one matron called me a troublemaking shrew and said I deserved to burn.

For almost a week I was afraid to eat what little food the barn boss saw fit to give to me, because one day I saw several women pulverize a light bulb with the heel of a shoe and sprinkle it over my portion of lunch. Each morning I washed my panties, petticoat and my bra and then I had to put them on soaking wet. If I'd hung them up to dry, they would have been stolen. Taking a shower was a nightly battle. There were only three overhead shower spigots for the 90 prisoners on the fourth floor. Twelve to 15 of us bathed at the same time. I was pushed, pinched, jostled and tormented. Gradually the other women began to leave me alone. I was so numb, so struck dumb by everything that I no longer fought. I didn't talk. I just moved around like a zombie. I suppose it wasn't fun anymore to pick on me. I just made up my mind to wait for my court hearing and try to keep from going insane.

Since there was no medical attention available after 8 P.M., one of my cell mates, who began hemorrhaging during the night, was taken to the infirmary where she was found dead the next morning. And another girl, badly in need of psychiatric care, put her head into a toilet bowl and tried to drown herself.

On Monday morning of the eighth week I was in the "joint," Ruby Yarbro lumbered over to where I was sitting. She was holding a dripping wet "kite"—a note that was tied to a string and passed between the tiers through a toilet pipe. "I got this from the boys downstairs," she said. "It says right here you was a girlfriend of Jack Penrith." (Jack Penrith, whom I *did* know, was an insurance executive who was shot down, gang-land fashion, in his own driveway.) Then Ruby said, "The boys say you're a stoolie, a state witness."

I laughed, maybe for the first time since I'd set foot in there. So I told Ruby, who was awaiting trial for murdering a "customer," "I'm as much a state witness as you are." And she said to me, "Watch your mouth, stoolie," and waddled back to her cronies. And then, quick as I'd laughed, I felt such a terrible fear that I got sick to my stomach right there in the dayroom. The next three days got tighter and tighter. Ruby and her group never took their eyes off me. Again I was afraid to eat the food. I could hear my name mentioned again and again. I was afraid to shut my eyes at night.

I went to the matron, Mrs. Fritz, and told her I thought I was going to be attacked, maybe killed. I explained about the men sending up the message that I was supposed to be a state witness on the Penrith murder. I told her the most I'd ever done was to have dinner with the guy, that he just liked girls to keep him company. Period. I begged her to put me in a cell I could lock, to keep Ruby and her gang away from me. She just said I was a silly girl, that I was perfectly safe, and that, anyway, she didn't know what I was talking about. She knew what I was talking about, all right. She just didn't give a damn.

Then it came. It was Thursday evening, the day before I was to go to court for my hearings. At just about six o'clock Ruby walked into my cell with seven of her friends.

Ruby's first blow caught me on the side of my head. As soon as she hit me, a scream went up from the others, "Kill the stool-pigeon bitch." All eight of them fell on me at once. Somebody set fire to my skirt, and my nylon petticoat went up in flames. I tried to beat at my burning legs, but they were banging my head against the bars. I felt my nose crumple and start to gush blood. I fell and they kicked me repeatedly in the left eye. They kicked my breasts and jumped up and down on me. Then somebody pulled off my panties, thrust them into my mouth as a gag, and I was raped. My hair was burning and I could feel the skin on my forehead crack and begin to peel. I'm told the beating went on for an hour.

When the matrons finally returned to the floor, they got me out of the cell. One of them called me "a troublemaker right from the start," and poured pure iodine all over my wounds. Pulling and dragging me, they got me upstairs and locked me into "the hole," a special detention cell located off the fifth-floor infirmary. At that point I was barely conscious.

The following morning at 5 A.M., Miss Mack, a sympathetic matron, dressed me in a black suit which a church had donated to the jail. She half-carried me to a van which took me to the courtroom for my hearing. I couldn't walk by myself. During the brief hearing, someone held me up. The judge gave me a suspended sentence and probation. Then he asked me what had happened. When I mumbled my story, he told me to file a complaint with Warden Johnson. Johnson simply dismissed my complaint by saying I was a nut and had hurt myself trying to commit suicide.

When I was helped out of the courtroom, I was given 35 cents—the amount allotted to every prisoner after a hearing. I used the money to get to the Salvation Army Emergency Lodge at 432 West Wisconsin Avenue in Chicago. I spent two months there recovering from the beating. I had bruises all over my body, sores, a broken nose, a bad concussion and infections from the burns. My eyes wouldn't focus for some time, and now I wear dentures. The Salvation Army Lodge didn't take one cent from me. Without exception, everyone there was wonderful and helpful.

I work now at a good-paying job. I'm useful.

I'm sure I'll never have to go to that jail again. But if something ever *did* happen, I'd make certain I'd be taken to the morgue instead.

man alone

WILLIAM DOYLE

William Doyle discusses some of the punishments to be found in prison beyond the custodian-inflicted physical pain described by Reynolds. The physical discomfort of prison life resulting from the noise, smells, extreme temperatures, loneliness, over-crowded conditions, and disagreeable food is recorded here.[1]

Everyone in McGraw carried a heavy burden, the short-termers and long-termers alike. The monotony, the same thing day in and day out, was deadly. The discipline was harsh, the tasks that accomplished nothing were onerous. The confinement of being locked in a cell fifteen hours out of every day, the noises, the smells, the loneliness—all combined to weaken a man's fiber. In summer the heat was terrific—115 degrees in the shade, and in the Stone Yard, working among the rocks, 130. Winter cold was intense. You were never warm. You went into your unheated cell and climbed into your bunk with your clothes on, dressed in two pairs of pants, two pairs of socks and with even your cap on—fully clothed. And in the morning you broke the ice crust from your pail to wash.

It was strictly the survival of the strongest. Not only must you be strong but you must be willing to fight on any occasion in which fighting was warranted. You must fight with your fists, with knives or hammers or anything you could lay your hand to. And you must inspire in others the knowledge that you mean to kill. Then and then only are you left alone.

The bad ones, the men who would shive you and take your life if you aroused them, were feared and respected by the other prisoners, even by the guards and officials. In the majority of cases they were the quiet ones, the old-timers, men who were serving long sentences.

The whole prison was divided up into gangs, and the tougher the gang the more it was respected. Sooner or later every young fish who came in was forced to submit to one gang or another. If one of them tried to hold out

Reprinted with permission of The Bobbs-Merrill Company, Inc. from Man Alone *by William Doyle (Indianapolis, Indiana, 1953), pp. 32–36.*

[1]Additional accounts of prison conditions include those of Cantine and Rainer (1950), Hankins (1956), Teale (1957), and Thomas (1967).

and was not protected by a gang or by a man strong enough to be feared, suddenly some morning four or five men would enter his cell, put knives on him, throw a blanket over his head and attack him. After this sort of treatment the young con looked for protection. And God help him if he snitched to the officials! From then on he was a marked man.

One of the greatest burdens was overcrowding. Owing to the lack of space it was necessary to place two men in a cell, and since the cells were very small it was desirable to be with someone you liked. Often it was impossible. Usually the turnkey for some reason wouldn't make the move and you had to cell with someone whose guts you hated. This resulted in fights and a trip to the hole for punishment. When you came out it was usually another move into a cell with someone you disliked or couldn't get along with.

You would come to your cell every day for fifteen hours of torture. You would lie down on your bunk and read your paper or magazine and put it under your pillow when you were through instead of passing it to your cell partner. And he would do the same. You watched each other like hawks to see that nothing of yours was touched. When the lights went out at nine o'clock and you were lying in your bunk, you would turn your back, as a gesture of contempt.

The first one up in the morning would wash, wipe the basin, dry himself and sit on the bunk. Then the other man would wash. In the meantime the first man would make his bunk and move over to the door and wait there for his cellmate to finish. The cells were so small that only one person at a time could move around without bumping his partner. This would go on for weeks and sometimes for months without a word being spoken. It didn't take much under these conditions to set off a bomb. One man might accidentally bump into the other, or disarrange his property, and the fight would be on.

I have known men who would go all night without a cigarette, lie on their beds and suffer, rather than ask their cellmate for a smoke, or a match when a box of them belonging to the other guy was sitting on the table. I have seen men purposely hide out, try escapes that would cost them their lives, rather than go to their cells under such conditions.

But the food was a torture, too, and not the least. During the first sixteen years of my life in McGraw it never varied. (Afterward a new regime came in and the food was better.) There were beans every meal, twenty times a week, year in and out, pale and watery. Monday and Tuesday mornings we had oatmeal mush, bread and coffee, and on Wednesdays corn-meal mush. Twice a month instead of the corn meal we had a round piece of hamburger, known as "jute balls," with brown gravy—and on Easter morning two eggs. Those were big events!

We ate only twice on Sundays because everyone was locked up at three, and the afternoon meal was a slice of beef, dry as blotting paper and about as thick, with potatoes and a piece of pie or cake. We were allowed to carry a lump to our cells, so we would either take the pie or make a sandwich of the meat. I used to give my meat away or trade it for a piece of pie, and all the men did the same, swapping for what they liked best. The waiters did a brisk business after the meal selling someone's pie or meat for a sack of weed. We were given six sacks of ducks a month, and some guys would rather smoke than eat.

The evening meals were always the same—beans, Monday through Saturday. On holidays such as the Fourth of July the Salvation Army would bring in ice cream. Thanksgiving and Christmas were big days: roast pork and apple sauce, pie, cake, fruit, and coffee with sugar and milk. It was too bad they came but once a year.

You were always hungry and everybody had the "chuck horrors." Many times all I would eat for supper was dry bread with salt on it, a cup of tea to wash it down. The meat in the stew, when you could find a piece of it, was black and streaked with green.

One day after I had been in McGraw several months the men rebelled against the stew and went on a hunger strike. Word circulated through the prison that no one was to eat it and no one was to work until it was changed. Everybody agreed and we all entered the mess hall and turned our backs on the stew. The guards watched us but didn't say anything. We marched to our jobs, refused to work and were immediately sent to our cells. Captain Crane came around with a bunch of guards and asked each man what he wanted to do—go back to work or go to the hole. Some went to work, the others were marched to the hole.

About sixty men were in the first day, fifty the next, then thirty, and after a week only twenty-six held out. Twenty of them were "Wobblies." I was one of the remaining six. A few days later Crane came back to the hole and asked us if we were ready to go to work. One of the Wobblies said no, and not until the stew was changed.

The Captain got red in the face. "You're a damn bunch of trouble-makers," he shouted. "And you can rot where you are. I'll change nothing. I don't give a damn whether you eat or not, but you'll work. I'm running this prison and not you."

We stayed in the hole for another week and then were taken out and placed on the line. We had been communicating with one another by tapping and had come to the conclusion, since there were too few of us to do any good, that we were foolish to hold out. When the Captain asked us if we had decided to go back to work we said that we had.

the deprivations of prison

NATHAN F. LEOPOLD, JR.

Nathan Leopold, one of two men who committed what has been called the "Crime of the Century," reacts to the discomforts of the prison setting. He discusses the problem of the psychology of the prison—in his view, more depressing than the physical deprivations. He further discusses the complicated question—whether or not to live out his sentence—which faced him early in his period of incarceration.

The long period of being locked into one's cell from Saturday afternoon until Monday morning is one of the most disagreeable experiences in prison. The physical surroundings, to begin with, are not particularly comfortable. The cells are, as I have said, very small: one can easily touch both side walls with outstretched arms. The bunk occupies well over half the available space; the stool and bucket account for almost half the remainder. The accumulated odors of nine hundred men confined in one building without plumbing facilities are definitely perceptible. Ventilation is poor; the light from the narrow windows in the outside wall, some thirty feet from the cells, is totally insufficient and the lights in the cells are always lit. There is a constant hum of talk and other incidental noise from the open cells.

But the psychological milieu is even more depressing than the physical. What to do with oneself, how to put in the long, dragging hours, becomes a problem. One can sleep only so many hours. One can pace three strides up and three strides back, but that soon wears thin. Pencil and paper are strictly forbidden, presumably to discourage the passing of "kites" from one prisoner to another. There is, indeed, a small slate and a slate pencil in the cell, but it is so small as to be useful only for working out problems in addition or multiplication. This early in my prison career I had no books of any kind, received no newspapers, had not even an old letter to reread.

The surroundings permitted, really, of only one kind of activity—thinking —and in this activity I indulged to a considerable extent that first week-end. I don't believe that I wallowed, then or later, in any great degree of self-pity. I had been brought up as the youngest in a household of four boys. Sometime, farther back than my conscious memory reaches, I had perhaps gone out and played marbles "for keeps." If I lost and then came home and whined about my losses, I feel very sure that I was taught the error of my ways, perhaps by a clout on the head. Not for losing—that was one of the expectable vicissitudes of life—but for being a poor loser. I remember no such incident, but the tradition of being a good loser goes back as far as I can remember. Above all, tears were taboo. Only babies cried; weeping was unworthy of a big boy. And this philosophy I applied to my present unhappy circumstances. Then, and many times during the years to come, I felt very sorry for what I had done. But I never, or almost never, felt sorry for myself. I had done something horrible and something unbelievably stupid, and this I regretted bitterly. I had lost my entire life, to say nothing of the grief I had caused others, but it still did not occur to me to weep over my loss.

My ignorance of prison life strikes me, on looking back, as well-nigh unbelievable. Yet I suspect that most people who have never had occasion to interest themselves in prisons have as little knowledge of them as I did. Certainly my few ideas on the subject were inchoate and disorganized. I had made no attempt in jail to acquaint myself with prison conditions; what few impressions I had, had apparently been culled from Byron's *Prisoner of Chillon* and similar romantic sources. I was faintly surprised to find that I was not to be chained in a dungeon or fed on bread and water. There were apparently no active, physical forms of punishment; the punishment was negative: it consisted of the things of which one was deprived.

The problem, then, resolved itself into the question of finding ways within oneself to supply the almost total lack of external stimulation characteristic of the prison environment. In later years I elaborated this thought into a more or less complete philosophy of trying to substitute, so far as is possible in the circumstances, element for element, for all the major areas that constitute life outside prison. But at the moment the problem was somewhat more simple. I had to make two decisions: whether I wanted even to attempt to serve my sentence and, in the event that I did try to serve it, how to occupy myself in the apparently enormous amount of leisure time at my disposal.

The first question—whether or not to serve my sentence—was complex and caused me considerable thought. The future looked anything but rosy and it seemed to me that the minimal degree of life—existence, really—that stretched before me was hardly worth the effort of living. It might be considerably easier, as it certainly would be quicker, to take a parole from the top gallery. Death would be almost certain and almost certainly instantaneous. Against this idea there militated primarily the thought of causing further anguish to my father and other members of my family. They had gone through indescribable grief over me and had put forth every effort to attain the very result that had eventuated: life imprisonment. Would it be fair for me to bring all those efforts to naught in a single leap? Besides, I had a perhaps unreasonably intense horror of being a weakling, of admitting defeat. I was determined, and all through my prison term I remained determined, to demonstrate that "they couldn't pitch 'em any faster than I could catch 'em." Stubbornness, willfulness, call it what you will, this trait of my personality buoyed me up more than once and carried me over periods which my sanity, at least, might otherwise not have survived. Finally, in allowing a defense to be offered for me in court and in co-operating with the alienists who had presented that defense, I had, in a sense, committed myself to a certain course of action. I felt that I should be less than consistent if I now took my own life in order to avoid the consequences of that course of action.

The arguments on both sides were so compelling that I felt myself unable to arrive at a sound decision. Accordingly, I temporized. I decided to do nothing for the moment and to put off the final decision for a period of three or six months. At the end of this time, I thought, I should be in a better position to make an intelligent decision.

If, then, I was to remain alive, at least for some months, I must face the second problem: how to occupy myself mentally in the interim. Monotony —sheer, utter boredom—is the bane of prison existence; one must find some way to combat it. Here the choice was simple, in view of the scarcity of alternatives. Obviously there wasn't much I could do in my spare time except read. The only question was whether to attempt some serious, organized study or merely to while away the time with light reading. I compromised. It was permissible to have books sent in from outside, provided they came directly from the publisher and provided they were acceptable to the censor, who at that time was the prison chaplain. Accordingly, at my first visit with my family I asked that certain books be sent me. First I asked for some of the books I had used as textbooks at college and others that I had wished I had time to peruse. These included, I remember, Cicero's *De Senectute*, which I had read in Latin class as a freshman in college. I thought that some of Cicero's examples of the compensations of old age might be applied with equal force to life in prison. He demonstrates that the pleasures lost in becoming old are chiefly the pleasures of the senses and that, in some cases at least, the decline of a man's physical appetites is to be regarded not as a loss to be bewailed but as a deliverance from thralldom that is positively to be welcomed. The deprivations of prison, in some ways, parallel the loss of physical prowess; here, too, one loses, among other things, the pleasures of the table and the bed, if for other reasons.

The analogy is not perfect, of course, for old age does not deprive one of the pleasures of friendship and intellectual companionship, except in so far as one's friends, with advancing age, die off. And with respect to sensual pleasures, in old age one's lessened indulgence is predicated upon waning desire; in prison, the appetites remain; it is only the possibility of their satisfaction that is lacking.

But Cicero's reasoning reinforced a thought I had had for some time in vague, undefined form. It seems to me that there are two possible ways of achieving satisfaction or contentment. The normal, and by far the preferable, way is by striving to attain what one wants. But in the face of insuperable handicaps, such as those presented by physical deformity and those inherent in imprisonment, there still remains a way to achieve contentment. One can train oneself to want only what one can obtain. The thirty-five foot wall that surrounds the prison becomes a barrier for me only if and when I attempt to cross it. There may be an unscalable cliff an uncrossable crevasse high in the Himalayas. But this does not constitute a barrier for me; it is a barrier only for those who want to get to the other side. And the difference between the deprivations of prison and the restrictions upon complete freedom in normal extramural society is one of degree only: there are few folks so fortunately situated as to be able to take a trip to Europe, for example, whenever the whim strikes them. The restrictions are economic and social rather than physical; they are none the less stringent.

sex roles in prison

HAYWOOD PATTERSON

A recent report on the Philadelphia prison system (Davis, 1968, pp. 8–16) documented 156 sexual assault cases for a 26-month period in that system. Prison officials in Philadelphia admitted that every young man of slight build convicted by the courts is sexually approached within days after admission. They further state that many of these men are raped; others, because of this fear, seek homosexual relationships. In this selection, prisoner Haywood Patterson, with the assistance of Earl Conrad, describes the pressures an inmate faces in this one-sex environment.[1]

For several months I had a soft job. I worked on the prison yard keeping it clean. I got up about four o'clock in the morning—like everyone—but I was through work four hours later. That was just when the others were beginning to sweat. My job, it was to take care of the front yard of the prison. The rest of the day I loafed. I got acquainted with prisoners, guards, and the things that went on. In the evening when the farm work was finished and the prisoners came in from the fields hell opened its mouth in the barracks. . . .

Before I got here I heard tell of the gal-boy life at Atmore. Gal-boy stuff went on at Kilby and at Birmingham jail too. All prisons all over, I guess, but I wasn't interested in it. I was a man who wanted women. But this was the main thing going on among the Atmore prisoners. It was on all sides, like the walls. They built "covered wagons" or "hunks" around the beds. That screened out what went on inside the bunks. I heard the boys talking about screwing someone or other. I thought that meant real women. I passed by some covered wagons. I looked hard.

I learned men were having men.

Old guys, they called them wolves, they saw me looking at this stuff

[1]Other autobiographical material on this subject includes Thomas (1967), and Martin (1952).

and thought I might be a gal-boy. One came up and propositioned me. I didn't like that none at all. I said, "If any of that stuff goes on with me in on it I'll do all the fukking myself. I been a man all my life." I doubled up my fists to show him I meant it.

Guys kept coming up to me. Saying no didn't stop them. I was being forced to be either a man or a gal-boy. They wouldn't hardly let you stay outside of this life. You had to prove you were a man or become a woman. I would say, "Leave off. I'm looking for a gal-boy myself." That was a hard-guy act I was putting on at first because at first I didn't look for no gal-boy.

It went on for weeks like that. The wolves gave me sweet talk. They told me I needed someone to live with, someone to take care of me. It hardened me up inside to see how rotten a man could get and it helped turn me against all people.

At night that went on in every cell. It made me think how any person who thinks he knows all the answers, he's a fool. Things happened there I never thought existed in the world. I never knew till then a man could use another man and get a thrill out if it. I didn't much want to know it even after I learned. The prison authorities, they were for it. It helped them to control the men. Especially the tough ones they called devils. They believed that if a devil had a gal-boy he would be quiet. He would be a good worker and he wouldn't kill guards and prisoners and try to escape. He would be like a settled married man. They especially wanted convicts who farmed to have gal-boys. The guards, they even matched up gal-boys with wolves. They liked to watch these goings on.

Some in prison, they did not take part in such stuff. They escaped being either husbands or gal-boys. That was a minority. Even a jive preacher, he would get up on a Sunday and preach to all the prisoners: "You must do right. You must do what the Good Book say. You must choose the way of the Lord and spurn off King Satan. You must leave off the sinning and the julep drinking and must not do this or that." That night you'd catch him all bedded up with a gal-boy.

Mostly teen-aged boys were used for this. Sometimes a gal-boy, he would be as much as twenty-five or thirty years old, but not so popular as a tender young boy. The state of Alabama had a school where they manufactured gal-boys. It was Mount Meigs Reformatory, a few miles from Montgomery. They called it the Alabama Reform School for Juvenile Negroes. A fine name for the worst place in the state. Far worse than Atmore State Prison Farm, from what all the graduates told me. Boys under fifteen who got in trouble, they were sent there. They were supposed to be taught trades. Also they worked on the farm that goes with Mount Meigs. Actually they were just got ready to be put out on the state prison farms or sent to Kilby Prison or Birmingham jail. All the gal-boys I ever talked with at

Atmore who came from Mount Meigs said they would rather be in prison than the reform school. The superintendent there at that time, he was named Morris. He is no longer there. The boys all spoke against Morris. He treated them so bad. He worked them hard. Made them go barefooted year around in all kinds of weather. Didn't feed them any more than just vegetables and corn bread. Just enough food to keep them existing. They called that reform. These boys, they sure spoke hard against Morris. They said he was the kind of a Negro that white folks want to have over Negroes. The kind that put one Negro against another to keep them all in an uproar. There was nothing there to make better citizens out of them. These youngsters, they came from povertied homes like mine. I know how they got there. At Mount Meigs they fought with each other. They fought over food, sex, friendships, and imprisonment. They rebelled. They got themselves made into permanent bad boys. Then they were shipped to Atmore or the other prison camps to be fought over by the wolves.

Many boys in from Mount Meigs, they tried not to get into this. But a fifteen-year-old stood no chance at Atmore. Prisoner and warden were against him and he was quickly made into a woman.

Soon after I got there I saw how a wolf would trick a young boy. They all worked the same way. First the wolf, he gave the new guy money and bought him what he wanted from the commissary. He told the boy he was a friend. He would protect him from the tough guys. He would fight for him. He didn't tell him right off what he was leading to. After he spent four or five dollars on the boy, he propositioned him. The boy was stunned, didn't know that was the pay-off. The wolf said, "What the hell I'm spending money on you for?" The boy offered to try to get the money back. The wolf didn't want the money back. The wolf knew where he could get help. He went to Warden Frank Kelly. To the warden he told that this boy was in debt to him and wasn't good to him. Kelly knew what that meant. He called in the boy. First he whupped him with his tongue. Then he had a guard give him a good lashing. Then the warden said, "You go back there and be good to the old man. He going to give you good protection out there and you going to need it. You be good to him." The warden wanted the old wolf quieted down. The Negro boy was nothing to him. The boy returned to the cell. The old wolf beat him up unmerciful. The other prisoners just looked on. They knew a young woman was being born. Some just looked forward to using her a little later themselves. If a man stepped in to take the boy's side and fight the wolf, there would be a murder. Often there was. After the boy was beaten up and lying on the floor the old wolf picked him up and brought him to his bunk. The covers went up over the old wolf's double-decker bed. The wagon was covered, the hunk set. The boy was broken.

I've seen young boys stand up and fight for hours for their rights. Some wouldn't give up. The prisoners and the guards, they just stood around and watched a fight like that. That was the way a man seduced a growing boy. Beat him around till he was weak, then took him inside the covered wagon. I have seen some young fellows with a determined mind, they wouldn't let anyone conquer them. I liked them for that and befriended them—even though I got to use the willing gal-boys myself.

Gal-boys didn't really like a man, but they did these things. After they were broken and became known as gal-boys, some carried on like real prostitutes. They sold themselves around on the week-ends just like whore women of the streets. Some guys gave them more money than they would a real woman, maybe five or ten dollars. Usually you could hunk up with a gal-boy for two or three dollars. Gal-boys got sold off to different men. If a guy had a gal-boy but didn't get along with him any more, he could put him up for sale. He could sell him for twenty or twenty-five dollars. News of a sale went through the prison pretty fast and bids came in every time. Once a gal-boy was sold, the husband couldn't touch him any more. There was always an uproar over gal-boys in prison. They sure were something. That was the root of most trouble—because they carried on like real women and pitted the men against each other. You take a good-looking, tender boy; the camp went for that. Always made a fuss. If a boy didn't soon decide and select a husband, there would soon be a killing. Mostly it was the wolves that killed one another over a gal-boy. Even when the boy made a choice, the others would still be after him. His man was supposed to defend for him, take his knife and fight for him. That's where the trouble began. That's why it was a murderers' home.

I once heard Deputy Warden Lige Lambert tell some state patrolmen that 50 percent of the Negro prisoners in Atmore were gal-boys—and 70 percent of the white.

But there was no reform school in Alabama for white boys that unloaded white youngsters into the hands of white wolves. That just went on among the Negro prisons. Young Negro boys were put in with the old Negro wolves. The whites took better care of their white truants. We colored didn't count. A gal-boy would spend a few years like that in Atmore. Then they would let him out, maybe when he was twenty-one or so. That is why, I later learned, the Negro sections of the Northern cities have so many gal-boys in the streets today. The Southern prisons breed them.

No one would ever take and beat me like some of those boys were beaten. No one would ever get the chance to go to the warden about me like that. If I had to be part of this life I would be a man. Soon I brought myself to try it out. I patronized one of the week-end whores. I didn't like it the first two or three times. It went against all my nature. But it set me as a man among the prisoners, not a gal-boy. I disliked the guys who acted like women. I called them fuk-boys. I called them all sorts of sorry names for doing that...but I was drawn more and more into this life. I saw so many weak human beings call themselves men. There were men who came into prison leaving wives and families on the outside, and they became gal-boys. I saw men learn to love boys harder than they could any woman. I saw beatings and jealousy and killings over it. I learned most of the killings at Atmore were over gal-boy stuff. It was war there. I would say to one of them, "You come here taking your mommy's and your sister's places. You rotten." I talked serious like that. . . and the next night I wanted them. Even after I had a regular gal-boy it didn't end my troubles with wolves who wanted to use me that way.

A wolf named John Peaseley, he was after me. He wanted to use both me and my gal-boy. He thought I was too young to have a gal-boy. First he tried to get my wife away from me, then he made a play for me. He got hold of my wife and said, "That's a *young* man you have for a husband. What you should do, you should have him for a buddy, and I'll take care of you both."

My gal-boy came back and told me what Peaseley said.

"How do you feel about it?" I asked my gal-boy. "Are you going to do what he says or what I say?"

"I'm not going to pay him any attention."

The wolf saw he couldn't make my gal-boy see it his way, so he decided to intrude on me. He came to my cell, sat down, and told me, "Listen, I got some talk for you."

"What kind of talk?"

"Listen, I know you can't live by yourself. You got to have someone see out for you."

I got blown up. "What you mean I can't live by myself and got to have someone see out for me? Now you listen to me! As long as you know me, don't you ever approach me again like that! If you do the place will be too small for us both! I want you to know I been a man all my life! You can't fuk me!"

He seemed to take it as a joke. But I was mad with him. This was the same sort of stuff he talked to my boy.

John Peaseley kept carrying on with my boy. He tried to take him away from me. Bought him whisky, tried to talk him out of me. My boy would come back and tell me what John Peaseley said. After a while I had enough of this and went to face Peaseley.

"John," I said, "now you're a man and so am I. Just between myself and you, you've gone a little too far. My little big-eyed boy that you get off with every Sunday, he tells me everything you tell him. And I don't like what you tell him. I don't want you to have anything more to do with him at all."

He got angry. "As long as he's here and wants to talk with me, I'm going to talk with him."

A few days later, out in the field, John Peaseley jumped me again and said, "I talked to that boy yesterday and he said he didn't want to have anything more to do with you. I want you to let him alone." Then he raised his voice up high so the guards and the squad heard him, *"You better not be caught in his face any more!"* That always meant a fight.

I didn't believe what Peaseley said. I told him I'd see my gal-boy about that. I would meet him after we got inside the prison. In there the guards wouldn't be able to stop a fight so quick.

He went back into camp that night and got himself a pair of shears somewhere. He put the shears in his pocket and went to his cell.

I had a switch-blade knife.

I went looking for him.

I found him up there in my kid's cell. He was sitting on the bunk talking to the kid.

I eased in on him with my knife cocked and up over my head. When John Peaseley looked up he saw me. I said, "Well, John, the devil's got you now. Don't you try to resist. Just take it easy and take what I'm going to give you. I'm going to put a lot of hell on you."

I didn't have to use my knife. I gave him a serious whupping. I beat on him like he was a snake. I kicked him with my heavy shoes.

Thereafter I didn't have any more trouble from him. He didn't try to take my gal-boy from me after that. Nobody did.

And Peaseley didn't try to make a girl out of me no more. Nobody did.

I had taken a gal-boy, whupped a wolf, and set myself up as a devil.

sex in a women's prison

ANONYMOUS

In the following interview, a female prisoner (a successful call girl in prison for possession of marijuana) relates her experiences with homosexuality in prison. In this interview conducted by Ward and Kassebaum she traces the course and problems of a prison love affair.[1]

What made you aware of homosexuality on campus?

I was brought here [from jail] with a homosexual and she had her people here [Frontera] and had had before she left [on parole], so she talked about her and kind of included me in the crowd that they were going to have when she returned here to kind of make me feel a little better. So I kind of learned through this and I observed. The only encouragement I received from these people in this crowd was that I was doing my time too hard and why didn't I find someone and make myself comfortable. Well, at this point (this was immediately after I arrived here), I had already met Lee and you know there was kind of an inclination in her direction. But I froze on myself.

How did you happen to meet her?

On the plumbing crew that we were working together on. I chose this because it was a free type thing and it wasn't in an area of police [staff] and I wanted to stay particularly away from them. I had hopes of doing my time where they didn't even observe me, good or bad. If they just hardly know you're here you have the least trouble, and that's how I came to get on the plumbing crew. Lee never knew for months that I had any inclination toward her at all because I covered it from myself and admonished myself for this, you know, I thought I was losing one of my marbles, which I may have done.

[1]For related materials, see Gagnon and Simon (1968, pp. 23–29), and Giallombardo (1966).

You said you were doing hard time when you first came here. What do you mean by "hard time?"

Well, I'm a tenacious person and I had just been alienated from Steve [her common-law husband] and we were very much in love and all this and everything happened so quickly, I didn't get to see him before I left, I went to court one day and I came down here that night, which was unusual. I didn't have time to adjust, you know, let me plant my feet for a minute, and the separation from him was something that really just drugged me. People wouldn't let me write for a while, I had to get a clearance, and this took a long time. So I did hard time because of this.

I couldn't come in off the streets, is the thing. You can do better time, if you just live in here and think about the things in here. . . . But if you insist upon every time the radio plays, in listening to the music wishing you were out there in the same bar or in the same area or with the same people, you're gonna kill yourself, which is what it amounts to. You're just dying a little inside all the time. So when I finally decided to just forget all that out there for a while and give it a break, and myself, I did better time.

We wrote while Steve was in jail and I was in jail here and then he got out and he wrote and he ran, but a man never runs for a woman as well as the reverse. Men just aren't too cool that way. They're too busy feeling sorry for themselves and going out and getting drunk and finding somebody else to occupy themselves with. You know—men! So he was arrested again and he was arrested on my charge, which was very unfair, not any evidence or anything, took to prison and he was very bitter about this and it was a Federal bust. So he decided that the best way that he could get out of prison sooner was to just tell them that he wanted nothing to do with me, which is just what he did. Well, this hurt me, but I could see what he was doing, but I never quite forgave him for it. So we never wrote, and that was it.

During this time, I'm probably half-ashamed of myself but this was part of the reason that I finally gravitated toward Lee. So what am I? How faithful am I to what? I don't know. That's why I don't know whether I'm homosexual, bisexual—or what. Was this a psychological thing? I have no idea.

In the beginning stages of your relationship with Lee, did you feel any anxiety or worry about what you were doing or getting into?

All the things I thought I would feel guilty about I didn't. I kept nagging myself about this, "Well, why don't you feel guilty?" The thing I really didn't want to think about was him and Lee along the same lines at all because I did feel guilt. So it was possible for me just to eradicate him completely from my thoughts. And I was pretty hung up on Lee so it really wasn't too hard at that, you know, when he would enter my mind,

I mean as far as our own relationship had gone, he and I. I could think about him, you know, just as a friend, as another person, and actually when Lee and I first got together she nagged me so much about Steve I didn't want to think about him. I was afraid she'd read my mind, so I would try and put him out of my mind whenever he would come in, because she was extremely jealous of Steve, and homosexuals are anyway—women are nothing but a hassle when it comes to jealousy, especially two women. So she nagged me so much about him that I didn't want to even consider thinking about him. We fought for quite a little while about this.

Do you feel that you initiated the affair with Lee, or did you respond to clues that she was giving to you?

I think it was just about fifty-fifty, but see because of pride I never told anybody that Steve put me down, I didn't want anybody to know this, this was a blow to my pride. She thought all along that everything was all right with Steve and I. So we were very close friends. We shared innermost secrets that she didn't even talk to the girl that she was with about, and it became difficult for me to work with her on occasion. I could feel this vibration between us but I kept telling myself it's just me—this is my imagination—until finally she just threw it at me one day and I discovered that all these things that I thought was my imagination she had been thinking too. So this frightened me and I decided no, I couldn't do this and she had guilt feelings because it meant turning a virgin out, as it were, and she didn't want to do this and I can now understand why. So I fought it and she fought it and then I decided to hell with it, I didn't feel like fighting it, I wanted to be with Lee. So then she fought me and we argued. Well this went on probably for two or three months and finally she just decided that she would go ahead despite her guilt complex and go through with this thing because she felt strongly enough toward me and it's something that she never did get over, this guilt.

Had you received a release date then or didn't you know when you were going to be released?

No, I hadn't gone to the Board yet for my time, and when I went to the Board I wanted to leave but I wanted to be with her, too. This was something that very few people cop to, really, but it's true. They want to go but they don't want to leave the people they're with—if they're pretty happy in this affair.

So when I got six months it was a drag because I had to do it, but I wasn't too unhappy because I was gonna do it with her. But Lee, three months prior to my going, kept nagging me about this, "You're gonna go pretty soon," and I'd tell her, "Well man, that's a long way off, you know, what difference does it make?" I couldn't understand why she was thinking about this. This was her insecurity. I see it now in this light, "She's going and I'm gonna be hung up here." I've seen this happen time and again since then, but I just didn't even recognize it. So this was what started some of our trouble and by the time I went to get my date she was just a mass of nerves, more so than I was, and not because she was worried about whether I would or would not get a date but because of my leaving her and we'd gone through this "never part" thing before and I realized later that this had a great deal to do with our breakup.

Were you living in the same cottage?

No. If we had been I don't think Lee and I would even be apart today—and she's agreed with this too. Doris finally asked her when I came back [as a parole violator] this same question: "If you two had been in the same cottage, would I have been able to interfere?" and Lee told her "no." But it's hassle. You can be together through the day if your jobs correspond and so forth, and even if they don't you can still manage to be together. But at five o'clock it's over and you don't have control of any situation that might come up.

How did getting your date affect you relationship?

At this point Lee had—Doris had been pursuing *her*. She succumbed, which was to me, "Okay, so you're weak, you've done this." It was convenient, she was attracted to the girl, and from what I understand it was physical more than spiritual, intellectual or anything else. It was convenient, they were in the house together, Lee was sick of hassling, being out on the campus. We used to sit through windstorms together, which was a drag, you know, I can understand her viewpoint. So by this time, they were pretty much together and all *we* did was fight most of the time. I don't know why, I'll never understand it. She couldn't see us being together any more at this time, yet it was because of her I changed my plans three times and I couldn't change them again. I was going to wait for her, and I just couldn't change them. The Board was liable not to let me out, you know, "unstable." So this was still going to be the plan. And she didn't want to cut me loose. She didn't want to be with me because I was going, I was going to leave her, she was miserable because she wasn't leaving, but she did not want to cut me loose. So I just never could understand it, you know, of course, I'm not a stud broad either, I just don't understand some of those things. I thought she was crazy, I still do. We fought a great deal, *I* fought *her,* I was the one who caused most of the trouble.

As this affair was terminating, did you find yourself looking for anyone else to take her place?

No. I was pretty disillusioned and, no, I didn't look for anyone else and I haven't since. Once in a while I get a little frisky and I go out and talk to all the little boys on campus (female boys, you know), but aside from that, nothing. I would never undertake—I'm almost sure I'd never undertake—another relationship unless it was with Lee. I don't know why. But of course I said that before I was with Lee. I said I would never turn out and I'm a pretty strong person in my beliefs and everything I say, and I think I held out for quite a long time, but I haven't played at all since I've been here this time, and won't. I'll leave here without having any kind of a relationship with anybody.

Do you feel that anything about your experience while hustling would be related to a willingness to give up males and turn to females?

Well for me that's a difficult question to answer because I can be sexually satisfied with a man if I'm lucky or with a woman, which isn't too difficult. But if I'm not emotionally satisfied with this person, then I'm going to blow 'em sooner or later anyway, they're going to go, it's just a matter of time. So, no, I don't think I'll ever give up men entirely. And it may just be that when I go out of here, if my life takes the turn that I'm going to try and manipulate it toward, I won't be with a woman either. The only woman I've ever wanted has been Lee on a future long-term basis, but I can't rely on her anymore either. So, no, I wouldn't. I don't think I would ever. I like men too.

In fact, I think I like men better than I do women at this point because I'm pretty disgusted with some of these homosexual scenes. For the most part they're all so damn crude and vulgar. Anybody's liable to walk up to you and ask you, "How much will you turn a trick with me for?" Because just the other night, the girl sitting next to me—a stud broad—somebody did just that. The femme sent her partner, her buddy, to ask the butch about it and it hurt her. Hell, what she told her was, "Christ, what do you think I am, a dog?" "No, that's not it, but we just thought you couldn't be approached." Well, she told her, "You're right. I can't be—in those terms or anything like that." So, she moved from our side of the house to the other side and she's very disillusioned. I don't think it'll be something that she'll get over for a little while.

I'm really disgusted with a lot of it. And there are very few affairs where, oh, you know all this. To me it's so much drivel. They say when you're with a woman you're completely loyal and you don't have to worry about them chippying. Hell, it's the biggest lie that was ever told. These women around here chippy maybe three times as much as a man will. There was a fight the other day in our house. This one girl was going home and luckily she went home on her [parole] date yesterday. Her people [lover] had gone to the release cottage. It's not enough that she's got a thousand women in her own house, that she might chippy with, but she decided to fool around. Her partner, the aggressor, her dad, whatever it is—*he*—why *he* was going home yesterday and she decided she couldn't wait to chippy, not even two days, so she went to the release cottage and chippied. What kind of a scene is this? I'm disgusted, really. And today's scene [window-smashing episode resulting from a spat between a butch and her femme]—I'm disgusted. There just is nothing in any of these things. It's always "forever," yes, each time, "I'm in love and this is forever." I've seen it for three years and I'm sick of it. It's a mass of frustration that's all. I don't care if the sexual and spiritual thing with another woman is perfect or can be perfect, it still doesn't last. There must be something wrong.

Do you think it's easier on the outside—you seem to be holding out some hope yet.

I guess I am. I don't know. I guess it is somewhat easier, everybody says it is who's been together on the streets, you don't have sixty females waiting for you to turn your back so that they can jump on your people and try and pull your people from you. You don't have this because there just aren't this many women looking for homosexual women outside. Just damn near all are femmes, and contrary to popular belief, half of these butch broads that run around here, they'll turn femme in a minute if there's a real butch that comes in. I've seen it happen over and over again. You don't really ever know who your people really are—you're not quite sure. For all I know, Lee could be with a man on the streets. I've heard that she isn't, but do I know for sure? She has a son, I have a daughter, how do I know?

But as I think I tried to explain to you before, a woman reaches beyond the core of another woman's soul; there aren't many men who can do this. This is, well I have to speak for myself, I can't say this happens to everybody. I've seen few relationships like the one that I had, but I know that I will never find again a man who can do the same for me and who would be capable of perhaps giving this so that I can give the same back. I don't think it's possible. I hope it isn't, really, because I don't ever want it to happen again and have it end like this. No, one time is enough. I've had quite a few relationships in my life, but this ruined it. I'd rather do the surface thing, and if I even married again, I would prefer that it not be too deep.

life on death row

EDGAR LABAT

The man who has been on death row longer than any other man in history—over fourteen years—presents in this interview his experiences in prison and the events leading up to his imprisonment. Here he discusses the psychological pressures of being locked in a cell and awaiting death for so long a period.[1]

You were on Death Row for more than 14 years. How does it feel to live that long under a death sentence?

I keeps myself prepared to die. I've learned not to fear death. I sometimes wonder how other people feel under a death sentence. Often, I dream what normal life would be like with my wife and children, but then I wake up, still here.

When I first came on Death Row, in 1953, there was another Negro, name of John Salomon, was killed here in the electric chair. From my cell, about 15 feet out front, you could see the Death Chamber. I could hear the fellows hooking up the chair, and I watched the men shave his head and legs and slitting the pants legs, and I talked with Salomon. He asked me to read the Bible to him. I read the Bible to him and sang some hymns out of a book he had, watched him eat his last meal, shook hands and watched him walk away with the priest and warden. I could hear the motors racing on the chair as it was getting the juice, and the flesh could be smelt. I stayed sick to my stomach for a long time after. I could feel a part of me dying with that man.

It was funny, but when my date was set in 1957, after they brought me to Angola, I didn't have the least fear. The uncertainty was hard to accept, though. I died many deaths at Angola. Little pieces of me died over the years.

Capital punishment is not good. It goes against God's Commandments. You not really punishing by killing. Dying is sometimes better than living.

Reprinted with permission of Pix Incorporated from Look 32 *(March 19, 1968), pp. 84, 86–88.*

[1]Similar experiences were related by Chessman (1954).

In 1957, you came within three hours of execution. How did you react?

They was fixing to shave our heads, me and the other boy, Poret. I seen the bowl and the razor, and when the captain ask me, "What you want to eat? You can have anything," I knew it was time. Mr. Gorret, who pull the switch, he was waiting. I never wanted no priest, because they just come around when the date is set, not in-between times when you in need of spiritual consolation. I was not afraid. The other boy, he say he not hungry, so I ate all mine and half of his too. It was something I really liked: fried chicken, potatoes, olives, pickled onion, lemon pie and real ice-cold milk.

My cousin, Emile Labat, is a undertaker, and he was waiting outside the gate for my body. The warden read the death warrant, and I kept on with my Bible. I read the Psalms, from the First on through. My hope was in Almighty God. He know I am not guilty of this, and I feel He will save me or give me strength to take whatever come.

How do you keep from going mad, locked up so long?

I read and I write and I exercise. I do 15 push-ups every day and some squatting and jumping things I made up. At first, I read trash, just trash. I ain't got much education, you know? But then, from people writing me and all, I started in reading good things, books about self-improvement and all. And my Bible. I've got two of them—a Douay, because I was raised a Catholic and it was gave me by John Michelle, who was electrocuted; and a Jehovah's Witness Bible, King James, sent to me by a lady, Mrs. Elizabeth Parsons of Christchurch, New Zealand. Her Daddy had it in the Second World War, and it say on it, "To Beth With Love." I got a whole stack of writing, sacks of it. Poems and the story of my life. Man, I have whole loads of that written. I use all kinds of paper, whatever I can lay my hands on, sometimes big hunks of wrapping paper, you know? On both sides.

The people was a big help, all over the world, writing me. Thousands of letters, seems like, and some never got to me. Some enclosed money, but the words was what counted, knowing somebody care, and I'm not alone. Like that lady in Sweden, name of Solveig Johansson, they made stop writing me.

I turned a lot to God, knowing He know I'm innocent. I say He, but I don't think of my God as belonging to no special church or even looking like a man. He a spirit, something that sustain me and succor me in my hour of need. I find him in the Bible: Isaiah, 41st Chapter—"Fear thou not; for I am with thee: be not dismayed; for I am thy God: I will strengthen thee; yea, I will help thee; yea, I will uphold thee with the right hand of my righteousness"—and the 14th Chapter of St. John—"Let not your heart be troubled: ye believe in God, believe also in me. In my Father's house are many mansions: if it were not so, I would have told you. I go to prepare a place for you"—and the 23rd Psalm—"The Lord is my shepherd; I shall not want." There's a lot more lift me up.

Edgar, how did you get in this fix? Tell me about your early life.

Well, I guess there not too much of the unusual about that. I was a regular happy kid, coming up in Bay St. Louis, Mississippi. A lot of white people from New Orleans had summer places there, and I used to cut their grass and work around their house. I dropped out of school after the eighth grade, and I worked around, in a shrimp-and-oyster canning factory for $3.50 a week, which was a lot for a kid because times was hard in the thirties, and we needed the money, especially after my stepdaddy broke his arm cranking up his old Model-T truck. My mom, everybody like her, white and colored. She favored me over my sisters, I guess, and I was always doing things to please her, trying to be good, you know?

When I was 17, me and two other boys struck out for New Orleans. I worked at the St. Charles Hotel, as a houseman, and at the Meal-A-Minit on St. Charles and Erato Street. I went to Texas, and I met this girl that I married, Mercedes Crawford. We left there and went to Bay St. Louis and Biloxi, Mississippi, and then New Orleans. That was around '47. I got a job at Lenfant's Sea Food on Canal Boulevard, $25 a week and overtime and tips. One day, my wife went to visit her sister in Texas, and she never came back. We have two fine daughters—Mercedes is 21 and Theresa is 19—which visit me since I got out of Angola.

The year 1950 started out rough for me. I was deeply in love with a young Creole Negro girl. We got in a argument over some money I had given her that we was saving together, and one word led to another and, first thing you know, we was fighting. She pulled a pistol, and I grabbed a knife, and I cut her. I ran out of the house and gave myself in to the 2nd Police Precinct. She went and had the charges dropped. Said it was all her fault.

But, being in jail like that and missing work, I lost my good job at Lenfant's. I got a job at Touro Infirmary—that's a hospital, you know? As a orderly. I guess I was feeling sorry for myself, because I started drinking pretty heavy. But I had no call to do that. I was 27 and had my good health and low rent at the housing project and all the friends and good times I wanted. Anyway, that's the way I was when they came and got me for this.

Tell me about that. Tell me about the arrest.

I was in bed. I heard a knock on the door, and I went downstairs to open it. I went to the front door first, and there was nobody there, so I went to the back door. I looked out the kitchen window and I seen some police and I thought, "Oh, oh, somebody been fighting in the project and here's the police." As I opened the door—I have a little extra lock on the inside, a little latch that you push, you know?—I opened the door, and the force of the police knocked me down. They were prying on the door, and the force of the police knocked me down. They came in there and started kicking me and going on about where's that nigger that raped that white woman—something like that. I didn't know what they was talking about. I'd been out drinking heavy the night before, and that make me even more confused. I tried to explain where I was and who I was with and so forth, but they wouldn't listen. They dragged me into the living room, mostly by my feet. They broke off a leg from a little table and was hitting me with it on the head and back and shoulders. They kicked me in the ribs and privates and they slapped handcuffs on me. They flashed a picture of a light-skin fellow didn't even look like me and said the lady picked my picture out of the police file when I didn't even have no picture there. They said a colored fellow name of Crip told them it was me, and I didn't even know nobody of that name. I pleaded with them, and they kept on hitting me, and I passed out.

How were you identified, linking you with the crime?

Later that same day, I heard the keys rattling, and they opened my cell door, and standing outside in the hallway was six or seven police with a young white couple in the middle. One of the police say, "That's him, isn't it?" And the lady say, "Oh, no he's not the one who raped me, it was a little short nigger; but he look a little like the one you gave the money to, Bob." I was so done in, I don't see how anybody could have identified me for anything. My face was so swollen and bloody, and my ear had been bleeding until they had me put a piece of toilet paper in there to stop it.

They told me the lady said she picked out my picture at 8 o'clock or thereabouts, but I wasn't brought in there until between 11 and 12 o'clock that day, and I never had a picture in the files. I was arrested that one time I told you about, but they never made a picture. They never made a picture until they stopped beating me and three weeks passed so I could heal up. And then they moved the numbers back so it look like they took the picture November 12th, the day I was arrested, or close to it.

They beat you some more? In the cell?

They beat me in the cell, out of the cell. It all came out the time Black Gal testified before Federal District Court Judge J. Skelly Wright, in 1957. Black Gal—they call her that, her name was Elenora Henderson—she testified she was with me from 2:30 until 7:30 that morning, and so I couldn't have did this thing, which they say happen at four-thirty.

The second day, they went and got Black Gal. They had me in a kind of little gymnasium, sitting on my hands, and they worked me over, shift after shift. One shift go off, another come on. They was punching and kicking, kicking my shins, working me over, threw some hot water on my arm they was boiling to make coffee, sat me on a round bench and hit me on the side with axe handles. When Black Gal was in there, I think she seen some of that. She started crying when she seen me bloody and swollen and saying, "Yes, that's Edgar—what have you all done to him? I was with him all night and he was so drunk he couldn't even wake up to be with me."

When I went to ask her to call my sister or a lawyer real quick, they drug her out, and one of them kicked me in the groin. I was all swollen up down there. Later, I was passing blood. My glands and everything, they was all swollen up. Man, I never thought anything like that—God never knows—I never thought, you know what I mean? That that could happen to me, what they put me under.

How long did that go on?

From Sunday until Wednesday or Thursday. They started off that last day by putting my genitals in a lemon squeezer and closing a little harder each time. Another time, they had did the same thing with the drawer of a table, closing it on me, not much, but keeping the pressure on. Black Gal seen that. They kept saying, "Sign these papers, and we'll move you to Parish Prison; and when we catch the fellows who committed this crime, we'll turn you loose." I asked what did the papers say, and that was a mistake because they tightened up the squeezer, and I passed out. They came and got me from my cell later and started to give me the treatment again, and I couldn't stand any more. So I signed the papers and never did know what I signed. I found out later it said I implicated Poret and admitted being at the scene of the crime.

What were you doing the night of the crime?

Well, I got off work at Touro, checked out about 11 o'clock. I got on a bus and I came back to the Little Harlem, the barroom where Black Gal work. It's on Fourth St., between Galvez and Johnson. The man that own it, Mr. Mac Hansberry, said that I was so drunk he quit serving me. I was drinking Scotch, and I turned to gin and then to beer. I was pretty well loaded, you know? I left out there at 12 o'clock, 12:15, maybe even one o'clock. I walked to a place not far called Breaux's on Thalia and Galvez and took some beer and went home.

You were with Black Gal then?

No, not then. She came to my house. She said on the stand it was 2:30. She had a key to my house, you know? I don't never remember Black Gal coming in, it's really vague. I knew she was in there. Next morning, I got up to go to the bathroom, and I seen bobby pins and her stocking laying around there.

Then all you know is you got loaded and went home with the beer?

That's right. Man, I couldn't even make love to Black Gal, how could I go out and rape somebody? She put some ice cubes on me to try to bring me to, but I couldn't snap out of it. I heard her husband beat her up, knocked out two front teeth, because she spent the night with me. She told me she would have come to testify at the first trial in 1953, but the police threatened to take away her kids because she was married and messing around and was a unfit mother.

Did they beat you at Angola?

No. But they mental-torture you. That's worse. No visitors, and they gave me a list of people I could write to. They narrowed that down finally to my daughter. I would write her or my lawyer, and they would keep it a week and then send it back saying I wrote the wrong things, too personal or something. Come back with big red writing on it, "too personal." How can you write too personal to your lawyer?

And I been in some awful cells up there, nine by ten feet and, on Death Row, seven by nine. The first 14 months, I was in a hole; they called it the Sweatbox. It used to be you could only take a bath and shave once a week, and then it was twice, and now it's Monday, Wednesday and Friday.

They'd do all kinds of ways. Take medicine. Say you taking medicine, and they tell you they run out and then, I hear, turn right around and give it to somebody else, some of the white boys. Or, when you go out to get your clothes, they give you old clothes with holes in them and give the white boys, you know, good clothes. Or when you exercising, they supposed to give you 30 minutes, but maybe give you only 20 or 25. They always find ways.

Or they come by your cell and keep talking about the charge against you. They say, "You know, nigger, you been living all them years after raping a white woman. I've seen the times when you never would be thinking about no appeal or anything like that." They say, "For raping a white woman, he'd been dead a long time ago. He'd been lynched."

The knot in your throat, when did you first notice it?

I first noticed it late in 1966. It was at Angola, and I complained right then. I thought maybe it was the thyroid glands. I read in some medical books where it could cause, you know, the glands to swell up in your neck because of thyroid deficiency. I asked them about penicillin. They wouldn't give you that. It's too expensive.

My lawyer at the time, Mr. Ben Smith, he agreed with me it might be cancer, and he asked the U.S. Circuit Court in January, 1967, to transfer me from Angola to New Orleans so his own personal physician could examine me. The petition say I might have "a tumorous or cancerous growth on his neck" and I was "not receiving adequate medical treatment for this newly discovered problem at the State Penitentiary." The Court said no. But they never looked at me up there. Years ago, they gave me a physical and X-rays. That was when Warden Ziegler was there. A fine man. Now, all they think about is how much corn grows, how much cane is cut, things like that. That's the feeling among the convicts up there and even some of the free people. They just try to make the farm make money. Profit.

Right after I finally come here to Parish Prison they examine me. They say I got a tumor, right here in the left side of my neck under my jawbone, and they operated and took out about 18 nodules, the main neck muscle and part of my tongue. They gave me radium and cobalt treatments. I may be cured or in remission until it flare up again. But I'm not afraid, not after what I been through.

What happened when they freed you at Angola?

Freed? We was never freed. They turned us over to the New Orleans sheriff's men, and they brought us here, 150 miles, in a Black Maria. Poret came later. We spent the first two nights together in the same cell. And that's funny, because they always seem like they trying to keep us apart, spreading rumors we at each other's throat and all. We have our little arguments, disagreements, but that happen even when you married. I never seen him before, until they brought us together for the trial in 1953. We been in this thing a long time together now, and we have had little arguments, but nothing serious.

They indicted us again and arraigned us again. I pleaded not guilty. They come and take me to court every now and then for preliminary hearings, and it's hard to say when the new trial will start.

Have you thought about making some sort of a deal? You know, copping a plea?

I was offered that when I was first arrested.

But I mean now. It has been so long. If you changed your plea to guilty and got out with time served?

I don't know. Be kind of hard to do, to say I am guilty. That would be hard on my conscience. I didn't do it. But sometimes, with time dragging on and nothing seeming to happen right, I do get some discouraged. Sometimes, I feel like saying anything just to get out to live free whatever days is left to me, even if I had to say I killed Lincoln.

Edgar, I can't understand why you're not bitter.

Well, I'll tell you about that. One of the other prisoners said the other day I should hate every white man. He said, "You should never even ever want to see any white devil." I told him I don't feel that way. Back in 1953, when I was on Death Row in Parish Prison, I was getting like that, but a nun came to see me, Sister Mary Harriet of the Sisters of Mercy, and she talked to me and put me on the right road. She visited me again last New Year's Day, and we went to Mass in the prison chapel.

I can't become bitter. That would destroy me.

Do you find that being light-skinned puts you in the middle, that white people won't accept you as white, and Negro people won't accept you as Negro?

Yes, very much. It has been a handicap, sort of. A lot of people, not all of them, but I'll just say a lot of them, if a light-skinned Negro try to dress and keep yourself neat and look to higher things, I learnt—mostly since I been in here, to be truthful, because I didn't experience it too much in my childhood—they shoot different lowering remarks at me about being light, or he thinks he's white. First thing they think, you see, he think he white or he look at their daughter too much. You know, might get funny ideas and so on like that. The Negroes, they are very prejudiced, more than the whites, maybe, because of the color. A lot of them will say you think you're better than them, you see, because you're light, and so on like that.

New Orleans is loaded with light-skinned Negroes. Around Bruxelles Avenue, they's a lot of them. Off to themselves. They know what I mean.

A person might not come straight out and tell you, but they will say it where you can hear it, you know? It get back to you, or they give you the feeling. Some white people really hates light-skin Negroes. They really hates them, more than the black. "Get that yellow thing away from me!" I found that out from some places I worked in, and here.

What will you do with the rest of your life if you get out?

Well, I don't know. I would like to write, follow some writing in college, take up some courses on journalism. I been working on a book.

And beyond that?

Beyond that, I would have to let it come as it goes. I would like to go somewhere just quiet, you know? Away away from here as far as I can go. I have some offers. From all over. I have to talk it over with my daughters. One of them's grown and married and is going to make me a grandfather in a few months; the other's in college up north.

I can't plan too far. I have to take it as it comes. Like in the poem I wrote on Death Row:

> Fourteen years on The Row
> Without knowing if I stay or go,
> Waiting from day to day
> To see what The Appeal would say.
> Bold letters on the wall spell out DEATH CELL.
> As if I couldn't tell.
> I look in the mirror each day,
> Watching myself decay.
> One day the Warden came

With the Death Warrant, and on it my name.
"Tonight," he said, "at 12 o'clock you must die."
Through my little window I tell the world goodbye.
Asked what I wanted to eat,
Said the State was willing to treat.
It was my last wish.
The State would give me any dish.
While I eat my last meal
I can only feel
The chill from the bars of steel.
The clock strikes ten
And the phone rings, the Warden again:
"Not tonight, Labat, but I'll tell you when."

PART THREE

Issues in Criminology

The proper disposition of criminals has long been a heated controversy among criminologists. Previous penal theory favored various punishments for offenders. Current penal practice, however, stresses reformation or rehabilitation. But this shift is still largely theoretical rather than actual. Many treatment techniques have been attempted, but recidivism rates are still very high (Vold, 1954, pp. 42–50; Glaser, 1964, pp. 13–35), and no clear or generally accepted evidence of successful implementation of rehabilitation methods is yet available (Gibbons, 1968, pp. 493–530; Gibbons, 1965). The picture is complex. Yet, the failure of the penal system has long been recognized by those occupying our prisons. We turn now to their reflections on these broad issues.

A central problem is the failure of contemporary penology to promote the self-respect of the prisoner as a necessary condition for successful rehabilitation. Prisoner No. 4000X and Alfred Hassler both argue that prison is a humiliation stripping the prisoner of his feelings of self-worth and making his treatment a practical impossibility. The third article by "Frisco" presents a more sociological and less psychological view of the problem. "Frisco" sees the average prisoner as a pawn in a kind of vast bureaucratic and political chess game played by what he calls the "Big Penology" of which "Scientific Penology" is a tool.

Finally the issue of capital punishment: though the trend in the United States clearly has been toward a reduction of executions, this ultimate punishment still exists in most states. Most criminologists supporting the abolition of the death penalty argue that it is ineffectively deterrent and morally wrong. Though the literature of criminology is full of pragmatic arguments on the failure of capital punishment (see Bedau, 1964; Sellin, 1967), it is the moral argument which is best presented by the prisoners themselves. Our final selection—by Caryl Chessman—vividly delineates the issue.

a criminal looks at crime and punishment

PRISONER NO. 4000X

Prisoner No. 4000X suggests that penology's principle of reformation has been a dismal failure. He attacks the basic methods of penology—still employed today—stating that they do nothing to outweigh the basic premise of most criminals—"Thou shall not get caught at it." He also suggests that for imprisonment to have successful results, reformers must effect changes in the inmate's conception of himself with the end result of building his self-respect.[1]

The following facts concerning myself are rehearsed only that the reader may understand what might be called my preparation for a discussion of crime and punishment.

As this is written I am completing a second term as an inmate of a penal institution; I have twice been convicted of felonies. In each instance I was guilty as charged; there were, I am now convinced, no extenuating circumstances. In the first prison to which I was committed I worked in shops for a few months and was then transferred to the offices, where I remained until released. In the prison where I am now confined I am assigned to the department dealing with newly received prisoners, one of my duties being to assist in the classification of prisoners after their mental, moral, and physical status has been determined. These details are pertinent because they serve to explain why I have come to look at crime and punishment as the law-enforcement forces look at them; my duties have given me the view-point of the official, while I remain, from the disciplinary standpoint, a prisoner.

It is likewise relevant to this discussion to add that during this present imprisonment I have "reformed," if I may be permitted to make use of that much-abused and misleading word. Of that, more later.

There is a wide gap between the opinions of those who advocate going after the criminal with the cat-o'-nine-tails and hell-fire, and the blubbers of those who would see him bedded in a hospital, psychoanalyzed, and

Reprinted from Scribner's Magazine 81 *(January, 1927), pp. 86–89.*

[1]For related statements, see Ex-con (1920, p. 36), and Hollister (1962, 14ff.).

coaxed back to the paths of rectitude, from which it is assumed he has been drawn by powers beyond his control. There seems to be scant reason to trust either of these extremes of opinion, and it becomes increasingly difficult to find judgments that may not be included with one or the other. Those who urge a return to the days of solitary confinement and the dungeon are uninformed; even more so are the too sympathetic ones.

The beginning of any criminal history is in the criminal's apprehension. A consideration of the methods by which he is searched out and apprehended has no place in this article; it is enough to say that the police are by no means as alert as they profess to be, nor are they at all as corrupt and as stupid as criminals like to describe them. When they fail to apprehend a criminal it is not that they have been outwitted by a master mind; they have gone down to defeat before the law of numbers. There are so very many more crooks than there are police officers; it is a pitifully unequal fight society demands be waged by its protectors.

To those who have knowledge of such matters I leave the consideration of how crime is to be prevented, and how the criminal is to be apprehended, brought to a speedy and completely fair trial, and placed under restraint. My interest is in the clumsy and wholly haphazard means by which his punishment is undertaken.

The aim of all modern penology is reformation. The State seeks for methods by which it shall regenerate the criminal so that when his last day shall have been served he can return to society as a reborn man. It is a noble aim; a high purpose; it is lamentable that it has so monstrously failed!

That it *has* failed is best attested by the lawlessness existing in these States to-day; the crimes that shock and terrify the law-abiding citizen are almost without exception crimes committed by graduates of our prisons, our jails, our parole systems. Of these, Chapman and Whittemore are notable examples; they are typical of a class whose technic has been developed and perfected in such institutions.

As a criminal, tucked away in prison, I am delighted to read the declarations of men like Warden Lawes, Warden Hulburt, and Thomas Mott Osborne, who wish to relieve the monotony of my confinement with additional moving-picture shows, with more ball games, with all the alleviatives that can be arranged to deaden the realization that I am in prison. I do very much admire the sincerity of those men, and I respect the intensity of their desire to experiment with means that they hope may aid in bringing about the reformation of their wards. I disagree with their methods only because through those methods they seek to *bestow* reformation, whereas I am wholly and absolutely convinced that reformation may only be *achieved;* that it may *never* be bestowed.

The prison inmate must be carefully and thoughtfully dealt with; he is the meat of our "crime problem" to-day. Unless we are for all time to remove him from society we must devise a method by which he may, at the expiration of his term, be returned to society so equipped as to minimize the possibility of his committing further crimes. If you need proof that he is not now so equipped, you need only talk with your local police officials; they can tell you what a great percentage of all crimes reported to them have been committed by ex-convicts. All the pretty theories of parole and pardon boards, all the sophistries contrived by sentimental reformers must give way before the smashing evidence of a thousand police blotters. That evidence is all in support of my contention that campaigns of crime are conceived and planned in prisons and are executed shortly after the parole boards have lopped off a goodly portion of the prisoner's original sentence, thus enabling him to proceed with the practical details of his profession.

Statistics such as are brought forward by every parole body to prove that seventy percent of all prisoners released on parole fulfil the terms of their parole and earn a final discharge mean exactly nothing. "Doing a parole," as the seasoned criminal refers to the process, is one of the functions he has learned to fulfil; he completes the term of his parole by use of the same negative sort of obedience to rules that made of him a "model prisoner," and thus hastened the day of his release on parole. Parole officials, in their anxiety to create justification for their release of the criminal, fix a not uncomfortably extended parole period and do not examine too closely into the daily doings of the paroled man. Parole supervision, as a matter of fact, becomes a routine matter; if the paroled man's monthly reports are received promptly with all the blank lines filled in, no individual inquiry is set up. Here, as with the police, exists the handicap of insufficient workers; in some States two hundred prisoners are assigned to one parole officer!

During the years of my own confinement I have talked with hundreds of prisoners drawn from every stratum of the criminal world. I have listened to exchanges of information on "jobs" of every imaginable kind. I have listened, fascinated, to tales of enormous exploits in which the relator was invariably rewarded for his cleverness with a "swag" of at least "ten grand." I have listened to proudly told stories of confidence built-up, betrayed, destroyed. I have observed all the manifestations of that honor popularly believed to exist among thieves. I have, on a thousand nights, given ear to conferences dealing with the criminal's attitude toward the reformers who work for his betterment, his attitude toward the parole system, his philosophy of life. I can offer no more eloquent opinion of my associates than to say that my own state of mind, which I have already described with the word "reformed," is the slowly built-up product of my experiences with these men undergoing "reformation."

I do not like generalities, yet I can think of no better manner of describing the composite criminal mind than to say that its only precept is: "Thou shalt not get caught at it." This is the rule the criminal applies to his "professional" duties; it is the standard by which he regulates his prison conduct; it is the still, small voice that causes him to be wary while on parole. Its presence in his mind breeds a warped series of mental processes that prevent his gaining the state of mind wherein he might begin to work for the achievement that is the only reform.

Has he been caught and placed in prison? Ah, well, for every one of him so caught and placed there are a thousand uncaught and active; ergo he is *not* a subject for reform, but an unfortunate lad betrayed by evil chance into capture. Better luck next time.

Has he an excellent record for regular attendance at the prison chapel services? Listen to *his* reason: "They tell me that this chaplain can git a guy a 'break' and he won't give you a tumble if you don't show up regular for church."

Is he penitent, aware of the seriousness of his crime, anxious to remould his character against the day of his return to society? I give you one example repeated to me within the past week, and it is rather more conservative than the average. "I got the gun, see, when the cops come in the room, and I throws it out into the hall. When they frisks me I ain't got nothing on me, then one of the bulls picks up the 'rod' in the hall and claims it's mine. That's the way they framed me, the blankety blank blanks. Why did I plead guilty? Because I could get a short bit by 'copping a plea' and you can't get by this parole board if you don't admit you're guilty."

I submit that the chances of that man's achievement of "reform" are lamentably few. He is not an exaggerated type, nor an exceptional one; in this institution with its population of nearly two thousand men I doubt if there are *one hundred* who do not, when expressing their innermost thoughts, display exactly the same mental attitude toward their present plight, the events leading up to it, and their plans for their careers after release. With all our elaborate welfare plans, with all our psychiatrists, with all our enthusiastic pleaders for a better understanding of endocrine disfunction with relation to crime, no one seems to be particularly concerned with the chore of bringing home to the individual criminal his true status, the extent of his wrong-doing, the impossibility of his ever remaining out of conflict with the law until he has started to bring about within himself a realization of his inability to survive unless he is a co-operating member of the community.

The newly received inmate of a penal institution is supplied with printed instructions telling him how to conduct himself in the prison so as to avoid infractions of its rules of discipline; he is told that his release will in large measure depend upon his obedience to those rules. He is cheered by predictions of moving pictures, baseball games, shows, reading matter, and whatnot to come. He is taken in hand by undergraduates who have preceded him into the institution and "tipped off" on the right way to "get by." A perfunctory official asks him which religious service he will attend; he is assigned to work. The rough edges of the shock of prison commitment are tenderly softened. I have listened on many an occasion to the opening remarks of the official who received new prisoners at the first institution in which I was a prisoner and he invariably stated: "Boys, there are men much worse than you running around free because they haven't yet been caught; since you *have* been caught, make the best of it, and keep your self-respect!" A well-meaning man he was, too, and deeply sincere in his desire to see men keep out of trouble. He did not know, he *could* not know, I suppose, that just about the most important thing a newly convicted criminal can do is to *lose* the "self-respect" which is the main factor contributing to the state of mind from which he sympathizes with himself as an unfortunate victim of circumstances.

Don't return, in your prisons, to the brutality of earlier years. Give prisoners clean surroundings, facilities to build up and maintain health in their too often abused bodies (self-abused); give them work in keeping with their capabilities to performance; give them the opportunity to study, to read carefully selected material; pay them, even, for their labor so that they may contribute to the support of their dependents. Such reforms are humane, intelligent, beneficial.

But stop the mental coddling, the tender back-pats, the sympathetic condolences that create self-pity; stick hatpins into their minds, and drive home the fact that *no* man can carry with him into prison any degree of true self-respect; his very presence there cries aloud the lack of anything to respect in himself. To think, to work, for the creation of a new self-respect, by all means, yes. To give him every facility *to* create that self-respect, yes. To place within his reach the boon of true reform, and to give him the opportunity to *achieve* that reform, yes.

These are not things impossible of accomplishment; they do not require new appropriations to finance; they are within the power of any prison administration to provide. If to provide them requires chopping off some official heads, let them fall. If well-meaning, but misguided, prison officials must give way to others equally well-meaning, but more intelligent in their application of reformative measures, let them go.

When you have cleaned house in your prisons, your jails, the problem of how and when to parole prisoners will have solved itself. The police blotters of a thousand towns and cities will shortly record the reform that has been achieved by our correctional agencies.

the futility of prisons

ALFRED HASSLER

Alfred Hassler, a conscientious objector who refused military service in World War II, wrote the very sensitive description of his imprisonment—in the Federal Penitentiary at Lewisburg, Pennsylvania—from which this selection was taken. Here he presents his feelings on the rehabilitative effects of prisons and on the conception that prisons are a deterrent to further crime.[1]

A dozen of us were sitting out on the stockade grass one warm September Sunday afternoon, listening to Slim hold forth indignantly on the subject of prison. After a while I interrupted him.

"But, look, Slim," I said, "granted all that you say, society still has to cope with the problem of crime somehow. What method other than prison can it use?"

His voice and his face both sobered.

"I don't know, Al," he said. "I don't know at all. All I do know is that prison doesn't protect society, doesn't reduce crime, and doesn't reform the criminal. Prisons are no good."

Before I finished my own stretch in prison I had come to agree with Slim. Prisons *are* no good. Not unless you are one of those who get some satisfaction out of seeing people punished when they do something wrong, regardless of the ultimate effect on them, on society, and even on yourself.

The immediate and overwhelming impression of prison, and one that continued through my sentence and beyond, was the feeling of humiliation. This is the reality of prison, more even than the all-too-frequent physical brutality, the occasional sadism of prison personnel, or the hopeful but frustrated system of rehabilitation. More than anything else, I think, the convict is infuriated and discouraged by the planned indignities and degradation that are his lot from the moment he gets into the hands of the prison authorities.

Reprinted with permission of Henry Regnery Company from Diary of a Self-Made Convict *by Alfred Hassler (Chicago, Illinois, 1954), pp. 177–82. (Footnotes omitted.)*

[1]Other autobiographical accounts by conscientious objectors include those of Cantine and Rainer (1950), and Nunnally (1948).

Totalitarianism always is characterized by this disregard of the individual human personality. The Nazis, hypnotized by the pagan vision of a world dominated by a pure German *Herrenvolk,* could find in their dream the justification for the indignities they heaped on millions of helpless humans. The Communists, peddling a more attractive vision of a society in which injustice and oppression would have disappeared, debase their dream and degrade themselves with the delusion that something good can be built on the humiliation and despair of more unhappy millions.

Prison—even an American prison—is fashioned on equally totalitarian lines, and the results in terms of its expressed aims are no less predictably dismal. The prisoner has no rights, but only privileges which may be taken away at the whim of the authorities. In every way the prison authorities can contrive he is deprived of his individuality. He stands in line to get the same drab clothes every other convict wears, which are handed out to him with a minimum of regard for size and condition. His cell must conform to every other cell in its complete sterility; his letters are read, his belongings pawed through every day or so, his movements regulated through the day by bells and whistles and observed by night by a flashlight-carrying guard who periodically peeks through the "judas-window" of his cell door. That some convicts still manage to evade this all-seeing observation long enough for the final contemptuous gesture of suicide must stand as a tribute to the indomitable ingenuity of man.

At several important points I did not have to endure the same kind of humiliation as most convicted felons. Partly this was because many of the men in authority with whom I came in contact recognized a deviation from the normal criminal personality, while a few even expressed a sneaking agreement. More important, probably, was the fact that considerable numbers of respected and influential people "outside," pacifists and nonpacifists alike, were indignant that conscientious objectors should be imprisoned at all and were alert and vocal about any attempts to add to their difficulties in prison.

At any rate, I was never formally arrested; I was free without bail both before and after my trial, and I never saw the inside of a jail until a week after my conviction and sentencing. Moreover, as a federal prisoner, and especially as a federal prisoner in the Southern District of New York, I escaped some of the more inhuman experiences of the men who do their time in the filthy, germ-ridden holes that so frequently serve as the municipal, county and state prisons of our country.

Yet in spite of this relatively easier time, I found myself sometimes shaken with rage at the insensitivity of those who had become the keepers of the keys of my life. Within days after my incarceration I found my sympathies heavily with the convicts and against the authorities, even though my natural inclinations were to support a law-abiding society and its rules.

It was to become clear to me in the months that followed how crucial this matter is, and how completely it nullifies all the really excellent intentions and insights that many professional penologists bring to their jobs.

The best of prisons does not reform or rehabilitate. It punishes, but punishment neither eradicates the original misdeed nor reforms the criminal. Neither does it serve as an effective deterrent, as is evident by the steadily rising rate of crime. It does not deter others from following a criminal career—for the simple reason that no man commits a crime expecting to be caught. Contrary to the highly publicized slogan, moreover, his chances of escaping apprehension are pretty good if he is reasonably intelligent. The jails are full of the unskilled workmen of crime; it is an event when one of the entrepreneurs of the illegal finds himself behind bars.

The institution of prison does take a few criminals out of circulation for varying periods of time, which some people like to call "protecting society." But since in most cases the criminal eventually is released again, equipped with some new prison-acquired skills and motivated by prison-enforced resentment, such "protection" is of doubtful value at best. The stark truth is that if the fundamental consideration is the protection of society against criminals, then the proper treatment is either life imprisonment or execution for every convicted criminal. Since both humanitarian and practical considerations of space and equipment make such a program impracticable, we come back to our original thesis that prison actually serves no useful purpose.

But this is the easier part. Serious students of penology have recognized for some time that prisons are a useless and expensive appendage to the apparatus of the community. Barnes and Teeters, in their authoritative *New Horizons in Criminology,* make clear their own conviction that even the "new prison"—of which Lewisburg is an example—eventually must go, to be replaced by some system of individual treatment. "For some," they write, "advice is all that this treatment or discipline should be; for others, strict supervision, kindly and understanding, may be necessary. . . . Each case will call for some special form of treatment."

It is a good comment and a good direction. Human beings *are* individuals; they cannot be treated as identical parts of a mass without further complicating the problem. The insights of modern medicine and psychiatry need to be brought extensively into the courtroom; the insights of psychology need to be absorbed and understood by those who deal in any way with the criminal individual.

But even these, administered with the best will in the world, will have only a minimum effect until psychiatry and psychology shift their focus from the "criminal personality" to the nature of the community itself, and the values to which it does homage. When these are examined, it becomes plain that the criminal is not so much a deviate from the norm as he is its mildly distorted reflection.

Tolstoi observed that "the criminal justifies his crime," and this continues to be the crucial fact of what we call anti-social behavior. Most of the men who land in prison are neither psychopaths nor schizophrenics. They are cynics. They observe a society in which wealth, the acquisition of things, ranks as the highest value. They are the products of a culture whose chief characteristics, as Margaret Halsey observed in *The Folks at Home,* are aggressiveness, competitiveness, and skepticism. Overwhelmingly, they come from the part of the community that has come off worst in the socially approved expressions of this competition, so that to their skepticism is added frustration.

The United States marshals who took us to Lewisburg in their car exercised their little graft on our meal on the way out. A guard at the penitentiary endured the unspoken jeers of the inmates when his wife was exposed as a black-market operator. Men who had connections with the underworld could, and did, tell which judges and district attorneys had paid how much for their jobs, and a former procurer was in the interesting position of having been sentenced by a judge who was a regular client of the house for which he worked. Another of my felon-compatriots, convicted of a minor embezzlement, entertained us for one stockade hour with stories of the bribes he had given over a period of ten years on behalf of the company that had preferred charges against him.

These are the facts of life as the "criminal" knows they exist, and they account for his contemptuous scorn for chaplains, parole officers, and every other official manifestation of society's hypocritical self-righteousness. So long as they continue to be the facts of life, they will continue to undermine every well-intentioned new approach to the problem of criminal behavior, even including the "kindly and understanding" individual treatment.

The problem of prison is indissolubly bound up with the morality of the culture of which it is a part. The criminal is our own reflection, staring out at us from the mirror of our own desires and ambitions. Our humanity drives us reluctantly to eradicate the more brutal aspects of prison life, and to make conditions inside the prison more tolerable for the wretches confined in them. But the problem of crime will not be affected seriously until we tackle it in our own lives, and put into our relations with all men the only thing that will work with any of them: love and forgiveness.

It was the Master who showed the answer long ago when they brought to him a woman caught in the very commission of a crime punishable by death.

"What shall we do with her?" they asked him, hoping to trap him.

"Let him that is without sin among you cast the first stone," he suggested mildly, and, when the whole crowd of accusers had slunk away, and none remained save him to judge the guilt of the "criminal," he said, "Neither do I condemn you. Go and sin no more."

a prisoner's views on scientific penology

"FRISCO"

"Frisco" expresses his ideas regarding the "New Penology" and its implications for prisoners. In his comparison of "Big Penology" with "Scientific Penology," he presents some striking and realistic views.

Old Mike took his time and read it carefully, stopping once to wipe his glasses and once to light his pipe. He's over seventy—been here since '24. Never hurries for anything, not even chow line—even the guards know that. His conversation is slow and deliberate and he won't talk at all unless he has something to say, but he's read everything in the prison library—two or three prison libraries, and he got around in his younger days. I waited quietly while he read.

We were in the print shop office behind the school where I help get out this rag, and he had come in on the off chance that we might have some coffee going. We didn't, but it was hot outside and he sat down.

That's how I happened to show him the circular. It had been lying on my desk in a pile of other stuff ever since the warden gave it to me. I'd made myself a half promise to knock out something and send it in—knowing perfectly well, of course, that I would never get around to it.

Mike said: "American Prison Association, eh? That's *scientific* penology—I remember when they started, back in the '30s, I guess it was—they've been going good. Lasted longer than most."

By the way he had accented that *"scientific"* penology, I knew he wanted me to react to it. Old Mike uses subtle gambits in his conversational excursions—so I did the straight for him. "Scientific penology? How do you mean, Mike; I thought *all* penology was based on scientific approaches. Is there any other kind?"

That's what I was supposed to ask. He kept a dead pan, but his eyes showed that he appreciated my picking up the cue.

"Scientific penology comes out of libraries, universities, laboratories, and clinics," he explained. "It reduces crime and the consequences of crime to

Reprinted with permission of the Raiford Record *from "Old Mike States the Case" by "Frisco,"* Raiford Record 12 *(August, 1950), pp. 10–13.*

charts and graphs and statistics—great stuff for the pamphlet publishing industry, and it's the number one hobby for people like statisticians and psychiatrists and dieticians and vocational guidance experts."

He lighted his pipe again, carefully and at length, then he sat back with his legs outstretched and closed his eyes meditatively. That was to see if the mood was right. If I had spoken it would have broken the spell. Mike had set forth a premise, now he chose to sound his audience before expounding. There may be a little touch of the ham in Mike, but the years have made him extremely wary of blunt-wits who know nothing of listening.

Satisfied that my attention was both valid and sincere, he resumed: "Scientific penology is the most harmless. They have a good time with it, and once in a while one of its followers gets into a spot where he can do a little good."

I asked him what kind of a spot.

"Some part of actual penology," he explained, "—in the big league. Probation officer or parole supervisor or prison psychiatrist. Even captain or warden. Scientific penologists go for schools and planned recreation and prisoner-classification, and they oppose strong-arm discipline and rank food."

He paused, leaning his head back and closing his eyes.

I remained silent, and presently he resumed, right on the beat, as though there had been no stop: "They make good conditions—especially when they're new and not discouraged yet."

"Discouraged?"

"You know—busted illusions. They get their heads and their hearts full of theory and ideals, then they get on the scene in one of these joints and gradually begin to learn what the score really is—the futility, the hypocrisy, all the rest of it; then they either turn bitter or quit, or they harden up and go along with Big Penology."

He paused expectantly, but he had confidence in me and I didn't disappoint him. I came in on cue: "Big Penology? what's that?" It wasn't altogether an act, either—I didn't know exactly what he meant. "Big Penology," said Mike patiently, "is the gag—the big-industry, heavy-money aspect of crime and imprisonment. It starts with the hustling bail bond broker who's shilling for a shyster lawyer on the side; it covers legions of bovine fat men with cigars, frustrated and threadbare lawyers, thin-lipped, untrained and fanatical Emissaries of Right—all of whom have in common a connection in the upper levels of a city or state administration."

"You mean special investigators, public defenders, and all them?"

"Those, and assistant D.A.'s and probation officers and county jail doctors and social and welfare workers—all the way up to the Boards and Committees and Commissions," he added. "It's the most powerful thing in the world, a foolproof gimmick for employment and production and political power. It's even better than a war, because there is practically no bloodshed and no danger of an armistice or surrender to interrupt or stop the action. The public is nuts about it."

It sounded pretty radical, but I'd seen a lot of it myself and knew that it was also pretty true. He leaned forward and pointed his pipe stem at me.

"Best of all," he went on, "there's no limit to it and no end to it. All they have to do is keep grabbing ignorant young punks who steal cars for joy rides and scared working stiffs who get out of work and broke and hungry and grab a spare tire or something in desperation. There are hundreds of them in every town everywhere. They run them through the mill and dress them into these joints by the dozen, then they scream to the public 'Crime increase...desperate criminals in overcrowded prisons...danger... more money...more prisons!'"

"What about the scientific penology you mentioned? Where do they fit in?" I asked.

"They throw it wide open—that's why I say they do good. They make better conditions for guys like us and they fatten up Big Penology. They have shown the big-business boys about classification...segregation...analysis ... custody ... treatment ... training ... parole preparation ... surgery...therapy...school...recreation...time and motion study—the works. All that takes wardens, associate wardens, doctors, psychiatrists, sociologists, instructors, engineers, sanitarians, dieticians, instructors, athletic directors—and college-trained guards who understand practical psychology and judo."

I started to answer, thought better of it, and let him go. He did. "It calls for more and bigger jails and penitentiaries, more prison farms, road camps, reformatories, industrial schools—more and more—because when one state sets up a machine like that and opens all those plum jobs to be tossed around for votes, other states catch on and start their own penal reform programs with multi-million dollar building schedules and the jobs and all the rest of it."

This time when he stopped he looked at me and I knew it was time for me to say something again. I asked, "What about the prisoners for all these joints? If Big Penology keeps setting up factories for reform and rehabilitation, and scientific penology keeps running down the causes of crime and correcting them, eventually there won't be enough convictions to populate the institutions they have now, let alone building more. Do you think crime is on the increase?"

Mike said gently, "The crime industry is on the increase. People, and the things they do, don't change much. In any given segment of population—a regiment of soldiers, a chapter of a fraternal organization, the congregation of a church, there will be a certain percentage of intellectuals and dullards and neurotics; some who are emotionally stable and some who are not. Those percentages will hold true in any region and they will change only as humanity changes through progressive generations."

"...and," I interposed, "there is always a certain percentage who are potentially criminal?"

"If by 'criminal' you mean potentially capable of breaking a statutory rule of conduct," he replied, "I'll have to ask you to remember that everybody who took a drink during prohibition was criminal, as is everybody who has ever driven an automobile faster than prescribed regulations."

Mike paused, it seemed to me that he sensed he was in danger of belaboring a trite point, then he switched his tack. "...but you mean felonious crime—murder, rape, assault, robbery, embezzlement. Every human being has within him or her certain basic instincts, dormant and suppressed, which, if heeded, would result in felonious crime. The influence that holds them in check is our civilization and culture. The more civilized and cultured the individual, the deeper are these atavistic instincts suppressed—but they are always subject to breaking through to the surface under the pressure of emotion, opportunity or circumstance. That is the reason it's considered shrewd business to paint up a worn out and broken down jalopy and palm it off on some sucker as an excellently-cared-for car formerly owned by an old maid school teacher. That's larceny by opportunity."

• •

I saw what he was leading up to. "A fraud, you mean, that isn't a fraud because there is no law describing it as such?"

He ignored me, continuing: "...likewise with circumstance and emotion —that's the reason respectable people of refinement get grabbed every so often for betting a chunk of their boss' dough on a cinch horse—or they throw a jealous wing-ding and murder their rivals. That's why nice clean-cut American college boys still get a kick out of telling how they shot Japs on Okinawa who had their hands up in surrender. Circumstances...Opportunity...Emotion—they can awaken instincts in anybody, anytime, that are usually good for headlines."

It was getting close to time for the bell, so I nudged him toward a conclusion. "So what's the answer, Mike? You've seen it all, in here and outside as well as in other joints—aside from the politicians with their Big Penology, what about the scientific penologists—the sincere ones, who are looking for the answer? What is their answer...?"

He was ready. First he prodded his pipe with a match stick, then he sat back and studied for a moment. Old Mike's innate sense of theater would never permit him to go into a second-act finale without first tensing up the scene with a brief stage-wait. "It would be easy," he said, "if the Big Penology boys would let it be done. First, they would have to cut down the field—eliminate that big seventy or eighty percent of harmless unfortunates who hate crime and are afraid of it, but yield to it in weakness because they have to live even if they are incapable mentally or emotionally of getting a job and holding it. Their only crime is that of being unable to manage their lives and themselves. Every joint like this is full of them."

"But how?" I couldn't tell whether he already had a solution in his mind or whether he was ad libbing as he went along.

"About half of them are mental defectives—psychopaths, mostly borderline paranoia. That's one of the first things the Scientific Penology boys discovered years ago. Big Penology could divert some of the budget that keeps these characters stumbling around prison yards and set up treatment clinics. Some could be cured, and others could be given gainful employment under normal conditions but with supervision—huge co-operative farms, canneries, various types of light industry. They could even coin a new name for it: Penological Socialism."

"How about competing with private industry?"

"State and federal agencies could use most of the output, saving the necessity of purchasing it with tax money. Private industry would lose some fat state and government contracts, but it would save correspondingly on the tax bill for supporting scores of over-crowded and unproductive prisons."

"How about your social misfits who aren't necessarily nuts, but resort to theft because they can't get into gainful employment and stay on the job."

"Big Penology again. An expanded probation and parole system, but with the emphasis on guidance and job placement. It's easy—during the war the Army grabbed up thousands of just such people, limited education, no special skills, unimaginative, drifters—and in swift months they were dynamited through training that taught them how to handle and service weapons and machinery, operate technical equipment, follow instructions and carry out orders. Similar methods in peacetime could qualify them in trades and crafts, special aptitudes could be discovered and developed."

• • •

I thought I saw a flaw and tried to nail it: "Where are all the jobs for these salvaged miscreants coming from?" I slipped in. "You know and I know that people in business want no part of ex-cons."

Mike brushed it off in stride. "They'll hire them if there is something to be gained by it. During the war when business was yelling for help ex-cons were doing everything from baby sitting to cashiering in banks. Give the average business man a tax discount for every state-sponsored man or woman he employs and he'll start putting on extra shifts."

"Swell," I said. "Now what are you going to do about the rest—the ones that insist on stealing—heavy guys who want the big dough and don't want any part of square shooting?"

"There are a few dozen or possibly a few hundred in each state," Mike answered. "One large institution—say as big as San Quentin—could accommodate all the professional thieves who are doing time right now. How many guys do you know in here—or in any other joint—who are actually able or inclined to support themselves exclusively from the proceeds of any sort of crime?"

I had to admit there were few, if any. Everybody I've ever talked to in prison has always been a working man of one kind or another whose experience with crime was incidental to his job.

"You see," Mike pressed on, "when you are in here on the scene you find there really isn't any crime problem at all—it's a social problem, the problem of what to do with uneducated, unskilled unfortunates who get hungry and steal a bag of groceries, and assorted neurotics who crack up under emotional stress, and perfectly normal people who get a bad break, like believing a girl is twenty when she is only a mature seventeen. Of course, if you blanket them all in under the label 'criminal' it looks pretty sordid and awesome—but actually it's just a matter of dealing with people... smart people and dumb people...psychopathic people and normal people —the same kind of people you find everywhere."

The bell rang then and Mike got up. "Nobody will change things much in our time," he said, "so don't worry too much about it. They'll keep bringing them in and they'll keep turning them out. Some will come back and some will not. Meanwhile, Scientific Penology will break it all down on charts and graphs, and Big Penology will use the charts and graphs to prove that more and bigger joints are needed, with more and bigger payrolls for people to handle classification...segregation...analysis...treatment...."

"See you later, Mike...."

"Yeh, so long."

a letter to the governor

CARYL CHESSMAN

Caryl Chessman spent almost twelve years under sentence of death. His ultimately unsuccessful struggle to regain his freedom and his fight against capital punishment received world-wide publicity. Chessman is well known for his writings, especially his book *Cell 2455: Death Row* (1954). On May 2, 1960, Chessman was executed at San Quentin Prison. In this remarkable letter to the governor of California, Chessman comments on the moral implications of capital punishment.

Name: Caryl Chessman
Box 66565, San Quentin, Calif.
Date: February 26, 1960

The Hon. Edmund G. Brown
Governor of the State of California
State Capitol
Sacramento, California

Dear Governor Brown:

As you know, at approximately 4:45 P.M. on Thursday, February 18, 1960, I was removed from the Death Row Unit located on the fifth floor of the North Block here at San Quentin and locked in the small holding cell, just a few feet from the State's lethal gas chamber, where California's condemned spend their last night on earth. The death watch began. So far as I knew, I would be put to death at ten o'clock in the morning.

I was permitted to see an early edition of a Friday newspaper. Its headlines were large and black: CHESSMAN MUST DIE, BROWN SAYS. Again, only an hour earlier, the members of the California Supreme Court had voted 4 to 3 against a recommendation to you for clemency. Thus, by

Edited and adapted unpublished correspondence. Reprinted with permission of Wadsworth Publishing Company and the editor from Contemporary Moral Issues, 2nd edition, *edited by Harry K. Girvetz (Belmont, California, 1968), pp. 140–48.*

a simple vote, you were foreclosed from exercising your commutation powers. The court had made its order "final forthwith." I had been notified of that action a few hours before being taken downstairs to the holding cell. In anticipation of it, I had put my affairs in order and executed a new will. . . .

And death appeared inevitable. I held out no feverish, desperate hope for a life-sparing miracle. On the contrary, what sustained me, what made it possible for me to await the morning and oblivion with a detached, almost clinical calm was hope of an entirely different sort: the burning hope that my execution would lead to an objective reappraisal of the social validity or invalidity of capital punishment, and that such a reexamination would lead, in turn, to an awareness on the part of all Californians that Death Rows, and death chambers and executioners were unworthy of our society, that the former, in fact, were gross obscenities, solving nothing but rather confounding solution.

The minutes passed, the hours. The prison's Catholic Chaplain, Father Edward Dingberg, visited me. Associate Wardens Walter D. Achuff and Louis S. Nelson saw me for a few minutes. Dr. David G. Schmidt, San Quentin's chief psychiatrist, came in. Attorney George Davis conferred with me hurriedly, intending to return later. Warden Fred R. Dickson dropped by for a talk.

Contrary to published accounts that I consumed the condemned man's traditional hearty meal of "fried chicken, French fried potatoes, vegetable salad, coffee and two kinds of pie—apple and chocolate cream," I am compelled to confess these reports, seemingly attesting to my capacity as a trencherman, are somewhat exaggerated. Actually, my wants were more modest. I had a hamburger and a coke about 7:30, and during the course of the evening I drank three cups of coffee. I also puffed on a cigar, although I normally do not smoke.

I waited. Midnight came. All my visitors had left but Warden Dickson. Then the telephone rang mutedly, and one of the death watch officers said, "It's for you, Warden." I watched Mr. Dickson disappear around a bend in the hallway. I paced the floor, my steps reduced to almost soundlessness by the cloth slippers. The radio outside the cell played quietly. Over it I had listened to a succession of newscasts. The news was all negative. One commentator reported Miss Asher* had been unable to see you but, in vain, had talked with two members of your staff. A second commentator solemnly quoted you as having said, "Only an act of God can save Caryl Chessman now."

My eyes fell on the newspaper I had been allowed whose stark headline I quoted above. One of its front-page lead paragraphs reads: "The world

*Editor's note: Chessman's attorney.

was disturbed last night as the hour for Caryl Chessman's execution drew near. Protests echoed from continent to continent." This San Francisco daily also reported: "There was little question that the Governor...was undergoing great emotional stress as Chessman's last hours ticked away," and: "The mail—most of it running about three to one for clemency—continued to pour in. So did the telegrams and the zero-hour telephone calls...."

On page two were pictures of the gas chamber and this account of how I would die in less than ten hours:

> ...He'll get a physical examination from the prison's chief physician, Dr. Herman H. Gross, at 9 A.M. and undoubtedly will once again be found to be in perfect condition.
>
> At 9:45 A.M. come the last, formal visits from Warden Dickson and his aide to hear any last requests. Once again the chaplains will wait silently. Over a carpeted floor, his stockinged feet should take the last walk at 10 A.M. on the dot.
>
> There have been 164 people in the gas chamber before him, and experience gives the prison staff an almost split-second foretelling of the rest. By 10:01 A.M. he should be in one of the two death chairs—chair B. in his case.
>
> Two straps for each arm and leg, one across the chest and another for the waist. That, and the final slamming of the great iron door—less than three minutes.
>
> At 10:03½, by schedule, Warden Dickson would nod at a guard and a lever will send the cyanide pellets into the sulphuric acid basins.

I smiled, grimly, I'm sure. I knew how it felt to be a dead man. Only the ritualized formalities of physically extinguishing my life with hydrocyanic acid gas remained.

"Has the Warden gone?" I asked one of the death watch. "No," I was told, "he's still on the phone."

I gave no thought to the significance of the call. Then, audibly, I heard Warden Dickson say, "All right, Governor." A few seconds later the Warden reappeared. I'd glanced up from the paper I was reading. As he approached the cell, the Warden's face was a thoughtful mask.

"I have some news for you, Caryl." Mr. Dickson paused. "Oh?" I responded. He nodded, smiled. "The Governor has just granted you a 60-day reprieve."

The words had been spoken softly—but they crashed and reverberated in my mind like thunder in an echo chamber. Except possibly in a mocking, sadistic nightmare, they were words I truly never had expected to hear up to the instant of their utterance. I had been prepared to die; now I must be ready to go on living, I realized, for at least another 60 days.

I drew a deep breath as my thoughts raced. My words have been reported in the press: "Thank you. This is a great surprise. I really didn't expect it. Tell the Governor I thank him. I am surprised and grateful."

The Warden said he would see me again later in the morning. We said goodnight. Swiftly I was taken back upstairs in the elevator to Death Row. Swiftly, in the office, I changed into my regular clothing. Accompanied by the officers, I was passed through the "Bird Cage"—with its double doors and multiplicity of bolts and bars and locks—into the Row proper. From most of the occupied cells, yellow light spilled out into the corridor. The condemned were awake, listening to their earphones, silent, waiting—for what? Somehow, even better than I, they had sensed their fate was tied to mine, and mine to a pressing social issue of far greater significance than what might, individually or collectively, happen to any or all of us. They had heard me say repeatedly that obviously the greatest hope for abolition of the death penalty lay with my death. They—even the tortured and troubled ones—knew this to be true. Their obvious course was to accept this fact and hope it might lead them out from the cold shadow of the gas chamber. But, as I later learned, they had sent you a telegram, urging your intercession in my behalf. They refused to believe that death—even another's—was a solution. I don't know whether that telegram ever came to your attention in the flood of messages you were receiving. I do know it had a profound effect on me. . . .

I continued along the corridor, stopping for a moment or two to speak to the occupant of each cell. The reaction was the same. Here was a genuine and spontaneous expression of brotherhood, commingled for them with a miracle. And make no mistake, Governor, I was for my doomed fellows no arrogant, swaggering hero returned after breathing defiance into the teeth of the cosmos. On the contrary, since they had come to know the man rather than the counterfeit black criminal legend, I was a flesh and blood human being whose appointment with man-imposed death had come to symbolize the critical and yet unresolved basic struggle of social man to rise above wrath and vengeance, to trust not the executioner, but their—mankind's—own reason and humanity in building a saner world for their children and their children's children. These men had been accused and convicted of homicidal violence, and so, better than any, they knew the futility of such violence. Now, after a bitter contest, life in my case had claimed at least a temporary victory. . . .

We got the word [that] you had granted the reprieve because, since the people of California were sharply divided on the issue, you wanted "to give the people . . . an opportunity, through the Legislature, to express themselves once more on capital punishment." . . .

And then, as well as in the hectic days to come, before there were calmer reflections and clearer analysis, the paradoxical evidence mounted: While the Chessman case had made evident the urgent need for a calm, careful and objective reexamination of the question whether capital punishment should not be discarded as a barbarous anachronism, productive finally of nothing but division and uneasy doubt among us, my continued existence, if only for another few weeks, and the fearful Chessman legend, which portrayed me as a cunning, fiendish, Cataline-like mocker of justice, threatened to throttle such a reexamination and reevaluation at the outset.

I remain haunted by that paradox. Beyond the descriptive power of words, these have been troubled and difficult days for me. I do not resort to hyperbole when I say they have been hell, even more than the past 11½ years have been hell. I cannot escape the fact I owe you my life for whatever days remain to me. I cannot forget that literally millions of people from nations around the world spoke out for me. In terms of the larger social good that is your goal, my obligation is a heavy one, and I refuse to try to rationalize it away. Over and over I have asked myself the questions. What possibly can I do, if anything, to divorce the ugly, emotion inflaming image of Caryl Chessman from the grave social issue of capital punishment? What can I say—and mean, and demonstrate?

. . . I decided I can and I do, without theatrics, offer them my life. If the hysteria and the mob wrath that surrounds the problem only can be propitiated by my death and if otherwise they agree that the death penalty should be abolished, then I earnestly urge the members of our Legislature to frame their bill in such a way as to exclude me. This can be done readily—for example, by a declaration in the law that anyone convicted of a capital offense during or subsequent to the year 1950, whose sentence of death remains in force and unexecuted, shall be treated as though serving a sentence of life imprisonment. I give my solemn word before the world that I will never challenge such a law in the courts and I will disavow any attempt by any attorney purporting to act in my behalf.

. . . If the legislators do not necessarily demand my death but do believe the final question of my fate, under the California Constitution, should be resolved by yourself and the majority opinion of the State Supreme Court, then I urge them so to indicate. This way, by the passage of the type of bill mentioned above, they can sever the two problems. . . .

Except for the days I was out to court, I have occupied a death cell continuously since Saturday morning, July 3, 1948. I have had eight dates for execution in California's lethal gas chamber fixed and then canceled, some in the very last hours. A ninth date soon will be set. Ninety-odd men have taken that last, grim walk by my cell to their deaths since I came to Death Row. If it gives them any satisfaction, Californians may be assured my prolonged half-life in the shadow of the gas chamber has been an indescribably punishing ordeal. The shock of it, I think, has brought me to maturity; it has forced upon me keen social awareness of the problem that, in exaggerated form, I am said to typify.

I am now 38 years of age. I was 26 when arrested. Behind me is a long record of arrest. I am a graduate of California reform schools and prisons. I have been called a "criminal psychopath." Certainly, as a young man, I was a violent, rebellious, monumental damn fool. I was at odds with my society; I resisted authority. I am ashamed of that past but I cannot change it. However, with my writings, I have tried to salvage something of larger social significance from it. Without shifting responsibility for my conduct, I endeavored in my first book to tell the story of my life and hence to explain how young men like myself got that way. I realized that Death Rows made sense only because people like Caryl Chessman didn't.

After being brought to the death house, the change in me and my outlook came slowly and painfully. Defiantly, I stood and fought in the courts for survival, asking no quarter and expecting none. But, ironically, to have any chance for survival, I had to turn to the law; I had to invoke the protections of the Constitution; I had to study, often as much as 18 to 20 hours a day; I had to learn to impose upon myself a harsh self-discipline; I had to think and to be ruthlessly honest with myself; in time, I forced myself to admit, "Chessman, you have been, and to some degree still are, an irrational, impossible fool. What are you going to do about it?"

At that juncture, the traditional thing, the conventional response almost certainly would have been for me to confess my past folly and to beg for mercy. But I hesitated, not out of pride or false pride. I couldn't escape the fact that such a response on my part would, in practical effect, amount to affirmation that gas chambers and a system of justice ultimately based upon retribution possessed a genuine—rather than a mistakenly conceived and defended—social validity. I knew they did not possess such a validity. Without mock heroics, I became aware then that the greatest contribution I could make was to cause people, all people, to become angrily aware of places like Death Row and the administration of criminal justice in general. This, in my own way, I did: by continued total resistance. I was told I could not write another line for publication and I wrote anyway. When concerted efforts were made to suppress my manuscripts, I found a way to smuggle them from the prison. I intensified my court fight, winning some battles, losing others. Vituperation was heaped upon me. I became known as a mocker of justice. Editorial writers and public officials roundly denounced me. The public clamored for "this cunning fiend's" execution. Often I was half-mad with doubt; often I was ready to collapse with a brutal fatigue; often I sardonically sneered at myself and my goal. But I kept on somehow. A remorseless voice within told me, "This is your penance, fool—to be reviled and hated. This, if you call yourself a man, is the price you must pay."

I had certain advantages, and almost impossible handicaps. Among others, I had been convicted of unsavory sex offenses, sordid acts that, when recounted, inflamed the mind of the listener. They had inflamed the judge, the prosecutor, the jury. A Red Light Bandit—so-called because the bandit had operated, according to trial testimony, with a car equipped with a red spotlight such as those on police cars. He had accosted couples in lonely lovers' lanes. Armed with a gun, he would sometimes rob the couples, if they had any money. On two occasions testified to at my trial, he took the woman to his car. In one of these instances, under threat of death, he compelled her, the victim, to commit an unnatural sex act before letting her out and driving off. On a second occasion, he drove off with a 17-year-old girl to another secluded area, compelled her, too, to commit a perverted sexual act and attempted to rape her. Then he let her off near her home. (This tragic young woman, who had a history of serious mental disturbance, was committed to a mental hospital some 19 months after her traumatic experience. "Today," the wire services have quoted her mother as saying, "she just sits and stares"—lost in the withdrawn unreal world of the schizophrenic.)

It is no wonder, then, that the Red Light Bandit crimes so aroused judge, jury and prosecutor and antagonized them against the man accused of their commission. They angered and outraged me to an equal or greater degree, to an extent where in a red haze of emotion, I was unable to defend myself as effectively as otherwise I might. Stupidly and stubbornly, as well, I had withheld certain vital facts about my involvement in a violent internecine struggle for control of an illegal but police protected book-making syndicate. The convict's code said I shouldn't talk, or name names. I didn't. Then, not by myself, other critical evidence got suppressed. Witnesses disappeared. And a damning net was drawn around me. The jury returned verdicts of guilty, doomed me. I was brought to Death Row, twice sentenced to death and to 15 consecutive prison terms. The question of guilt or innocence was closed unless I could convince an appellate court I had been convicted illegally. Otherwise, branded a loathsome sex predator, I would die. I would have no chance to establish California had convicted the wrong man. It would make no difference that the description furnished the police of the bandit didn't remotely fit me; that the 17-year-old girl said her attacker had been "shorter than the usual man" and had weighed nearly 50 pounds less than the evidence showed I did, while I was six feet tall; or that she said the bandit had spoken with a slight accent, had appeared to be Italian and had a linear cut scar extending back from his right ear; or that this bandit usually gave his victims a look at his face before pulling up a handkerchief mask, while I just had been released from prison on parole and knew that my photographs almost certainly would be the first shown robbery victims; or that I had absolutely no history as a sex offender; or that I had been refused the right to produce witnesses at the trial who would testify to my reputation for sexual normality as well as to produce expert psychiatric evidence that I did not possess the psychological disposition to commit sexual crimes, particularly those involving force or violence, and that I was not a sexual psychopath.

All this made no difference. In the eyes of the law, I was guilty and would remain guilty unless I could win a new trial and acquittal. This galled but it also drove and sustained me. . . .

I wait to die. I remain locked in a death cell. More than 12 years have passed since my arrest. The State has spent nearly a million dollars in trying to kill me.

Now, in a few days, the California Legislature will be called into special session to consider abolition of capital punishment. Disturbed that a vote against the death penalty will be a vote for me, the man they believe has embarrassed their State and made a mockery of their laws, many legislators have vowed publicly to see that capital punishment is retained. I do not presume to tell them what to do; I do pray they will reconsider and reevaluate. . . . I am more than willing that they separate me decisively from the greater issue. I am quite willing to die if that will bring about this desperately needed social reform. I do suggest that if our positions were reversed and they had found themselves occupying a death cell under the conditions I have they too, and honorably, would have done as I have done, even though it meant bringing the wrath of the State down upon them. Happily, they will never know what it means to be doomed, to be within hours and minutes of execution, to feel the full, terrible impact of mob wrath, to have a claim of innocence brushed impatiently aside, to be called a "monster" and vilified, to seek redemption, not through hypocritical groveling, but by a harder, perhaps impossible road, to win friends and want desperately to justify their friendship and their faith, to want to live and to believe, humbly, that within them is a gift for words that can enrich our literature and, their own case aside, contribute significantly to the pressing social problems of our day.

I do not overstate when I say I gladly would die ten thousand gas chamber deaths if that would bring these truths into the hearts and minds of those who make our laws: A vote for either abolition or a moratorium is not an indication of approval of murder or other capital crimes, for the death penalty does not deter; it does not protect society. On the contrary, it leaves it defenseless, since as long as we have an executioner and a gas chamber, we will be content to believe that we can bury the problem with the offender. We will think that revenge is enough. It isn't. We must find why men kill and we must learn to prevent killing. We must become as intensely concerned with tomorrow's prospective victims as yesterday's actual ones. We must learn how to save lives and to salvage lives.

As long as the death penalty is on our statute books, there will be too much emotionality and circus atmosphere tainting our administration of justice. And for those who doubt this, there is a ready and rational test at hand: Let a moratorium be ordered on the supreme penalty for a period of, say, five years. I am certain during that period there will be no rise in the per capita crimes. Rather, I am convinced the crime rate will drop appreciably, and that justice will function in a far more even-handed and fair way. The sensationalism inevitably attending capital cases will vanish. The citizen will be reassured. He will know that the man who has killed has been isolated. The accused is more likely, if he is guilty, to plead guilty. Our courts thus will be able to perform their duties more efficiently. And if an innocent man is later found to have been mistakenly convicted, it will not be too late to correct the error.

Unfortunately, as investigation will confirm, too often it is the friendless and the fundless upon whom the death penalty is imposed. The man with means or who knows the angles does not come to Death Row. As well, under our outmoded tests for legal sanity or insanity, too often the man who is executed is one who, while not legally insane, suffers from some serious mental disability. It needlessly demeans our society to engage in killing the mentally ill. Still further, among this group, as psychiatrists and penologists will attest, is the type of personality who is inflamed by the thought and threat of the gas chamber. His response to it, his overt expression of defiance, is to strike out homicidally. In effect, he gets his revenge in advance, and we in turn get ours after the tragedy.

That is why so many thoughtful citizens advocate abolition or a moratorium. They feel, as I do, a sense of guilty responsibility at a lethal act that is both more than futile and less than futile when the State takes a life. They want their laws to express humanity's ideal of nobility, compassion, understanding and social awareness. They know that our laws can do so without endangering the citizens of California. The basis for their opposition to man's government killing man is thus, in the highest sense, ethical, social, practical and religious. They do not want to see their society needlessly degraded, their system of justice compromised.

I must close, and in closing I again earnestly urge you to ask the Legislature to consider the question of capital punishment apart from Caryl Chessman and the Chessman case. I urge you to request that they consider framing their bill as suggested above, to exclude me. You can do this honorably by taking my life back into your hands alone. You can let me die. Indeed, as the matter now stands, you are powerless to do otherwise because of the present 4–3 vote against me in the California Supreme Court. But, at the same time, you can give your proposal to the Legislature a chance.

It deserves that chance. It deserves your forceful leadership. You are right in the position you have taken. It is time to speak out, for too seldom does unenlightened humanity in this age of fear and awesome nuclear devices have a spokesman with the courage to advocate that death and hate are not and never can be an answer to the problems that beset our civilization. Mankind and future generations ever will remain in your debt and ever will honor your name.

Yours respectfully,
/s/ Caryl Chessman

Bibliography

Autobiographical

Adler, Polly. *A House Is Not a Home*. New York: Holt, Rinehart & Winston, Inc., 1953.

Alvarez, Walter Clement. *Minds That Came Back*. Philadelphia, Pa.: J. B. Lippincott Co., 1961.

Anonymous. "A Day in my Double Life by a Homosexual," *20th Century* 173 (Summer, 1964): 44–52.

Anonymous. "Annie the Cop Fighter," from *Alcoholics Anonymous,* 2nd. ed. New York: Alcoholics Anonymous World Services, Inc., 1955, pp. 514–22.

Anonymous. " 'Discipline by Rape' at U.S. Prison." *National Catholic Reporter* (April 23, 1969).

Anonymous. "Drug Addict—Inactive," from *Readings in Criminology and Penology,* edited by David Dressler. New York: Columbia University Press, 1964, pp. 116–26.

Anonymous. *The Dying Speeches and Behavior of the Several State Prisoners That Have Been Executed the Last 300 Years.* London: F. Brotherton and W. Meadows, 1720.

Anonymous. "Gang Boy," from *Readings in Criminology and Penology,* edited by David Dressler. New York: Columbia University Press, 1964, pp. 149–63.

Anonymous. "How It Feels To Be A Convict." *American Mercury* 58 (April, 1944): 472–79.

Anonymous. "Military Versus Marijuana." *Los Angeles Free Press—Other Scenes* (January 5, 1968): 7.

Anonymous. "My Life in the Pententiary." *The Independent* 56 (February 4, 1904): 255–60.

Anonymous. "Notes From a Campus Pot Smoker." *Yale Alumni Magazine* 31 (1967): 27–28.

Anonymous. "On Selling Marijuana," from *Marijuana,* edited by Erich Goode. New York: Atherton Press, Inc., 1969, pp. 92–102.

Anonymous. *Opium-eating: An Autobiographical Sketch by an*

Habituate. Philadelphia, Pa.: Claxton, Remsen & Haffelfinger, 1876.

Anonymous. "The Smoker's View," from *Marijuana,* edited by Erich Goode. New York: Atherton Press, Inc., 1969, pp. 52–57.

Anonymous. "Some Thoughts on Marijuana and the Artist," from *Marijuana,* edited by Erich Goode. New York: Atherton Press, Inc., 1969, pp. 177–83.

Anonymous. "Soul in Prison: The Poems and Letters of X107." *Harper* 133 (October, 1916): 722–38.

Anonymous. "A Straight Adult." *Time* 94 (September 26, 1969): 73.

Anonymous. *Streetwalker.* London: The Bodley Head, Ltd., 1959.

Anonymous. "A Teen-ager's Trip." *Time* 94 (September 26, 1969): 72–73.

Anonymous. *Twenty Years in Hell, or the Life, Experience, Trials, and Tribulations of a Morphine Fiend.* Kansas City, Mo.: 1903.

Anonymous. "Why I am a Life Prisoner in Sing Sing Prison." *Ladies Home Journal* 27 (March, 1910): 15, 93.

Anonymous. "Why Students Turn to Drugs." *Reader's Digest* 92 (April, 1968): 173–78.

Bamberg, Robert D., ed. *The Confessions of Jereboam O. Beauchamp.* Philadelphia, Pa.: The University of Pennsylvania Press, 1966.

Behan, Brendan. *Borstal Boy.* New York: Alfred A. Knopf, Inc., 1958.

Benton, Roger. *Where Do I Go From Here? The Life Story of a Forger.* New York: L. Furman, Inc., 1936.

Benuto, Rita. *Mistress of Cuba.* Los Angeles, Calif.: Holloway House Publishing Company, 1967.

Black, Jack. "A Burglar Looks at Laws and Codes." *Harper's Magazine* 160 (February, 1930): 306–13.

———. *You Can't Win.* New York: The Macmillan Company, 1926.

Bone, Edith. *Seven Years Solitary.* New York: Harcourt Brace Jovanovich, 1957.

Booth, Ernest. *Stealing Through Life.* New York: Alfred A. Knopf, Inc., 1929.

———. *My Life in Prison.* New York: Grove Press, Inc., 1966.

Branch, Margaret. "My Outcast State." *20th Century* 173 (Summer, 1964): 88–96.

Brown, Claude. *Manchild in the Promised Land.* New York: The Macmillan Company, 1965.

Bruce, Lenny. *How to Talk Dirty and Influence People.* Chicago, Ill.: HMH Publishing Co., Inc., 1963.

Burns, Robert. *I'm A Fugitive From a Chain Gang.* New York: Vanguard Press, 1932.

Burns, Vincent G. *Out of These Chains.* Los Angeles, Calif.: New World Books, 1942.

Burroughs, William. *Junkie.* New York: Ace Books, *subs.* of Ace Publishing Corp., 1953.

Byrnes, Thomas. "Criminal Life and Experiences," from *Darkness and Daylight,* edited by Helen Campbell. Hartford, Conn.: A. D. Worthington and Co., 1891, pp. 641–740.

Cacopardo, J. J. and Don Weldon. *Show Me a Miracle: The True Story of a Man Who Went From Prison to Pulpit.* London: Victor Gollancz, Ltd. 1962.

Cantine, Holley R. and Dachine Rainer, eds. *Prison Etiquette: The Convict's Compendium of Useful Information.* Bearsville, N.Y.: Retort Press, 1950.

Carpenter, Ed. *Prison Ex: Revelations of a Former Inmate.* Las Vegas, Nevada: M-T Publishers, 1969.

Carter, Marshall. "Buttons, Buttons." *Moderator* 4 (October, 1965): 14.

Charrière, Henri. *Papillon.* New York: William Morrow & Co., Inc., 1970.

Chessman, Caryl. "A Letter from Death Row." *Psychology Today* 2 (February, 1969): 38–41.

———. *Cell 2455, Death Row.* Englewood Cliffs, N.J.: Prentice-Hall, Inc., 1954.

———. *The Face of Justice.* Englewood Cliffs, N.J.: Prentice-Hall, Inc., 1957.

———. *Trial by Ordeal.* Englewood Cliffs, N.J.: Prentice-Hall, Inc., 1955.

Clark, Charles L. and Earle Edward Eubank. *Lock Step and Corridor; Thirty-five Years of Prison Life.* Cincinnati, Ohio: The University of Cincinnati Press, 1927.

Cleaver, Eldridge. *Soul on Ice.* New York: McGraw-Hill Book Company, 1968.

Cluverius, Thomas J. *Cluverius: My Life, Trial and Conviction.* Richmond, Va.: Andrews, Baptist & Clemmitt, Printers, 1887.

Coffey, John. "The Autobiography of An Ex-thief." *Outlook and*

Independent 154 (February—April, 1930): 421–23, 478–79, 502, 519–20, 538–39, 583–84, 598, 620.

Contant, George C. *A Pardoned Lifer.* San Bernardino, Calif.: The Index Print, 1909.

Cory, Donald Webster. *The Homosexual in America.* New York: Greenberg Publisher, Inc., 1951.

Crowe, Patrick T. *Spreading Evil, Pat Crowe's Autobiography.* New York: The Branwell Co., 1927.

D., M. "The Personal Experiences of an Ex-opium Habitué." *Medical Record* 13 (May 18, 1878): 399–400.

Dahl, Robert. *Breakdown.* Indianapolis, Ind.: The Bobbs-Merrill Company, Inc., 1959.

Deming, Barbara. *Prison Notes.* New York: Grossman Pubs., Inc., *subs.* of The Viking Press, Inc., 1966.

De Quincey, Thomas. *Confessions of an English Opium-eater.* London: W. Scott, 1886.

Doyle, William. *Man Alone.* Indianapolis, Ind.: The Bobbs-Merrill Company, Inc., 1953.

Ex-con. "A Convict's Defense of 'Prison Cruelty'." *Literary Digest* 66 (August 28, 1920): 36.

Ex-con. "Judges as the Criminal Sees Them." *Outlook* 124: 588–90.

Feldman, Gene and Max Gartenberg, eds. *The Beat Generation and the Angry Young Men.* New York: Citadel Press, Inc., 1958.

Fiddle, Seymour. *Portraits From a Shooting Gallery.* New York: Harper & Row, Publishers, 1967.

Flynn, Elizabeth Gurley. *I Speak My Own Piece; Autobiography of "The Rebel Girl."* New York: Masses and Mainstream, 1955.

———. *The Alderson Story: My Life as a Political Prisoner.* New York: International Publishers Co., Inc., 1963.

Frankfurter, Marion Denman and Gardner Jackson, eds. *The Letters of Sacco and Vanzetti.* New York: The Viking Press, Inc., 1928.

"Frisco." "Old Mike States the Case." *Raiford Record* 12 (August, 1950): 10–13.

Gage, Leona. *My Name is Leona Gage, Will Somebody Please Help Me?* Los Angeles, Calif.: Holloway House Publishing Company, 1965.

Genêt, Jean. *Miracle of the Rose.* Lyon: L' Arbalète, 1946.

———. *The Thief's Journal.* Paris: Olympia Press, 1954.

Ginsberg, Allen. "The Great Marijuana Hoax: First Manifesto to End the Bringdown." *Atlantic* 221 (November, 1966): 104–12.

———. "Playboy Interview: Allen Ginsberg—Candid Conversation." *Playboy* 16 (April, 1969): 81ff.

Goosen, William. *On the Run.* Cape Town: Howard Timmins, 1964.

Gouzer, Dr. "Journal of a Morphine Addict." *Archives of Anthropological Criminology* 11: 75–94; 220–28; 313–32; 432–44.

Goy, Carl. "Report from the Asylum." *Neurotica* (Spring, 1950): 33–41.

Grey, Peter. "Look at Me." *The New Yorker* 39 (March 23, 1963): 133–43.

Guerin, Eddie. *I Was a Bandit.* Garden City, N.Y.: Doubleday, Doran & Co., Inc., 1929.

Haggart, David. *The Life of David Haggart.* Edinburgh: 1821.

Hambly, Charles R. *Hold Your Money: A Sucker's Handbook—Con Games Exposed.* Los Angeles, Calif.: Monitor Publishing Company, 1932.

Hamilton, Charles., ed. *Men of the Underworld: The Professional Criminal's Own Story.* New York: The MacMillan Company, 1902.

Hankins, Leonard. *Nineteen Years Not Guilty.* New York: Exposition Press, 1956.

Hapgood, Hutchins. *The Autobiography of a Thief.* London: G. P. Putnam's Sons, 1904.

Harris, Sara and Lucy Freeman. *The Lords of Hell.* New York: Dell Publishing Co., Inc., 1967.

Hassler, Alfred. *Diary of a Self-made Convict.* Chicago, Ill.: Henry Regnery Co., 1954.

Heckstall-Smith, Anthony. *Eighteen Months.* London: Allan Wingate, 1954.

———. *Crime Without Punishment.* London: Allan Wingate, 1955.

———. *Company of Strangers.* New York: Coward-McCann, Inc., 1960.

Henry, Joan. *Who Lie in Gaol.* London: Victor Gollancz, Ltd., 1952.

Hirsch, Phil, ed. *Hooked.* New York: Pyramid Books, 1968.

Hodge, Raymond. "The Rehabilitation Process: A Prisoner's Point of View." *American Journal of Correction* 26 (March-April, 1964): 12–16.

Hollister, Hal. "I Say Prisons Are a Failure." *The Saturday Evening Post* 234 (August 26, 1961): 13, 40, 44.

———. "An Ex-convict's Scheme for More Practical Prisons." *Harper's Magazine* 225 (August, 1962): 14, 16, 19–20.

Horan, James D. *The Mob's Man.* New York: Crown Publishers, Inc., 1959.

Horsley, J. W. "Autobiography of a Thief, in Thieves' Language." *MacMillan Magazine* 40 (1879): 500–506.

Hughes, Helen M., ed. *The Fantastic Lodge.* Boston, Mass.: Houghton Mifflin Company, Riverside Press, 1961.

Irwin, Will. *Confessions of a Con Man.* New York: B. W. Huebsch, 1909.

Jennings, W. O. *The Morphia Habit and Its Voluntary Renunciation (A Personal Revelation of a Suppression After 25 Years Addiction).* New York: Wm. Wood & Co., 1909.

Jones, Richard. " 'Up' on Psilocybin." *The Harvard Review* 1 (Summer, 1963): 38–43.

Klein, Alexander, ed. *The Double Dealers.* New York: J. B. Lippincott Co., 1958.

Krassner, Paul. "Paul Krassner on LSD." *Realist* 60 (1965): 1–2.

Krim, Seymour. "The Insanity Bit," from *The Beats,* edited by Seymour Krim. New York: Fawcett, 1960.

Labat, Edgar. "My Fourteen Years on Death Row." *Look* 32 (March 19, 1968): 80, 84, 86–88.

Lacenaire, Piere-Francois. *The Memoirs of Lacenaire,* translated by Philip John Stead. London: Staples Press, 1952.

Leary, Timothy. *The Psychedelic Experience.* New Hyde Park, N.Y.: University Books, 1965.

———. "Playboy Interview: Timothy Leary—Candid Conversation." *Playboy* 13 (September, 1966): 93ff.

———. *High Priest.* New York: World Publishing Company, 1968.

———. *The Politics of Ecstasy.* New York: G. P Putnam's Sons, 1968.

———. "Episode and Postscript." *Playboy* 16 (December, 1969): 221ff.

——— and Richard Alpert. "The Politics of Consciousness Expansion." *The Harvard Review* 1 (Summer, 1963): 33–37.

———, *et al.,* ed. *The Psychedelic Reader.* New Hyde Park, N.Y.: University Books, 1965.

Leopold, Nathan F., Jr. *Life Plus 99 Years.* New York: Doubleday & Company, Inc., 1958.

Little, Jim. "I Care, You Care, He Cares." *Harper's Magazine* 228 (April, 1964): 169–70.

Lowrie, Donald. *My Life in Prison.* New York: M. Kennerley, 1912.

Ludlow, Peter. "In Defense of Pot: Confessions of a Canadian Marijuana Smoker." *Saturday Night* 80 (October, 1965): 28–29, 32.

MacIssac, John R. *Half the Fun Was Getting There.* Englewood Cliffs, N.J.: Prentice-Hall, Inc., 1968.

MacKenzie, Donald. *Occupation: Thief.* Indianapolis, Ind.: The Bobbs-Merrill Company, Inc., 1955.

McCaghy, Charles H., James K. Skipper, Jr., and Mark Lefton, eds. *In Their Own Behalf: Voices From the Margin.* New York: Appleton-Century-Crofts, 1968.

McGrath, Edward F. *I Was Condemned to the Chair.* New York: Frederick A. Stokes Co., 1934.

McLeod, J. "I Stole Cameras for a Living." *Modern Photography* 26 (February, 1962): 88.

McManus, Virginia. *Not for Love.* New York: G.P. Putnam's Sons, 1967.

Macfarland, Charles Stedman. *I Was in Prison.* New York: Fleming H. Revell Company, 1939.

Malcolm X. *The Autobiography of Malcolm X.* New York: Grove Press, Inc., 1964.

Marlowe, Kenneth. *Mr. Madam: Confessions of a Male Madam.* Los Angeles, Calif.: Sherborne Press, 1964.

Martin, John Bartlow. *My Life in Crime: The Autobiography of a Professional Criminal.* New York: Harper & Row, Publishers, 1952.

Mol, Albert. *Memoirs of An Amsterdam Streetwalker: Conversations with Greta.* New York: Award Books, 1967.

Moore, Langdon W. *His Own Story of His Eventful Life.* Boston, Mass.: L. W. Moore, 1893.

Moray, Alastair. *The Diary of a Rum-runner.* London: Philip Allan and Co., Ltd., 1929.

Morrison, Majbritt. *Jungle West 11.* New York: Universal Publishing, 1967.

Nemo, Stephen. "Letter to the Editor." *Avant Garde* (March, 1968): 3–10

Newland, Constance A. *Myself and I.* New York: Coward-McCann, Inc., 1962.

No. 49049. "Writing the Hard Way." *Saturday Review* 46 (September 11, 1965): 34.

Nunnally, Joe Frederick. *I Was a Conscientious Objector in Camp, in Prisons (and) on Parole*. Berkeley, Calif.: Sooner Publishing Co., 1948.

Orwell, George. *Down and Out in Paris and London*. New York: Harper & Row, Publishers, 1933.

Palmer, Stuart. *A Study of Murder*. New York: Thomas Y. Crowell Company, 1960.

Parker, Tony and Robert Allerton. *The Courage of His Convictions*. London: Hutchinson & Company (Publishers) Ltd., 1962.

Parkhurst, H., ed. "My Road to Crime." *Saturday Evening Post* 231 (March 21, 1959): 23–25ff.; (March 28, 1959): 36ff.; (April 4, 1959): 36ff.

Parmelee, Lucius A. *The Confessions of a Bank Swindler*. Waterloo, Quebec: Duval Press, 1968.

Parton, Margaret. "I'm Going to be in Prison a Long Time." *Reader's Digest* 67 (September, 1955): 27–29.

Patterson, Haywood and Earl Conrad. *Scottsboro Boy*. Garden City, N.Y.: Doubleday & Company, Inc., 1950.

Price, Charles. *Memoirs of a Social Monster; or the History of Charles Price*. London: G. Kearfley, 1786.

Prince, Virginia "Charles." *The Transvestite and His Wife*. Los Angeles, Calif.: Argyle Books, 1967.

Prisoner #4000X. "A Criminal Looks at Crime and Punishment." *Scribner's Magazine* 81 (January, 1927): 86–89.

Rashleigh, Ralph. *Adventures of an Outlaw*. New York: Jonathan Cape and Harrison Smith, Inc., 1929.

Raynor, Darrel G. *A Year Among the Girls*. New York: Lancer Books, Inc., 1968.

Reid, Calvin G. "The Phone Call." *Harper's Magazine* 228 (April, 1964): 164–66.

Reynolds, John N. *The Twin Hells*. Chicago, Ill.: The Bee Publishing Co., 1890.

"Ric." "I Turned On 200 Fellow Students at the U. of Michigan." *Esquire* 68 (September, 1967): 100, 190–93.

Rice, George G. *My Adventures with Your Money*. Boston, Mass.: R. G. Badger, 1913.

Riddell, Patrick. *I Was an Alcoholic: The Story of a Cure*. London: Victor Gollancz, Ltd., 1955.

Robinson, James. "Open Letter to the Governor of Ford Prisons." *Spectator* No. 7094 (June 12, 1964): 789–90.

Rubin, Theodore Isaac. *In the Life*. New York: Ballantine Books, Inc., 1961.

Rudensky, Morris "Red." "After the Stretch." *Harper's Magazine* 228 (April, 1964): 180–82.

Sands, Bill. *My Shadow Ran Fast*. Englewood Cliffs, N.J.: Prentice-Hall, Inc., 1964.

———. *The Seventh Step*. New York: The New American Library, 1967.

Schiffer, David. "I Stole a Million." *Colliers Magazine* 123 (February 5, 1949): 13, 42–43; (February 12, 1949): 34, 35, 72–73.

Shaw, Clifford. *Natural History of a Delinquent Career*. Chicago, Ill.: The University of Chicago Press, 1931.

——— *et al. Brothers in Crime*. Chicago, Ill.: The University of Chicago Press, 1938.

———. *The Jack Roller: A Delinquent Boy's Own Story*. Chicago, Ill.: The University of Chicago Press, 1945.

Shelby, Gordon. *I Take the Rap*. New York: Frederick Fell, Inc., 1957.

Shoda, Akira. "Memoirs of a Man Sentenced to Death." *ACTA Criminologie et Medicinae Legalis Japonica* 30 (February, 1964): 30–37.

———. "Memoirs of a Man Sentenced to Death." *ACTA Criminologie et Medicinae Legalis Japonica* 30 (April, 1964): 27–34.

Slim, Iceberg. *Pimp: The Story of My Life*. Los Angeles, Calif.: Holloway House Publishing Company, 1967.

———. *Trick Baby: The Biography of a Con Man*. Los Angeles, Calif.: Holloway House Publishing Company, 1969.

Smith, Edward H. *Confessions of a Confidence Man*. New York: Scientific American Publishing Company, 1923.

Sontag, Linda. "The Eyes of the Child-corpse Were Open Wide," from *The Ecstatic Adventure,* edited by R. Metzner. New York: Macmillan Company, 1968, pp. 176–82.

Stanford, Sally. *The Lady of the House*. New York: G. P. Putnam's Sons, 1966.

Steffens, Lincoln. *The Autobiography of Lincoln Steffens*. New York: Harcourt Brace, 1931.

Street, Leroy. *I Was a Drug Addict*. New York: Random House, Inc., 1953.

Su-Ling. *The 9 Holes of Jade*. Los Angeles, Calif.: Holloway House Publishing Company, 1967.

Sutherland, Edwin H. *The Professional Thief by a Professional Thief*. Chicago, Ill.: The University of Chicago Press, 1937.

Sutton, Willie. *I, Willie Sutton.* New York: Farrar, Straus & Giroux, Inc., 1953.

———. *"My Story," Scoundrels and Scalawags: 51 Stories of the Most Fascinating Characters of Hoax and Frauds.* Pleasantville, N.Y.: The Reader's Digest Association, 1968, 542–59.

Teale, Christopher. *Behind These Walls.* New York: Frederick Fell, Inc., 1957.

Thomas, Piri. *Down These Mean Streets.* New York: The New American Library Inc., 1967.

Thompson, Walter William. *Time Off My Life.* London: Rich & Cowan, 1956.

Trask, Robert A. "The Waiting Time." *Harper's Magazine* 228 (April, 1964): 168–69.

Tufts, Henry. *The Autobiography of a Criminal.* New York: Duffield and Company, 1930.

Tyler, Betty. "A Parolee Tells Her Story." *Federal Probation* 32 (June, 1968): 54–56.

U.S. Congress-Senate, *Hearings Before a Special Committee to Investigate Organized Crime in Interstate Commerce.* 81st Congress, 2nd Session, 1950.

U.S. Congress-Senate, Organized Crime and Illicit Traffic in Narcotics, *Hearings Before the Permanent Subcommittee on Investigations of the Committee on Government Operations.* 88th Congress, 1st Session, 1963.

U.S. Senate, Subcommittee to Investigate Juvenile Delinquency, *Exploitation of Minors in Interstate Confidence Racket.* 84th Congress, 2nd Session, 1956.

Vaux, James Hardy. *The Memoirs of James Hardy Vaux,* edited by Noel McLachlan. London: William Heinemann Ltd., 1964.

Victor, Sarah M. *The Life Story of Sarah M. Victor.* Cleveland, Ohio: The Williams Publishing Co., 1887.

Warren, Paul. *Next Time Is For Life.* New York: Dell Publishing Co., Inc., 1953.

Washington, Kipp. *Some Like It Dark.* Los Angeles, Calif.: Holloway House Publishing Company, 1966.

Watts, Marthe. *The Men in My Life.* London: World Distributors, 1962.

Weil, Joseph R. *"Yellow Kid" Weil—Con Man.* Chicago, Ill.: Ziff-Davis Publishing Company, 1948.

West, Dorothy. "I Was Afraid to Shut My Eyes." *The Saturday Evening Post* 241 (July 13, 1968): 23.

Whalley, W. "Confessions of a Laudanum-drinker." *Lancet* 2 (July 14, 1866): 35.

Whelan, Kenneth E. "Benny and His Brothers." *Harper's Magazine* 228 (April, 1964): 166–67.

Wilde, Oscar. *De Profundis.* New York: G. P. Putnam's Sons, 1909.

Willard, Josiah Flynt. *My Life.* New York: The Outing Publishing Company, 1908.

Williamson, Henry. *Hustler!* Garden City, N.Y.: Doubleday & Company, Inc., 1965.

Willis, Aubrey. *I Was an Alcoholic.* New York: Vantage Press, 1956.

Wilson, Herbert Emerson. *I Stole $16,000,000.* New York: The New American Library, Inc., 1956.

Witherspoon, Bill, ed. *Death Row.* New York: Pyramid Books, 1968.

Zimmerman, Isidore. *Punishment Without Crime.* New York: Clarkson N. Potter, 1964.

Theory, Research, and General Interest

Allen, Francis A. "Offenses Against Property." *The Annals* 339 (January, 1962): 57–76.

Anderson, Nels. *The Hobo.* Chicago, Ill.: The University of Chicago Press, 1923.

Anderson, Robert T. "From Mafia to Cosa Nostra." *American Journal of Sociology* 71 (November, 1965): 302–10.

Baird, Russell N. *The Penal Press.* Evanston, Ill.: Northwestern University Press, 1967.

Barnes, Harry Elmer and Negley K. Teeters. *New Horizons in Criminology.* Englewood Cliffs, N.J.: Prentice-Hall, Inc., 1951.

Barrows, Isabel C. "Periodicals in Prisons and Reformatories," from *Correction and Prevention,* edited by Charles R. Henderson. New York: Charities Publication Committee, 1910.

Becker, Howard S. "Becoming a Marihuana User." *American Journal of Sociology* 59 (November, 1953): 235–43.

Bedau, Hugo Adam, ed. *The Death Penalty in America.* Garden City, N.Y.: Doubleday & Company, Inc., 1964.

Bennett, James V. *I Chose Prison.* New York: Alfred A. Knopf, Inc., 1970.

Block, Herbert A. "The Sociology of Gambling." *American Journal of Sociology* 57 (November, 1951): 215–21.

——— and Gilbert Geis. *Man, Crime, and Society: The Forms of Criminal Behavior.* New York: Random House, Inc., 1962.

Bryan, James H. "Apprenticeships in Prostitution." *Social Problems* 12 (Winter, 1965): 287–97.

———. "Occupational Ideologies of Call Girls." *Social Problems* 13 (Spring, 1966): 441–50.

Cameron, Mary Owen. *The Booster and the Snitch*. Glencoe, Ill.: The Free Press of Glencoe, 1964.

Cavan, Ruth Shonle and Eugene S. Zemans. "Marital Relationships of Prisoners in Twenty-eight Countries." *Journal of Criminal Law, Criminology and Police Science* 49 (July-August, 1958): 133–39.

Chambliss, William J. "A Sociological Analysis of the Law of Vagrancy." *Social Problems* 12 (Summer, 1964): 67–77.

Chein, Isidor, *et al. The Road to H*. New York: Basic Books, Inc., Publishers, 1964.

Clemmer, Donald. *The Prison Community*. New York: Holt, Rinehart & Winston, Inc., 1958.

Clinard, Marshall B. and Richard Quinney, eds. *Criminal Behavior Systems: A Typology*. New York: Holt, Rinehart & Winston, Inc., 1967.

Cloward, Richard A. and Lloyd E. Ohlin. *Delinquency and Opportunity: A Theory of Delinquent Gangs*. Glencoe, Ill.: The Free Press of Glencoe, Inc., 1960.

Cohen, Albert K. *Delinquent Boys: The Culture of the Gang*. New York: The Free Press of Glencoe, Inc., 1955.

———. *Deviance and Control*. Englewood Cliffs, N.J.: Prentice-Hall, Inc., 1966.

——— and James F. Short, Jr. "Research in Delinquent Subcultures." *Journal of Social Issues* 14 (Summer, 1958): 20–36.

Conrad, John P. "Violence in Prison." *The Annals* 364 (March, 1966): 113–19.

Cressey, Donald R. *Other People's Money*. New York: The Free Press of Glencoe, Inc., 1953.

———, ed. *The Prison: Studies in Institutional Organization and Change*. New York: Holt, Rinehart & Winston, Inc., 1961.

———. *Theft of the Nation: The Structure and Operations of Organized Crime in America*. New York: Harper & Row, Publishers, 1969.

Davis, Alan J. "Sexual Assaults in the Philadelphia Prison System and Sheriff's Vans." *Trans-action* 6 (December, 1968): 8–16.

Davis, Kingsley. "The Sociology of Prostitution." *American Sociological Review* 2 (October, 1937): 744–55.

Dees, Jesse Walter, Jr. *Flophouse.* Francestown, N. H.: Marshall Jones Co., 1948.

Deutscher, Irwin. "The Petty Offender: A Sociological Alien." *Journal of Criminal Law, Criminology and Police Science* 44 (January-February, 1954): 592–95.

Dressler, David. *Parole Chief.* New York: The Viking Press, Inc., 1951.

Duffy, Clinton T. *88 Men and 2 Women.* Garden City, N.Y.: Doubleday & Company Inc., 1962.

Ennis, Phillip H. "Crime, Victims, and the Police." *Trans-action* 4 June, 1967): 36–44.

Finestone, Harold. "Narcotics and Criminality." *Law and Contemporary Problems* 22 (Winter, 1957): 69–85.

Gagnon, John and William Simon. "The Social Meaning of Prison Homosexuality." *Federal Probation* 32 (March, 1968): 23–29.

Galtung, Johan. *The Prison Community.* Oslo: The Oslo University Press, 1959.

Giallombardo, Rose. *Society of Women: A Study of a Women's Prison.* New York: John Wiley & Sons, Inc., 1966.

Gibbons, Don C. *Changing the Lawbreaker: The Treatment of Delinquents and Criminals.* Englewood Cliffs, N.J.: Prentice-Hall, Inc., 1965.

———. *Society, Crime, and Criminal Careers: An Introduction to Criminology.* Englewood Cliffs, N.J.: Prentice-Hall, Inc., 1968.

Glaser, Daniel. *The Effectiveness of a Prison and Parole System.* Indianapolis, Ind.: The Bobbs-Merrill Company, Inc., 1964.

Goode, Erich, ed. *Marijuana.* New York: Atherton Press, 1969.

Healy, William and Augusta F. Bronner. *New Lights on Delinquency and Its Treatment.* New Haven, Conn.: Yale University Press, 1936.

Hall, Jerome. *Theft, Law and Society,* 2nd. ed. Indianapolis, Ind.: The Bobbs-Merrill Company, Inc., 1952.

Hentig, Hans von. "The Pickpocket: Psychology, Tactics, and Techniques." *Journal of Criminal Law, Criminology and Police Science* 34 (May-June, 1943): 11–15.

Hirschi, Travis. "The Professional Prostitute." *Berkeley Journal of Sociology* 7 (1962): 33–49.

Hopper, Columbus B. *Sex in Prison.* Baton Rouge, La.: Louisiana State University Press, 1969.

Humphreys, Laud. *Tearoom Trade: Impersonal Sex in Public Places.* Chicago, Ill.: Aldine Publishing Company, 1970.

Irwin, John and Donald R. Cressey. "Thieves, Convicts, and the Inmate Culture," from *The Other Side,* edited by Howard S. Becker. New York: The Free Press of Glencoe, Inc., 1964, pp. 225–45.

Irwin, John. *The Felon.* Englewood Cliffs, N.J.: Prentice-Hall, Inc., 1970.

Jackman, Norman R., Richard O'Toole, and Gilbert Geis. "The Self-image of the Prostitute." *Sociological Quarterly* 4 (April, 1963): 150–61.

Kinzel, Augustus F. "Violent Behavior in Prisons." Paper read before the annual meeting of the American Psychiatric Association Division Meeting, Chicago, Ill., November 16, 1968.

Korn, Richard R. and Lloyd W. McCorkle. *Criminology and Penology.* New York: Holt, Rinehart & Winston, Inc., 1961.

Landesco, John. *Organized Crime in Chicago,* 2nd ed. Chicago, Ill.: The University of Chicago Press, 1968.

Lawes, Lewis E. *Twenty Thousand Years in Sing Sing.* New York: Ray Long and Richard R. Smith, Inc., 1932.

———. *Life and Death in Sing Sing.* Garden City, N.Y.: The Sun Dial Press, Inc., 1937.

Lemert, Edwin M. *Social Pathology.* New York: McGraw-Hill Book Company, 1951.

Lewis, Norman. *The Honored Society.* New York: G. P. Putnam's Sons, Inc., 1964.

Leznoff, Maurice and William A. Westley. "The Homosexual Community." *Social Problems* 3 (April, 1956): 257–63.

Lindesmith, Alfred R. "Organized Crime." *The Annals* 217 (September, 1941): 76–83.

———. *Opiate Addiction.* Bloomington, Ind.: Indiana University Press, 1947.

Lombroso, Cesare. *The Criminal Man,* 4th. ed. Bocca, Torino, 1889.

McCall, George J. "Symbiosis: The Case of Hoodoo and the Numbers Racket," from *The Other Side,* edited by Howard S. Becker. New York: The Free Press of Glencoe, Inc., 1964, pp. 51–66.

Maas, Peter, *The Valachi Papers.* New York: G. P. Putnam's Sons, 1968.

Mannheim, Hermann. *Comparative Criminology.* New York: Houghton Mifflin Company, 1965.

Maurer, David W. *The Big Con.* Indianapolis, Ind.: The Bobbs-Merrill Company, 1940.

———. *Whiz Mob: A Correlation of the Technical Argot of Pickpockets with Their Behavior Pattern.* New Haven, Conn.: College and University Press, 1964.

Miller, Walter B. "Lower Class Culture as a Generating Milieu of Gang Delinquency." *Journal of Social Issues* 14 (Summer, 1958): 5–19.

Morris, Albert. "Criminals' Views on Crime Causation." *The Annals* 217 (September, 1941): 138–44.

Murtagh, John M. and Sara Harris. *Cast the First Stone.* New York: McGraw-Hill Book Company, Inc., 1957.

Peterson, W. Jack and Milton A. Maxwell. "The Skid Road 'Wino'." *Social Problems* 5 (Spring, 1958): 308–16.

Pittman, David J. and C. Wayne Gordon. *Revolving Door: A Study of the Chronic Police Case Inebriate.* New York: The Free Press of Glencoe, Inc., 1958.

Polsky, Ned. "The Hustler." *Social Problems* 12 (Summer, 1964): 3–15.

Reckless, Walter C. *The Crime Problem,* 4th. ed. New York: Appleton-Century-Crofts, 1967.

Reimer, Hans. "Socialization in the Prison Community." *Proceedings of The American Prison Association* (1937): 151–55.

Reiss, Albert J., Jr. "The Social Integration of Queers and Peers." *Social Problems* 9 (Fall, 1961): 102–20.

Roebuck, Julian B. and Ronald C. Johnson. "The Short Con Man as a Professional Criminal Type." *Crime and Delinquency* 10 (July, 1964): 235–48.

Rogers, Joseph W. and Elizabeth Smith Alexander. "The Penal Press: Research Opportunities." Revision of a paper read before the annual meeting of the Midwest Sociological Society, 1968. (Mimeographed.)

Rubington, Earl. "The Chronic Drunkenness Offender." *The Annals* 315 (January, 1958): 65–72.

Schur, Edwin M. *Crimes Without Victims: Deviant Behavior and Public Policy.* Englewood Cliffs, N.J.: Prentice-Hall, Inc., 1965.

Scudder, Kenyon J. *Prisoners Are People.* New York: Doubleday & Company, 1952.

Sellin, Thorsten. *The Death Penalty.* Philadelphia, Pa.: American Law Institute, 1959.

———, ed. *Capital Punishment.* New York: Harper & Row, Publishers, 1967.

Shaw, Clifford R., *et al. Delinquency Areas.* Chicago, Ill.: The University of Chicago Press, 1929.

Skolnick, Jerome H. *Justice Without Trial.* New York: John Wiley & Sons, Inc., 1966.

Smith, Ralph Lee. "Cops as Robbers." *The Nation* (February, 1965): 102–7.

Solomon, David, ed. *The Marihuana Papers.* Indianapolis, Ind.: The Bobbs-Merrill Company, Inc., 1966.

Stoddard, Ellwyn R. "The Informal 'Code' of Police Deviancy: A Group Approach to 'Blue-coat Crime'." *Journal of Criminal Law, Criminology and Police Science* 59 (June, 1968): 201–13.

Sutherland, Edwin H. *White Collar Crime.* New York: Holt, Rinehart & Winston, Inc., 1949.

——— and Donald R. Cressey. *Principles of Criminology,* 7th ed. Philadelphia, Pa.: J. B. Lippincott Co., 1966.

Sykes, Gresham. *The Society of Captives.* Princeton, N.J.: Princeton University Press, 1958.

Thomas, William I. and Florian Znaniecki. *The Polish Peasant in Europe and America.* Chicago, Ill.: The University of Chicago Press, 1918.

Thomas, William I. *The Unadjusted Girl.* New York: Little, Brown and Company, 1923.

Thrasher, Frederic M. *The Gang: A Study of 1,313 Gangs in Chicago,* abr. ed. Chicago, Ill.: The University of Chicago Press, 1963.

U.S. Department of Justice. *Uniform Crime Reports.* Washington, D.C.: U.S. Government Printing Office, 1968.

Vold, George B. "Does the Prison Reform?" *The Annals* 293 (May, 1954): 42–50.

———. *Theoretical Criminology.* New York: Oxford University Press, Inc., 1958.

Ward, David A. and Gene G. Kassebaum. *Women's Prison: Sex and Social Structure.* Chicago, Ill.: Aldine Publishing Company, 1965.

Wilson, Donald Powell. *My Six Convicts.* New York: Holt, Rinehart & Winston, Inc., 1951.

Yablonsky, Lewis. *The Violent Gang.* New York: The Macmillan Company, 1962.

Zemans, Eugene and Ruth Shonle Cavan. "Marital Relationships of Prisoners." *Journal of Criminal Law, Criminology and Police Science* 49 (May-June, 1958): 50–57.

Zola, Irving Kenneth. "Observations on Gambling In a Lower Class Setting." *Social Problems* 10 (Spring, 1963): 353–61.